The Marlborough (Spencer-Churchill) line of descent

Sir Winston Churchill b.1620= Elizabeth Drake of Ashe, Devon

John
b.1650 or Duke of Marlborough *
and KG 1702
or Prince of the Holy Roman
Empire 1705 d.16 June 1722

= Sarah
dr. of Richard Jennings of
St Albans
b.1660 m.1678 d.18 Oct 1744

* Duke of Marlborough a title which John
Churchill is believed to have taken in consequence
of a connection on his mother's side, with
the family of Ley, earls of Marlborough,
extinct ten years previously.

Henrietta
b.1681 suc. as
Duchess of Marlborough
1722 s.p.m. d.1733

= Francis
2nd Earl of
Godolphin

Anne = Charles Spencer
b.1684   KG 3rd Earl of
d.1716   Sunderland

Elizabeth = Scroop
b.1687   1st Duke of
d.1714   Bridgewater d.1751

Mary = John
b.1689   2nd Duke of
       Montagu

Diana Spencer = John
b.1708 d.1735   4th Duke
              of Bedford KG

John Spencer
(Ancestor of the
Earls Spencer)

John
Marquess of Blandford
b.1686 d.1703

Robert Spencer
b.1701 suc. as Earl of
Sunderland 1722
d. unmarried 1729

Charles Spencer
b.1706 suc. as Earl of Sunderland
1729 and as 3rd Duke of
Marlborough 1733 KG d.1758

= Elizabeth
dr. of Earl
Trevor

George Spencer
4th Duke of Marlborough
KG, LLD, FRS
b.1739 suc. 1758 d.1817

= Caroline
dr. of Duke of Bedford
b.1743 d.1811

Georgina = George
dr. of Earl
Granville

† The fifth Duke was authorized in 1817
to 'take and use the name of Churchill,
in addition to and after that of Spencer...
in order to perpetuate in his Graces
family a surname to which his illustrious
ancestor, John, first Duke of Marlborough,
added such imperishable lustre'.

George Spencer-Churchill †
5th Duke of Marlborough
b.1766 suc. 1817 d.1840

= Susan
dr. of 7th Earl of Galloway
b.1767 d.1841

George Spencer-Churchill
6th Duke of Marlborough
b.1793 suc. 1840 d.1857

= 1. Jane, dr. of 8th Earl of Galloway d.1844
   2. Charlotte, dr. of Viscount Ashbrook d.1850
   3. Jane, dr. of Hon. Edward Stewart d.1897

General of Ireland 1876-80 d.1883

George Charles Spencer-Churchill 8th Duke of Marlborough b.1844 suc.1883 d.1892
= 1. Alberta dr. of Duke of Abercorn
2. Lilian dr. of Cicero Price (USA)

Randolph Henry Spencer-Churchill b. at Blenheim 1849 PC, LLD, etc d.1895 buried at Bladon, Oxon
= Jennie dr. of Leonard Jerome (USA) d.1921

Charles Richard John Spencer-Churchill 9th Duke of Marlborough KG b.1871 suc.1892 Secretary of State 1903-5 d.1934
= 1. Consuelo dr. of William Vanderbilt (USA) m.1895 d.1964
2. Gladys dr. of Edward Parker Deacon (USA) m.1921 d.1977

Winston Leonard Spencer-Churchill KG, OM, CH, MP, etc b. at Blenheim 30 Nov 1874 d.24 Jan.1965 buried at Bladon, Oxon
= Clementine dr. of Sir Henry Montagu Hozier KCB. d.12 Dec 1977

Ivor Charles Spencer-Churchill b.14 Oct.1898 d.1956

John Albert Edward William Spencer-Churchill 10th Duke of Marlborough JP b.18 Sept.1897 Suc.1934 DL, etc Mayor of Woodstock 1937-42 Lt Col Life Guards (ret.) d.1972
= 1. Alexandra Mary Cadogan dr. of Viscount Chelsea m.1920 CBE JP Chief Comdt ATS 1938-40 d.1961
2. Laura dr. of Hon. Guy Charteris m.1972

Sarah Consuelo Spencer-Churchill b.17 Dec.1921 m.1) 1943 Edwin F Russell (USNR) 2) 1966 Guy Burgos 3) 1967 Theodorous Roubanis

Caroline Spencer-Churchill b.12 Nov 1923 m.1946 Major Charles Hugo Waterhouse

Rosemary Mildred Spencer-Churchill b.24 July 1929 m.1953 Charles Robert Muir'

Charles George William Colin Spencer-Churchill b.13 July 1940 m.1) 1965 Gillian Spreckels Fuller 2.) 1970 Elizabeth Jane Wyndham

John George Vanderbilt Henry Spencer-Churchill 11th Duke of Marlborough DL JP b.13 April 1926 Suc 1972
= 1. Susan Mary dr. of Michael Hornby m.1951
2. Athina Mary dr. of Stavros G Livanos m.1961
3. Dagmar Rosita dr. of Count Carl Ludwig Douglas m.1972

Charles James Spencer-Churchill Marquis of Blandford b.24 Nov.1955

Henrietta Mary Spencer-Churchill b.1958 m.1980 Nathan Gelber

David Aba Gelber b.1981

Richard Spencer-Churchill b.1973 d.1973

Edward Albert Charles Spencer-Churchill b.1974

Alexandra Elizabeth Mary Spencer-Churchill b.1977

John David Ivor Spencer-Churchill b.1952 d.1955

THE CHURCHILLS OF BLENHEIM

By the same author

BLENHEIM PALACE
SARAH DUCHESS OF MARLBOROUGH
QUEEN ANNE
THE BATTLE OF BLENHEIM

John, eleventh Duke of Marlborough by La Fontaine

David Green

THE CHURCHILLS
OF BLENHEIM

Constable London

First published in Great Britain 1984
by Constable and Company Limited
10 Orange Street, London WC2H 7EG
Copyright © 1984 David Green
ISBN 09 465420 4
Set in Monophoto Ehrhardt 12pt by
Servis Filmsetting Ltd, Manchester
Printed in Great Britain by
BAS Printers Ltd, Over Wallop

For Audrey Russell MVO

HEREDITY

I am the family face;
Flesh perishes, I live on,
Projecting trait and trace
Through time to times anon
And leaping from place to place
Over oblivion.

The years-heired feature that can
In curve and voice and eye
Despise the human span
Of durance – that is I;
The eternal thing in man
That heeds no call to die.

Thomas Hardy (1840–1928)
Moments of Vision

Contents

	Illustrations	8
	Foreword	11
	Introduction	13
	Acknowledgements	20
1	John Churchill first Duke of Marlborough (1650–1722)	23
2	Sarah first Duchess of Marlborough (1660–1744) and her children	50
3	The Grandchildren	73
4	George fourth Duke of Marlborough (1739–1817)	88
5	George fifth Duke of Marlborough (1766–1840) George sixth Duke of Marlborough (1793–1857)	100
6	John Winston seventh Duke of Marlborough (1822–1883) George Charles eighth Duke of Marlborough (1844–1892)	109
7	Charles Richard John ninth Duke of Marlborough (1871–1934)	124
8	John Albert Edward William tenth Duke of Marlborough (1897–1972)	160
9	Interlude in the Sun	204
10	The Winston Churchills at Blenheim	225
	Appendix	245
	Select Bibliography	248
	Index	250

Illustrations

Marlborough in armour by Kneller, at Blenheim Palace
(*His Grace the Duke of Marlborough. Photo: M R Dudley*)   25

Sarah Duchess of Marlborough at cards with Lady Fitzharding by
Kneller (*His Grace the Duke of Marlborough*)   32

Statue of Queen Anne (detail) by Rysbrack in the Long Library at
Blenheim (*His Grace the Duke of Marlborough. Photo: Edwin Smith*)   36

Anne Countess of Sunderland by Kneller
(*His Grace the Duke of Marlborough*)   43

Sir Samuel Garth by Kneller (*National Portrait Gallery*)   45

The Marlborough monument in the chapel at Blenheim Palace
(*His Grace the Duke of Marlborough. Photo: Thomas Photos*)   48

The Ladies Henrietta and Anne Churchill (*The Earl Spencer*)   61

Elizabeth Countess of Bridgwater by Kneller
(*His Grace the Duke of Marlborough*)   62

Lady Henrietta Godolphin by Kneller, at Blenheim
(*His Grace the Duke of Marlborough. Photo: Jeremy Whitaker*)   63

Francis second Earl of Godolphin, attributed to Kneller
(*National Portrait Gallery*)   65

Mary Duchess of Montagu by Kneller
(*His Grace the Duke of Marlborough*)   67

William Congreve (*National Portrait Gallery*)   69

The eighth Duke and his family (*Hugo Vickers*)　　118

Consuelo ninth Duchess of Marlborough with the infant Marquis of
Blandford (*His Grace the Duke of Marlborough*)　　128

Charles ninth Duke of Marlborough with his younger son and the heir,
Lord Blandford (*His Grace the Duke of Marlborough*)　　129

The Royal shooting-party outside High Lodge 1896
(*His Grace the Duke of Marlborough*)　　131

The gatekeeper, with Blenheim spaniels, at Flagstaff Lodge
(*His Grace the Duke of Marlborough*)　　133

Blenheim Palace: The Venus fountain outside the Bow Window Room
(*His Grace the Duke of Marlborough. Photo: M.R. Dudley*)　　136

The Sphinx bearing the features of Gladys Duchess of Marlborough
on the Water Terraces (*His Grace the Duke of Marlborough. Photo: M.R.
Dudley*)　　153

Mary tenth Duchess of Marlborough in Red Cross Uniform
(*His Grace the Duke of Marlborough*)　　166

The author with Richard Dimbleby (*Photo: A.M. Illingworth*)　　179

The tenth Duke of Marlborough on his 70th birthday
(*His Grace the Duke of Marlborough. Photo: Ray Williams*)　　196

Woodstock House, Montego Bay: the Duke at his front door, 1971
(*His Grace the Duke of Marlborough*)　　208

Woodstock House, Montego Bay: Lady Churchill in the swimming-
pool with the tenth Duke of Marlborough, 1965
(*His Grace the Duke of Marlborough*)　　210

Sir Winston Churchill at Blenheim
(*His Grace the Duke of Marlborough*)　　230

Lady Churchill beside the croquet lawn at Blenheim
(*His Grace the Duke of Marlborough*)　　232

Mary Duchess of Marlborough at cards in her sitting room at
Blenheim with Sir Winston Churchill
(*His Grace the Duke of Marlborough*)　　233

The Freedom of Woodstock: the Winston Churchills with Mary tenth
Duchess of Marlborough (*Photo: Westmoreland Studios*)　　234

At the Temple of Diana: the Duke of Marlborough and David Green
assist Lady Churchill to her car (*Photo: Oxford Mail and Times*)   241

Hanborough station, dressed overall for the funeral of Sir Winston
Churchill (*Photo: Norman Vincent*)   243

IN COLOUR
John, eleventh Duke of Marlborough by La Fontaine
(*Jeremy Whitaker*)   *frontispiece*

The first Duke of Marlborough and his family by Closterman   *facing page*
(*His Grace the Duke of Marlborough*)   64

Lady Diana Spencer, fourth Duchess of Bedford attributed to Thomas
Hudson
(*The Marquess of Tavistock, and the Trustees of the Bedford Estates*)   65

The fourth Duke of Marlborough and his family by Reynolds
(*His Grace the Duke of Marlborough*)   96

The ninth Duke of Marlborough and his family by Sargent
(*His Grace the Duke of Marlborough*)   97

The Venus Statue in the Italian Garden at Blenheim
(*The Alden Press*)   176

The Water Terraces at Blenheim   *between pages*
(*The Alden Press*)   176/177

Mary, tenth Duchess of Marlborough   *facing page*
(*His Grace the Duke of Marlborough*)   177

Foreword

by his Grace the eleventh Duke of Marlborough

'I can't deny but that there is a possibility of the world's being destroyed, but for God's sake, my dear, don't afflict yourself for possibilities.'*

Faith in the future – a confidence that in some civilised form the world will continue – has always been an intrinsic part of man's make-up and belief. Without it there would be no sense at all in living and planning.

At Blenheim we have seen this in men's minds and actions when Marlborough and Vanbrugh rose to the challenge of creating a park and a palace where the site was then a marshy chasm with only a ruined manor-house overlooking it. And we see this again when the fourth Duke and Capability Brown re-landscaped the park and made the lake. In fact this has happened again and again. In 1902 my grandfather replanted a two-mile avenue with elms because those planted by Queen Anne's gardener in 1710 had naturally died. But thanks to Dutch elm-disease I have had to replant yet again with lime trees . . . and so it goes on in the park; while in the palace the work of restoration (and its cost) has in the past thirty years been colossal – and it continues today. Our climate sees to it that the toughest stone available sooner or later begins to crumble and has to be renewed.

There's a text we all of us know – 'Ye shall hear of war and rumours of war; see that ye be not troubled' – and how sensible that is. In the meantime

*Charles third Duke of Marlborough to his wife Elizabeth (*c.* 1750)

[11]

we pay heavily for the defence of our own country, while responding to every kind of urgent appeal from those in distress at home and abroad.

Sir Winston Churchill, writing of Blenheim where he was born, said that Marlborough 'sought a physical monument which would certainly stand, if only as a ruin, for thousands of years'. As Blenheim's owner I must confess that the idea of trying to live in a ruin has little appeal for me. On the other hand, if the worst came to the worst, I'm not sure that we couldn't put up some pretty tough resistance from the undercroft which runs for half a mile or so beneath this house.

But to be serious, rural estates of this nature will only survive if firm business principles are applied throughout. I have a traditional management structure, with departments or cost centres, each budgeted separately. We use a computer for the farm records; and throughout the estate, including the Palace, the departmental results are monitored against budget predictions. This enables me to note any major variations and to react accordingly before any disastrous situation arises.

My desire is for Blenheim to be in a healthy financial state – but I can do this (particularly the major tasks of the palace and park restorations) only by applying the latest twentieth-century management principles to the eighteenth-century work of Vanbrugh and of Brown.

Without the willing co-operation of my wife, my staff and the visiting public, my task of maintaining Blenheim as Marlborough and his architects planned it would be quite impossible. I am lucky indeed to be able to count upon them.

MARLBOROUGH

Introduction

As with the rest of us (if we knew as much of our own predecessors as we now know of theirs), the Churchills and Spencer-Churchills have in the past been a mixed bunch, some outstandingly brilliant, some fashionably rakish, some – not many – just plain virtuous and dull.

Sarah Jennings the first Duchess was strong and fluent enough to steal any stage, even in competition with her phenomenally patient and heroic husband; and so of course could the late Sir Winston Churchill, whose monopoly of any conversation (he counted upon playing Hamlet and everyone else) might have been insufferable had it not been for the originality of his language which poured from him like smoke from his cigars but with far more meaning.

It can indeed be hard on a family when its first astonishingly brilliant member, John Churchill, becomes, like his successor Sir Winston, an international hero; because that standard is superhuman and so, for men of goodwill but not of genius, must prove one all but impossible to emulate.

Even so, for that one fantastic house called Blenheim to have produced in nine generations two saviours of the civilised world is not, as the most cynical will admit, bad going. Between the two we have of course extremes, from Henrietta Godolphin, second Duchess in her own right, who in her day raised eyebrows, to the stern and self-righteous seventh Duke, who thought it of far more consequence to prevent a widower's marrying his dead wife's sister, than to preserve most of the Sunderland Library he had inherited, and was, quite needlessly as time proved, anxious to sell. And among them too we find at least one man typical of the Spencers' devotion to culture: George Spencer, who succeeded to the dukedom in 1758 and died in 1817. He it was who with Brown was responsible for the lake as we know it. But the ninth Duke too, dedicated as he was to Blenheim's setting, comes into that picture.

As for the sixth Duke, one can but admire his discretion – married three times though he was – in directing that all his papers, at his death, should be destroyed. What, one mischievously wonders, had he to hide?

Approaching our own time we find healthy infusions of foreign blood – from America, from Sweden – which help to revitalise the strain and reverse any trend there may have been towards staleness and apathy.

In the tenth Duke's time, for the switch to personal reminiscence, after the last war, I make no apology except to his own family, where feelings may still be tender since his death in 1972. I knew him for twenty-five years and believe that those who got to know him as well as I did will agree that he took a great deal of knowing.

Dukes are, thanks to their status, constantly plagued by the serious and the less serious – by scholars, by historians, by the lunatic-fringe – and there must have been times when the tenth Duke of Marlborough became bored beyond endurance by my stream of questions about Blenheim and its history. Nature had not endowed him with the patience and diplomacy of the first Duke; but I can vouch for his tolerance and generosity in my own case when I had been asked to write a series of books (including his own memoirs) which involved a great many more or less tedious sessions between the two of us at Blenheim and abroad.

Not everyone found him as entertaining as I did; but I laughed with him rather than at him, and I hope I have made that clear in this book.

In his long last illness he showed extraordinary courage; but then courage seemed second nature to him. The one thing I think he feared was showing emotion, so that at times even a show of gratitude was smothered rather than that he should appear sentimental. In some of his keenest interests I could take no share: hunting, for example, and croquet; but excepting that one hilarious croquet-game in Jamaica, he never forced such things upon me. As with most of us, he had strong aversions: he hated to be stared at – a shyness which at Blenheim, wide open to public gaze, was for him unfortunate. He made a private garden to hide in and found some solace there, calling it in jest his mausoleum; though he decided it would be unfair on his family to insist upon being buried there.

It has been said that a man is best known to his valet; and if that be so, as it well may be, it says much for the tenth Duke that when he died I never saw anyone more upset than that retainer of his who, after long service, must have known him better than anyone else.

With his memoirs there were obstacles which proved insurmountable. Would he state his father's case, as he knew it, in answer to all his mother had written in *The Glitter and the Gold*? No, he would not. ('That, I think,' said the present Duchess, 'was out of loyalty to his mother.') But more serious, from the reader's point of view, was his extreme caution which, admirable though it was, looked like making a much duller book than he and his public deserved. I dreaded the day when a publisher might have to tell him so; but at his death barely half the manuscript had been written.

When I first saw Blenheim and was asked by *Country Life* to write a book on it, I found it, as a gargantuan building set in a two-thousand-acre park, so overwhelming that I decided then and there to make no attempt to write about its owners, with the exception of the first Duke and Duchess for whom it was built. As time went on however I was tempted to devote another full-length book to that first Duchess who, as she said, had herself been a kind of author; and that of course led to more books, including guidebooks, all rooted in Blenheim.

Even then it was never my intention to climb as it were to the topmost branch of the family tree. With the *Battle of Blenheim*, which Collins persuaded me to write in 1974, I had, as I thought, made 'positively my last appearance'. Yet how was I to resist an invitation to write for the last time about Blenheim, even as a background for the Churchills, when as Gerald Horne had said, 'Blenheim was our world'? It was irresistible.

Above the proscenium of the fourth Duke's private theatre ran the legend: 'Laugh where you may, be candid where you can'. I hope sincerely that in this book about people I have not been candid enough to offend anyone; and that goes above all for the kind and distinguished family now living at Blenheim or closely connected with it. Before agreeing to write the book I of course approached the present Duke and outlined my hopeful intentions; to which he was good enough to make no objection. On the contrary, as with his parents, I have met with nothing but interested and helpful co-operation from himself and from the Duchess, for which I am more than grateful.

'Many things are impossible to believe', wrote Hardy, 'but nothing is too impossible to have happened'. In the history of the Churchills one is twice reminded of this: when in Sarah's time her good turn to Abigail (Cinderella) recoils on her at the cost of Queen Anne's favour; and again when, some one-and-a-half centuries later, Winston Churchill, as though by miraculous chance, happens to be born at Blenheim Palace.

I am not likely to forget the kindness of the tenth Duke and Duchess in asking us to meet the Winston Churchills at Blenheim; nor that of their successors in inviting me to join them when Lady Churchill unveiled a plaque in the Temple of Diana (where Winston had proposed), with Lady Soames. Those were indeed red-letter days, and I have tried to describe them.

Sir Winston, heir-apparent to the Marlborough dukedom for a number of years, although anything but the conventional type of aristocrat, might at times have seemed to hold an ambivalent attitude towards Blenheim. As Chancellor of the Exchequer he did not hesitate to impose heavy taxation upon the owners of such houses. Yet when he was given the Freedom of Woodstock he said of Blenheim: 'This great house is one of the precious links which join us to our famous past, which is also the history of the English-speaking peoples, on whose unity the freedom of the free world depends. I am proud to have been born at Blenheim, and to be an Honorary Freeman of Woodstock.'

For *The Churchills of Blenheim* I have, with authors' and publishers' consent, shamelessly quoted from the two-volume edition of Sir Winston's *Marlborough* (Harrap, 1947), which the author was generous enough to give me; as I have also from Dr A.L. Rowse's invaluable books on *The Early Churchills* and *The Later Churchills* (Penguin, 1969 and 1971); from Consuelo Balsan's *The Glitter and the Gold* (Harpers, 1952); and from Hugo Vickers' *Gladys Duchess of Marlborough* (Weidenfeld & Nicolson, 1979); and of course from many another to whom in due course I hope to make some acknowledgement.

I was lucky indeed to have access to the Blenheim manuscripts before they were transferred to the British Library, where of course they are properly cared for and invigilated: a job which calls for a fully qualified and full-time staff. I must own that in the tenth Duke's time, while I was studying ninety-one drawers labelled 'Sarah Duchess of Marlborough', it came as an unpleasant shock when his agent, my friend Bill Murdock, discovered that all the Sunderland Papers, concerned with our American colonies in the reign of Anne, were missing. Naturally the police were called in and a number of people (including an earl) questioned. It was not until 1983 that, with the help of the Curator of Manuscripts at the British Library and his counterpart at Sothebys, it was discovered that the ninth Duke of Marlborough had had those manuscripts auctioned in 1920.

That, as time proved, was needless enough; and the sales sanctioned by the seventh and eighth Dukes were nothing less than deplorable. 'However,' as I heard Sir Winston at Blenheim reassure the tenth Duke, 'you still have a nice lot left.' And that, with its tapestries and staterooms (the Red Drawing-room, for example, with the great Sargent and the still greater Reynolds), the incomparable grounds and all the relics of Sir Winston himself, Blenheim undoubtedly has. And as for Bladon . . . 'You know', I remember saying to the tenth Duke, 'one dead lion can sometimes be worth more than a pride of live ones'. There was a pause, and then: 'Did I say that?' 'No, but you may say you did if you like.' But he was far too straightforward for such subterfuge; although there were times when what he called trivial detail I thought very funny indeed. A sense of humour, as all of us know, can be a tricky thing. To take but one example, I thought Vanbrugh's *Relapse*, superbly acted in the Long Library in 1964, one of the most uproariously funny plays I had ever enjoyed; but a few were shocked by Vanbrugh's bawdy. The Duke, returning from America, said,

[17]

'I hear I missed something. I might have enjoyed it.' I am quite certain he would.

Of one thing he was determined and that was not to turn Blenheim Park into a fun fair, nor indeed into anything out of character; and in that of course I was entirely with him. Without confessing it he had a deep-rooted love of his home and wanted no change in it. This had but one drawback and that was that urgent restoration, of which he had small knowledge, had to be left to his heir.

Looking up at Marlborough's statue, skyed atop the Column of Victory, one is reminded of Addison's line (from *The Campaign*): 'rides in the whirlwind and directs the storm'; itself echoed by Cowper in his great hymn:

God moves in a mysterious way
His wonders to perform;
He plants his footsteps in the sea
And rides upon the storm.

At Blenheim there are bound to be mysteries, some of which may never be solved; and perhaps not the least of them is the way, year after year, the public besieges it to the tune of more than 300,000 visitors. Yet perhaps that is not quite such a mystery after all, for Blenheim has every kind of appeal from its lakeside setting and its water-terraces to its challenging architecture ('emphatic as an oath', as someone called it), its treasures, its history . . . And how long may this continue? That is a mystery indeed and one for optimists to solve. As a nation – it happened in Marlborough's time and has been repeated in our own – we have a lamentable habit of winning a war and losing the peace, of relinquishing carelessly our greatest treasures. But emphatically it will be no fault of its owners if this should ever happen to Blenheim. No one felt this more keenly than the ninth Duke when he wrote:

Blenheim is the most splendid relic of the age of Anne, and there is no building in Europe, except Versailles, which so perfectly preserves its original atmosphere . . . It may be that the time will come when

[18]

democracy, in the nation's name, will try to recall the nation's gift. Meanwhile, on behalf of the family to whom this trust was committed, I offer my tribute of gratitude to the memory of the Queen by whose hand it was bestowed.

Acknowledgements

I have already referred to the invaluable help and encouragement I have had from the present owners of Blenheim, who have most kindly allowed me to reproduce photographs not only of their family portraits but of prints from their private albums. I hope too that in the second part of this book I have made it clear how tremendously indebted I was, in their lifetime, to the tenth Duke and Duchess; and since to their eldest daughter Lady Sarah, now living in Jamaica, where she and the dowager Duchess Laura were most helpful with the tenth Duke's memoirs, and with reminiscences of his mother, née Consuelo Vanderbilt, whose *The Glitter and the Gold* has, for a would-be historian, proved a goldmine.

The Marlborough Papers at Althorp were referred to by kind permission of the late Earl Spencer, who agreed also to my reproducing his Kneller portraits.

I am grateful to Lady Soames for allowing me to quote her mother's priceless story about the beetle in Blenheim's Temple of Diana; and to Sir Sacheverell Sitwell for similar favours in connection with the ninth Duke's water-terraces.

In the sad case of the ninth Duke's second wife, Gladys Deacon, no one could have been more generous than her biographer, Hugo Vickers, who after research in depth has put all his published and unpublished material at my disposal.

As to my own researches, I was lucky enough to have kept all my index cards and notebooks from the years I spent as archivist at Blenheim when the manuscripts were there; and these included notes made at the Bodleian Library, the British Museum (now the British Library, where Mr Hudson has been most helpful), and the Public Record Office where, in the face of total bewilderment and frustration, Noel Blakiston saved my reason.

At Blenheim I have had the assistance of the Duke's agents (notably Bill Murdock and now Paul Hutton, and their secretary Liz Thomas); from the retired Chief Guide Jock Illingworth, and from the present Administrator Paul Duffie and his deputies, Bill Parncutt and Ray Huggins; not forgetting Mrs Moore, also retired; Harold Fawcus, the Education Officer and the private secretaries.

But indeed my friends and helpers at Blenheim have formed such a multitude — butlers, chauffeurs, keepers, gardeners, and so on — that I cannot hope to name them all. Freddie Brammall, valet and chauffeur, to whom the tenth Duke meant so much, died a few months ago. For myself I can only say that he made the Duke's house in Jamaica a happy place which, thanks to his master's illness, must have been mournful without him.

And then how to begin or end with my debts to authors and publishers? Without the scholarship and research of Dr A.L. Rowse, author of *The Early Churchills* and *The Later Churchills*, this book would have been twice as laborious for me and probably more tedious for the reader. I am indeed grateful to him and to his publishers for letting me quote from his works. To the publishers (Harrap) of Sir Winston Churchill's definitive biography of his ancestor the first Duke of Marlborough, and to Sir Winston's executors, I am again more than grateful for allowing me to quote from that incomparable work.

Audrey Russell, the best commentator England has yet produced, I met for the first time at Blenheim twenty years ago. Since when I have had the benefit of her wisdom and advice, her encouragement and interest in every book I have written.

It only remains for me to thank my publishers and my literary agent, Richard Simon, which I most warmly do.

[21]

The Churchills, from Duchess Sarah to Sir Winston, with possibly two exceptions (the sixth and seventh Dukes), have never been dull; and if I have made them so, then I am entirely to blame.

D.B.G.

John Churchill first Duke of Marlborough
———— 1650–1722 ————

'I have determined', wrote Sarah first Duchess of Marlborough, 'to give the materials in my possession to the gentlemen that are to write the Duke of Marlborough's history. (They are Mr Glover and Mr Mallet). For it will take a great deal of time only to sort the papers and read them over . . . I remember to have read somewhere a great author that I would have imitated . . . beginning in the same style: "I write the history of the Duke of Marlborough"; and I would have it throughout in that manner, for it will require no flourishes to set it off, but short plain facts . . . I would have no thing in it but what is the real truth . . .' None of it was to be in verse; and it was to begin in 1688 when James II fled to France, leaving our throne vacant until his daughter Mary (the future Queen Anne's sister) ascended it to reign jointly with her Dutch husband William III.

Sarah makes it sound simple; yet Glover withdrew before the book had been begun, while of his colleague, Dr Johnson was to write: 'Mallet, I believe, never wrote a single line of his projected life of the Duke of Marlborough. He groped for materials and thought of it till he had exhausted his mind.' In August 1745 Mallet did in fact send to Marlborough House for 'the books and papers relating to the Duke of Marlborough's life'; but one feels for the amateur writer called upon to

[23]

disentangle the intricate complications of Marlborough's military career; and, still more difficult, to penetrate the motives of a mind belonging to one who had deliberately set out to remain forever an enigma, defying posterity to solve a score of problems, some of which, once clarified, might have set his reputation on an even higher pedestal than that now graced by his statue on the Column of Victory in the park at Blenheim.

Greatness and goodness here at once are seen
Sweetly enthroned in his majestic mien:
How mild, yet awful, piercing, yet serene!

Thus Lediard (1736) upon the portrait of Marlborough reproduced as the frontispiece to the first of those innumerable biographies. And yet the closest study of Marlborough's portraits leaves us with a mask, majestic, serene, impassive and impenetrable. From high forehead to chin the features are unexceptionable and well balanced. The mind keeps its secrets.

Very well, by their fruits ye shall know them; and the fruits of his victories – the conquest of France, the opening of Europe's gates to England – we know well enough; not to speak at this stage of his posterity, which in our time has produced a second saviour of the free world, and a highly popular Princess of Wales!

'Of the making of many books there is no end', and here is yet another; but at least it is not a thousandth attempt to write a biography of the first Duke of Marlborough. That gargantuan task has for all time been determined, dared and done by his great descendant Sir Winston Churchill who, as it might seem almost by chance, was born at Blenheim in the house Marlborough himself had commissioned, and is buried in that village churchyard which lies within sight of it.

To the present writer, having read and re-read those volumes, which he gave me, some half-dozen times, it seems astonishing that writers of far less calibre as historians than Sir Winston continue to plod in that titan's footsteps and still find publishers to print the same now familiar material and readers prepared doggedly to wade through it.

No, the title of this book is *The Churchills of Blenheim* (eleven dukes and

Marlborough in armour: Kneller's portrait at Blenheim Palace

not a few duchesses and their families), with 'Blenheim' standing for the palace (originally called a castle); not for the battle, which has a book to itself; not for the wars of the Spanish succession (a labyrinth far more complex and less interesting than the Fair Rosamond's); not for speeches in the Lords as to whether or not it was right for Victorian widowers to marry their dead wife's sister; but about those who, for eleven generations or nearly, have spent part or much of their time at Blenheim. Visitors too of course must play some part, whether they be famous – Voltaire and Pope, Winston and the Windsors – or, like oneself, one of a large and curious crowd.

It would be hypocrisy to apologise to the shade of that formidable Duchess Sarah for not beginning with the bloodless revolution of 1688; although from her point of view it would mean dodging such awkward times as when John Churchill, her husband-to-be, was the lover of Barbara Villiers (later Lady Castlemaine, later Duchess of Cleveland). Nor did Sarah care for the fact that John's sister Arabella had by James II (then Duke of York) what she (Sarah) called 'a train of bastards', which included the Duke of Berwick. Even more embarrassing perhaps had been Churchill's desertion of James II for William III; but that, as Sarah herself explained, had been 'with great regret and with hazard to himself; and if he had been like the patriots of present times', she added later, 'he might have been all that an ambitious man could have hoped for by assisting King James to settle Popery in England'.

But 'short plain facts'? Better perhaps to skim over them; although in my youth every schoolboy knew them only too well, and how boring they could be.

One small point sometimes forgotten is that those we think typical of the reign of Anne were in fact born in the seventeenth century: John Churchill plumb in the middle of it. He was baptised on the 26th of May (in the cusp of Gemini and Taurus), though he may have been born some days earlier. Sarah, a typical Gemini if ever there was one, was born ten years later, on May 29th, and not baptised until nearly a month after that. Princess Anne (Queen in 1702) was junior to Sarah by five years, and to her own sister Mary by three. Their father was James II, then Duke of York, their mother

Anne Hyde.

John Churchill, born at Ashe in Devon in the year after Charles I's execution, was the son of Sir Winston Churchill who had married Elizabeth Drake, daughter of Sir John Ashe. John Churchill was the second son of eleven children, only four of whom survived. (It was an age when smallpox was responsible for the deaths of an appalling number of infants and not a few adults.) His brothers, Admiral George Churchill and General Charles Churchill, were of relatively small historical importance and since neither of them knew Blenheim they must play minor parts in this book.

Sir Winston, John Churchill's father, was obsessed with genealogy, one of the more enervating topics known to man. Sarah's comment is typical: 'This history (Lediard's) takes a great deal of pains to make the Duke of Marlborough's extraction very ancient. That may be true for aught I know; but it is no matter whether it be true or not, in my opinion, for I value nobody for another's merit'. The one thing the first Sir Winston never tells us is why he chose Spanish for his motto: Fiel Pero Desdichado (Faithful but unfortunate); with an uprooted oak for his crest. The oak is obvious: like many another loyal cavalier he had lost a fortune in the royal cause; but no link with Spain has as yet been established. He has left on record that after Charles I's execution he had no other weapon than his pen; and indeed, though his book on genealogy is as a whole unreadable, his paragraph on the King's execution is worthy of his namesake and descendant at his best:

Here seemed to be the *consummatum est* of all the happiness of this kingdom, as well as of the life of the King. For upon his death the veil of the Temple was rent and the Church overthrown. An universal darkness overspread the state, which lasted not for twelve hours only but for twelve years. The two great luminaries of law and gospel were put out. Such as could not write supplied the place of judges, such as could not read of bishops. Peace was maintained by war, licentiousness by fasting and prayer. The commonalty lost their property, the gentry their liberty, the nobility their honour, the clergy their authority and reverence. The stream of government ran down in new–cut channels whose waters were always shallow and troubled.

[27]

In or about 1664, when the first Winston received his knighthood, his son John attended St Paul's School in London where he was, according to Sarah, whipped for not reading his book. Even his descendant, Sir Winston Churchill, with his team of experts, was unable to trace anything more of Marlborough's early life save that he lived for nine years in his grandmother's house and, after leaving St Paul's, joined the army. He then became page to the Duke of York (King James II to-be), his sister Arabella having already for some time been comfortably installed as James's mistress.

In fact the plot becomes interesting only when the Sir Winston we knew conjures his readers to 'brace themselves' for the profoundly shocking affair between John Churchill and Barbara Villiers, one of the more notorious of Charles II's women, which resulted in the birth of a daughter, who is said to have been sent to a convent. This slip, pleads John's champion, must be blamed on those 'compulsions which leap flaming from the crucible of life itself'. Sarah of course would have liked this suppressed, but in Charles's Court everyone knew about it and thought of it, if at all, as fashionable, normal and natural. If the King could make light of it, so could they. The one shocking corollary was that the strumpet gave her lover considerable sums of money, which he carefully invested.

Sarah however had good reason to take the liaison more seriously, for John Churchill had fallen in love with her – and there can be no doubt but that she was radiantly attractive – and pursued her with note after note, not one of them mentioning marriage. His parents had what they considered a far better match in mind; while Sarah's mother Mrs Jennings, who looked like a witch, had taught Sarah the value of that stratagem now vulgarly known as playing hard-to-get, a lesson she had learned so well that her own cold replies sound as loveless as laundry-bills. Later she was to describe herself as 'of the simple sex', but it is impossible to imagine that after, say, the age of six she was ever anything of the kind. Her early experiences at Court, where she too and her elder sister (later to be married to an Irish Roman Catholic the Duke of Tyrconnel) had become installed in the Duke of York's household, had taught her to be elusive and calculating. Even the date of her marriage to John Churchill, when at last it came about, was kept secret. It is thought to have been some time in the winter of 1677–8. In October 1679 Sarah gave birth to a daughter Harriet, in John's Jermyn Street apartments where they were then living, but she died in infancy. As time went on she was to have two sons and four daughters . . . but that may be kept for the next chapter.

In Sarah's defence it needs to be stressed that for some years the young married couple had to live in Devon with John's mother, Elizabeth Drake, who was a Roundhead of the most virulent type. This was a lasting trial for them both and at one stage John had to remind his wife, in a loyal attempt to excuse the jealous tantrums of a maddening mother-in-law, 'After all, she is my mother'.

The switch from incompetent James to frigid William and Mary, important though it was to the Churchills and to the nation, may for present purposes be passed over, since the revolution happened long before Blenheim was heard of. The population then numbered less than six millions, most of them faced with dull diets, short lives and with little if any influence on their means of subsistence or government. Our country, as now (though nominally democratic), was run by a handful of people; but at least it was not overpopulated, poisoned by insecticides and threatened with nuclear war. As for medicine, the only painkiller for those who could afford it was laudanum; and for education? For girls it was not favoured; while for boys, if their parents were Persons of Quality, they might go to Eton and then to Oxford or Cambridge, before embarking upon the Grand Tour of the Continent; and this most of the later eighteenth-century Churchills did. Culture, as now, was for the few. The mob were useful as hewers of wood and drawers of water, while weeders, usually women, could be hired for fourpence a day.

After Monmouth's Rebellion James II had been so brutally vindictive and cruel (he had supported Judge Jeffreys), and so inadequate and tactless as a king, that few pitied him in his flight to Louis XIV. There was far more sympathy for his second queen, Mary of Modena, who when the marriage had been arranged, after the death of Anne Hyde, was fifteen and had never heard of England nor of her chosen bridegroom the Duke of York. She preceded him into exile, drifting down the Thames with her baby the

Pretender [sic], who had given rise to one of the least credible myths in history, that of the 'supposititious prince' smuggled into the royal bed in a warming-pan. At least, let us flatter ourselves, we are a little less credulous than that.

On John Churchill's account a thing that must not be regarded too lightly was his religion. More than once he was heard to vow that should James try to change it, he would leave him to stay Protestant. In these cynical days this may sound specious; yet it has to be owned not only that his biographer and descendant make a very strong case for his sincerity, but in Marlborough's letters and indeed in his whole life, even on his deathbed, he appears to have been genuinely devout. Sarah was agnostic ('I think 'tis unnatural', she wrote, 'for anybody to have so monstrous a notion as that there is no God'), but that again is another story, which has little to do with Blenheim.

At first, on King William's accession, John Churchill appeared to be in royal favour. William himself was so distressingly unamiable – cold, plain, bellicose, asthmatical – it was hard for a good Englishman to know whether he was friend or foe. However, in Churchill's case, trimmer though he might be, he had clearly backed the winning side. Moreover he now added to this by helping to persuade the Princess Anne that, should her sister Mary predecease her detestable husband, he should continue to reign as king for his lifetime, although Anne in fact had the prior claim. For all of which even William realised that Churchill should be rewarded; and so it was that his rank of Lieutenant-Colonel was confirmed and, at the coronation in April, he was made an earl. Churchill chose the title of Earl of Marlborough because of a family connection with James Ley, first Earl of Marlborough. The title had become extinct and he now decided to revive it.

Even so, contemporaries may not have been altogether surprised when, four years later, William dismissed the soldier he had made an earl and, without trial or reason, had him thrown into the Tower. For this sudden loss of favour the generally accepted reason is that William knew of Marlborough's correspondence with the deposed King in Paris and that he had even pleaded for a pardon not only on his own behalf but on that of James's treacherous daughter the Princess Anne. Interesting if true. Sir Winston of course leaps to the barricades and, all the way through – for there are volumes of seemingly damning evidence in the Stuart Papers and in Hanover – insists that Marlborough was crafty enough to play a double game and to fool the Stuarts for two reasons: first, just in case the Pretender or his son might one day claim his rightful throne, and secondly, to coax more information out of the Jacobites than he was prepared to give. After all, the Duke of Berwick, now in Louis XIV's army, was his nephew; and the Duchess of Tyrconnel, exiled as a Roman Catholic, was Sarah's sister. What could be more natural than that they should correspond?

However, there were other reasons. William had his Dutch favourites and too obviously preferred men to women. This to Marlborough was of no consequence; but when Dutch officers were promoted over the heads of far more deserving Englishmen, this was more than he could stand without protest. Who knows? One guffaw in an officers' mess may have cost him much. Moreover, William and Mary had a most reliable spy in Sarah's camp in the plump person of Lady Fitzharding, sister of Elizabeth Villiers, the titular mistress of King William. At Blenheim there is an excellent Kneller of Sarah at cards with Lady Fitzharding, who is showing us, but not Sarah, the nine of diamonds. In the game known as Pope Joan this was the vital card, representing His Holiness; so that it might possibly refer to the suspected collusion of the Marlboroughs with the Roman Catholic Jacobites.

In another much larger painting, between the Great Hall and Sir Winston's birthroom, Closterman shows the whole Marlborough family – Blandford, Henrietta, Anne, Elizabeth and the baby Mary, with Sarah, wearing a sour expression, in the middle; but Marlborough himself, on the left, is half hidden by a curtain; his portrait is said to have been added later because during the family sittings he was still in the Tower. As for Sarah, she was so disgusted with her own representation, she vowed she would have a flowerpot painted in instead. The only one missing is the baby Charles, who had died at the age of two. In Kneller's 'mantilla' portrait of Sarah, in the Green Drawing-room, she is thought to be in mourning for him.

Heartless though William was, he could not by the laws of his adopted country keep Marlborough in the Tower indefinitely, without trial; and

Kneller: Sarah Duchess of Marlborough at cards with Lady Fitzharding

[32]

knowing this, Sarah as she tells us kissed the Act of Habeas Corpus. There were plots of course and no paucity of false witnesses. Marlborough as always remained calm. 'I am certain they have nothing against him', Anne assured Sarah, 'but methinks it is a dismal thing to have one's friends sent to that place.' After six weeks it was proved that there was absolutely no case against him and he was released.

As a regular rule Sarah insisted that her letters to her husband be destroyed, but Marlborough's biographer suggests that it was while he was in the Tower that he received from his wife the one moving love-letter of hers that has survived: 'Wherever you are whilst I have life my soul shall follow you, my ever dear Lord Marl, and wherever I am I shall only kill the time and wish for the night that I may sleep and hope the next day to hear from you.'

Since the times of the Tudors, few kings had been slower to pardon offence than William. For six years Marlborough was banned from office and from favour. But change came at last with the death of Queen Mary, from smallpox, in 1694. William had treated her wretchedly, but at her deathbed he collapsed and became distracted.

The whole scene then changed. Mary had had no child; so that now her sister Anne, ignoring her exiled father and brother, was in direct line to the throne. Moreover Anne had a pathetic son (he had water on the brain), known as the Duke of Gloucester, who must, if spared, succeed her. With the luckless Anne, hatchets had now to be buried. Quarrels were patched up and in the summer of 1698 Churchill was appointed Gloucester's 'governor' (guardian), while for his spiritual care and education the nine-year-old was put into the hands of Bishop Burnet. This latter appointment was misguided, since although Burnet was as a churchman sound enough and by no means unintelligent or unkind, he believed in cramming a child with mountains of history and politics, as well as with 'ghostly advice', which must surely have helped to addle his already waterlogged brain.

Marlborough, for his part, made it his duty to induct the boy into the tactics and manoeuvres of military art, lessons which were to prove useful in Gloucester's games with Churchill's only surviving son John, now twelve; although by 1703, one year after Anne's accession, both playmates were dead.

[33]

On March 24th, 1698 the Marlboroughs' eldest daughter Henrietta married the Earl of Godolphin's son Francis. He was twenty, she was eighteen. Sidney Godolphin, Henrietta's father-in-law, was the Marlboroughs' closest friend and remained so for life; but he was never to occupy the suite reserved for him on Blenheim's garden front. The Godolphin Rooms have been closed and shuttered since his death in 1712, their only occupant his portrait, as Lord Treasurer. When he died Sarah wrote of him in her Bible: 'The best man that ever lived'.

As so often happens with the great and the famous, the son Francis was a nonentity: honest, unexceptionable and dull. In startling contrast Henrietta was almost as self-willed and eccentric as her mother; but since she was, on Marlborough's death in 1722, to become second Duchess of Marlborough in her own right, it will be best to deal with her and her sisters in another chapter. In the history of Blenheim, which she disliked as much as her mother did, she plays no part; but as we shall see, she was interesting in herself.

In January 1700 Marlborough's second daughter Anne married Charles Spencer, who was to become the third Earl of Sunderland. Of their sons Charles was one day to be third Duke of Marlborough and the owner of Blenheim, while his brother John kept Althorp, the family home in Northamptonshire. The present Earl Spencer is his direct descendant.

But for Princess Anne, who had offered the brides £10,000 each (Sarah graciously accepted half), 1700 was a year of grief, for on July 30th her only surviving child the Duke of Gloucester died swiftly of smallpox. Anne's unenviable record of no less than seventeen still-births, infant deaths and miscarriages (she even miscarried twins) has puzzled doctors ever since she died in 1714. At one time it was thought that she must have inherited syphilis from her father who, it was said, 'went the rounds of the Maids of Honour'; but modern medicine finds against this theory, the pattern fails to fit. All that need be said is that her sufferings from these and other causes, including the want of an heir, must to that extent excuse her from some of her shabbier actions; although as Sir Winston found, she was 'not averse to lying her way out of a tight corner, nor to putting on a convincing act when it suited her'. Abigail Masham, when Anne was dying, had the grace to say,

'This poor lady deserves pity'.

When in 1702, after his horse Sorrel had stumbled on a molehill in Bushy Park and thrown him, King William died, one might have thought that that sunshine day to which Anne and her intimate friends, the Marlboroughs and Godolphin, had at last arrived; and indeed she made a brave show of her coronation, even though she had to be carried to it. In soft tones that pleased all hearers she assured the Lords that her heart was entirely English; and it soon became obvious that nothing pleased her more than to reward those she loved and trusted with every honour a queen could think of. Marlborough she created a duke, Sidney Godolphin Lord Treasurer, while her special favourite Sarah was made Groom of the Stole, Mistress of the Robes and Keeper of the Privy Purse; her two elder daughters, Henrietta and Anne, being Ladies of the Bedchamber.

Naturally the new duke became Captain-General and Master of the Ordnance. Could there be any limit to the Queen's bounty? True, there was some slight check from Parliament when she ordered £5,000 a year 'out of the Post Office' to help support the dukedom, but even that was later to be allowed.

As Sir Winston has written,* 'Anne was devoted to England and to the English people; and in spite of poor health she was as tough on her throne as Marlborough was on the battlefield . . . Her intellect was limited, but her faith, her conscience, her principles and her prejudices were for ten years a factor in the life of England and in the fortunes of Europe, which held its own with the growing power of Parliament and the victories of Marlborough.' Her chief interests were the Church, Marlborough 'her faithful servant, guide and champion, and Sarah, her dear bosom friend from childhood onward. Besides these she cared intensely about the glory of England, which mattered a great deal, and about her husband, Prince George of Denmark, who mattered very little except to her.'

In Sir Winston's view Anne's consort was 'a good, brave, soldierly simpleton'. It was not easy to keep Anne from showering every kind of princely post and honour upon him too. He was typical of the person of

* *Marlborough, His Life and Times,* volume I, pp. 504-5

[35]

Rysbrack's statue of Queen Anne (detail), in the Long Library at Blenheim

[36]

importance (a few of them occur in every age including our own) who for the nation's sake needed to be shunted into some sinecure where he could do only a modicum of harm. It was one of Marlborough's few mistakes to let him share with his own brother George the management of the Admiralty. Admiral George Churchill could, he felt sure, be counted on to keep his royal namesake on the right lines. Slight hope! Both Georges took to the bottle and, between toasts to each other, to the Queen, to England . . . they 'sent languid orders', or so they were eventually accused, to British captains, ordering them to stop those bloody pirates from plundering our bloody ships at *once*. In such cases a surprisingly large amount of scandal can and always has been brushed under the carpet; but inevitably, as our shipping losses grew and rumour persisted, questions were asked in Parliament and they were questions which embarrassed the Queen. It was not until 1708 that Marlborough and Providence stepped in. Marlborough curtly told his brother to retire (he did and kept caged birds at Windsor); while Prince George, so dear to Anne though so worthless to England, obligingly died.

But that is racing ahead. We have yet to fight the battle of Blenheim in 1704; but there again, as with Marlborough, Sarah and Anne, they all have books to themselves; and we have military experts too (of the kind that play the War Game) on every one of Marlborough's campaigns, so much so that exhausted readers have been heard to sigh, as Anne did after Oudenarde (1708), 'Oh Lord, when will all this dreadful bloodshed cease?'

No, for the purpose of this book, and that indirectly, we are concerned only with the small Bavarian village called Blindheim, which until August 2nd, 1704 (or by our calendar August 13th), no one outside its immediate neighbourhood had heard of. However, by a set of curious chances and by dint of superhuman planning, marching and fighting, it was there that Marlborough, with his reliable brother Charles to head the infantry, his fat and faithful Quartermaster-General Cadogan, his incomparable secretary Cardonnel, and above all his fearless and devoted ally Prince Eugene, with platoons of the Grand Alliance, won their most famous victory over the French and the Bavarians; and it is after that obscure little village that Blenheim Palace, in its anglicised version, has been named.

[37]

But what should be done for the man the Queen delighted to honour? Duty kept him abroad until December 14th, when Anne welcomed him with a diamond sword and installed him at Windsor as a Knight of the Garter. But what else? After much discussion of more or less worthy alternatives (a statue? A London square?) Anne decided to make over to the Duke and his posterity 'the hundred of Wootton': the royal estate at Woodstock in Oxfordshire, its manor house half-ruined, and with several villages surrounding a wild park originally walled by Henry I. Henry II had built an elaborate retreat there, with colonnades and bathing-pools, for Rosamond Clifford; while king after king had hunted deer in the park and had added courts, gardens, chapels, a gatehouse (in which Elizabeth I was confined by Mary for two years), until the manor, once a hunting-lodge, had become a fair-sized palace with walls thick enough to withstand much battering by Cromwell's troops.

It went without saying or writing that something worthier of a Prince of the Holy Roman Empire (as Marlborough now was) than that crumbling manor house should be built not only to commemorate a great victory but also as a monument to the Queen's glory and as a noble token of the nation's gratitude. At the time there must have seemed no question but that the Queen, who loved giving, should pay for Blenheim Castle, as it was at first to be called, no matter what the cost; and indeed it was her own Board of Works who built it and her own Treasury which for some years footed the bills. Later, as the flowers of friendship faded, supplies wilted too; but that again is a long and unedifying story which has been told at length elsewhere.

At Blenheim's foundation in June, 1705, celebrated as it was with free beer and bucolic junketings, only one royal stipulation had been heard of: on every anniversary of the victory a replica of the captured standard of France was to be delivered, as quit-rent, at Windsor to the reigning sovereign – surely a delightful idea, typical at that time of a munificent queen.

As for the architect (then called surveyor), it has been claimed by one of Marlborough's countless biographers that Vanbrugh was chosen by the Queen. That is nonsense. One has but to refer to Vanbrugh's letters and to the documents formerly at Blenheim to learn that, after meeting

[38]

Marlborough at the playhouse (probably the Haymarket theatre Vanbrugh had built and launched with Congreve), Vanbrugh had shown him a wooden model of Castle Howard, the mansion he and Hawksmoor were building for the Earl of Carlisle in Yorkshire. Godolphin, who was with Marlborough when they viewed that model, advised him to look no further; for that, with modification and enrichment, was just what was needed; and Marlborough was pleased to accept his advice. From their first meeting Marlborough and Vanbrugh, fellow-members of the Kit-Cat Club, took to each other and, but for Sarah's 'extremely prying-into habits' (as Godolphin described them), her parsimony, lack of vision and infinite capacity for trouble-making, all would probably have gone far more smoothly, swiftly and well.

Tremendous as the victory at Blenheim was (so shattering to Louis XIV that he forbade all mention of it), it proved but the beginning of a series of victories – at Ramillies, Oudenarde, Lille, Malplaquet, Bouchain – for all of which Marlborough was mainly responsible. He never knew failure. It was only after his disgraceful dismissal by Anne, when his enemies at home had undermined him, that for England the tide turned. To all of which Sarah, in protest at least, was an outraged and frustrated witness. 'If I had been a man . . .' she was always saying; and indeed she had twice offered to join her husband on the battlefield and had twice been gently thanked and refused.

Apart from the care of her children, about whom Marlborough constantly and tenderly enquired, there were her duties at Court in attendance upon the Queen. Courageous as she was, it was certainly not fitting that she should witness such carnage as Marlborough saw at the Schellenberg, at Ramillies and at Malplaquet; all of which made her compassionate husband ill and brought on those violent headaches which prostrated him. Though she wrote and rewrote her own *Conduct* – hard-hitting stuff, heavily prejudiced – she unquestionably calls for a chapter to herself and she shall have it.

But first to follow Marlborough into his retirement, after Anne had forsaken him and sent her note of dismissal, which he flung into the fire. For two years then – 1712–14 – the Duke and Duchess stayed abroad, first at

[39]

Aix, then at Frankfurt and later at Antwerp. They even visited their little princedom of Mindelheim, given to Marlborough by a grateful Emperor for rescuing Vienna. A prophet is not without honour save in his own country. Wherever Marlborough went he was acclaimed, while secretly as always – for he was never without foresight – while keeping on good terms with nephew Berwick and the Jacobites, he sedulously cultivated the Court at Hanover, where the future of the Protestant Succession now seemed all but certain to lie. That Court was then headed by the Electress Sophia who, partly thanks to her chief counsellor Leibnitz, was one of the wisest women in Europe. She had long since recognised the merits of Marlborough, as well as his superlative charm, and was now heard to say that if Queen Anne had made an ape her general and that ape had won so many victories, she would still be on the side of the ape. It was a grievous loss for England that she died less than two months before Anne did, leaving the English throne vacant for Sophia's dim-witted son. Anne, as everyone knew, loathed the whole Hanoverian family; and when asked if Sophia's death upset her, said it was so much 'chipping-porridge, it would neither give more ease nor more uneasiness'.

At Antwerp, where they settled, the Marlboroughs were joined by Cadogan, who was cheerful company and had been asked by Marlborough to invest for him £50,000 in Holland, in case of need. Sarah at first was delighted with everything, including of course the honours publicly staged for 'that glorious man' her husband. After some months however she found herself longing for 'a clean sweet house and garden though ever so small' – but it must be in England. In the Netherlands she had failed to notice one woman, except for the dowager Lady Albemarle, that resembled a human creature; while as for heating, 'their manner is stoves which is intolerable and makes my head ache'. Far more serious was that crushing blow when the news reached her that her third daughter, Elizabeth Countess of Bridgwater, had died from smallpox. Marlborough is said to have fainted.

But some relief was on the way. Marlborough, alert to many of the secrets of Europe, realised that it was time for them to make tracks for England. At the Hague they were fêted at the Mauritshuis, already familiar to them; and eventually, though kept waiting a week for a 'Protestant wind' to take them

[40]

to England, they arrived back on August 2nd, 1714, the day after Anne's death. A week before Anne died, Harley (Lord Oxford) had been dismissed at a Cabinet meeting. He then flung such accusations at St John (Lord Bolingbroke) that a violent quarrel broke out – shattering enough, it was said, to have brought on the Queen's last illness – and the whole Tory structure fell to pieces. Oxford went to the Tower, Bolingbroke to France as secretary to the young Pretender, the Mashams (Abigail and her husband) to Langley in Buckinghamshire, where she died in obscurity in 1734.

Although George I could not be bothered to learn English he was, through his interpreter, affability itself towards Marlborough when, landing at Greenwich with his two German mistresses, he said, 'My lord Duke, I hope your troubles are now all over'. Naturally they were not, but at least Marlborough was restored to his former offices and was treated with respect.

Blenheim was far from ready for him. Sarah and the Queen had stopped all progress there, and none had been attempted for the past four years. Large sums were owing and the Edward Strongs, who owned Taynton quarries and had been Wren's chief masons at St Paul's, successfully sued the Duke for debt.

In the meantime the Marlboroughs contented themselves with Holywell, the St Albans house they had rebuilt, after pulling down the one where Sarah had been born; or with Windsor Lodge (Sarah's favourite); or if they had to be in London, with Marlborough House, overlooking St James's Park. On ground leased from the Crown – it had once been part of Anne's long garden – Sarah had ordered Wren to build her a house that should have nothing about it resembling 'that known as Blenheim'. He did it in three years (1709–11), and it was, she declared, the strongest and best house that ever was built. Before it had been finished, however, she rid herself of Wren as she later did of Vanbrugh, having found that 'the poor old man', as she described him, was being imposed upon by the workmen to charge prices that were unreasonably high. The house, given two more storeys, at the death of the fourth Duke in 1817 reverted to the Crown.

In 1716 it was decided that Blenheim should be finished at the Duke's expense on the understanding that the castle or palace and the estate it stood on should for ever stay in the possession of the Marlborough family and its posterity; but of course there were still difficulties. Craftsmen, including master-masons and that greatest of all carvers Grinling Gibbons, had left in 1712 and nothing would induce them to return. Still, the private wing was all but habitable and Vanbrugh was as anxious as Marlborough to make it so. Building had restarted in 1716 when disasters happened.

On April 15th Anne Sunderland, the Marlboroughs' second daughter, died of a 'pleuritic fever', leaving three sons and a daughter to be cared for by her mother. This was at a time when Sarah's disputes with Vanbrugh were nearing their zenith; and so, from one cause or another, on May 28th Marlborough suffered his first stroke, resulting in partial paralysis and loss of speech. By summer however his speech had returned, and with Sarah and his gargantuan doctor, Sir Samuel Garth, he was able to be moved to Bath, a spa Anne had damned as 'stinking' and Sarah thought 'most disagreeable'. One pictures them in separate sedan-chairs and envies least those who had to carry Garth who weighed at least twenty stone.

In desperation Sarah was prepared to consider any remedy her friends recommended, the latest being broth of vipers, which the Duchess of Shrewsbury assured her must come from France. With astonishing speed they were sent for and popped into the post; by which time Sarah had been told that 'they that took the broth complained that their loathing of the vipers made their other food less useful', and so her order (too late) was countermanded.

In November Marlborough's second stroke was more serious. This occurred at High Lodge near the western boundary of Blenheim Park and at that time a small farmhouse to which Vanbrugh, on its eastern side, had added a wing. It was there that in 1680 Bishop Burnet had heard the deathbed confession of John Wilmot Earl of Rochester, who wrote scurrilous lampoons on Charles II and then rusticated himself to Woodstock Park, where he was Ranger, until pardoned. The lodge was rebuilt in the eighteenth century as a gothick folly; but at the time of Marlborough's illness it was so packed with doctors and apothecaries that when the eldest daughter, Henrietta Godolphin, arrived, Sarah feared that she herself might die of grief and claustrophobia.

[42]

Kneller: Anne Countess of Sunderland

[43]

Once again Marlborough recovered, although he was never completely to regain his power of speech. In 1717 he voted for Lord Oxford's impeachment (he was acquitted); and attended the House of Lords until 1721. The Duke and Duchess with Dr Garth might occasionally be seen at Tunbridge Wells, where Marlborough recognised no one, but they were more often at St Albans, Marlborough House or Windsor Lodge. Yet, as Sir Winston found, 'all of Marlborough's active interest was in Blenheim'. He would ride to what Sarah mockingly called 'that bridge in the air' and repeatedly ask whether it could ever be joined to the sides of what was still called a chasm (the Glyme valley). He was assured that it would be, even if it meant levelling the hill upon which some remains of Woodstock Manor still stood.

For the palace itself – in Sarah's phrase 'a chaos which only God Almighty could finish' – the Duchess had taken over when, after their final *fracas*, Vanbrugh had withdrawn. Sarah opened her husband's letters, reading aloud to him only what she considered suitable; so that he was kept in the dark not only about Vanbrugh's disappearance but about Sarah's lawsuit with Cadogan over what she considered his misappropriation of the funds Marlborough had asked him to invest in Holland. In hopes of better interest Cadogan had transferred the money to Austria, with disappointing results.

In 1719, at long last, Marlborough and his Duchess were able to move into Blenheim's private wing on the east front. His rooms were at the south end, hers at the north, their two suites meeting in what is called the Bow Window Room, a delightful apartment now used as a dining-room, but at that time said to be the only sitting-room where Sarah felt at ease. It was there, in the bow or apse, the small 'stage' framed by Corinthian columns carved in wood by Grinling Gibbons, that, for the ailing Duke's benefit, his grandchildren acted Dryden's *All For Love* in a version carefully bowdlerised by Sarah to ensure that, in spite of the title, there were no kisses or cuddles. The children wore silks and brocades from Italy, intended for the staterooms, and glittered with jewels, Anthony wearing Marlborough's diamond-hilted sword. The surest sign of its success was Marlborough's cheerfulness. He had clearly enjoyed it.

Kneller: Sir Samuel Garth

[45]

Sir Winston as a writer found it hard to understand how Marlborough, with so much time on his hands and so much to explain, had preferred to play at ombre or piquet rather than write his memoirs; but as Marlborough himself had said, he believed that a man should be judged by his deeds alone; and besides that, after two severe strokes he was beyond writing or even dictating. In one of his finest passages Sir Winston wrote of Blenheim:

Marlborough had set his heart upon this mighty house in a strange manner. Sarah considered it as his 'greatest weakness'. It certainly gives us an insight into the recesses of his being. There is no doubt that the desire for posthumous fame, to 'leave a good name to history' . . . was in these years his strongest passion. At his age he could not hope to enjoy Blenheim much himself. Several years must pass before it could even offer the comforts of Holywell. It was as a monument, not as a dwelling, that he so earnestly desired it. Hence the enormous thickness of the walls and masses of masonry in Vanbrugh's plan had appealed to him, and had probably been suggested by him. As the Pharaohs built their pyramids, so he sought a physical monument which would certainly stand, if only as a ruin, for thousands of years. About his achievements he preserved a complete silence, offering neither explanations nor excuses for any of his deeds. His answer was to be this great house.

This mood has characterised dynasts in all ages, and philosophers in none. Remembrance may be preserved to remote posterity by piling great stones on one another and engraving deep inscriptions upon them. But fame is not to be so easily captured. Blenheim cost him dear. It weakened him in his relations with hostile Ministers. It exposed him to mockery and malice. The liability for its expense was turned as a weapon against him . . . In his will he had to leave £50,000 to complete the work otherwise derelict. Indeed, his happiness lost much and his fame gained nothing by the building of Blenheim. However, Blenheim stands, and Marlborough would probably regard it as having fulfilled its purpose if he returned to earth at this day.*

*   *Marlborough*, volume II, pp. 754–5

About Marlborough's all-too-short stay at Blenheim there is but one slight story and that is how, old and frail as he felt, he tottered up to Kneller's portrait of him as a noble looking young officer in armour and muttered, 'That was once a man'.

Mrs Clayton (later Lady Sundon), an obsequious woman, wrote to Sarah in August, 1721:

> I hope the Duke of Marlborough is well since he came to Blenheim and I am sure he is pleased, for one may see he takes great delight in that place; and indeed I don't wonder at him, for I think 'tis a glorious place to be in and must be much more so to the Duke of Marlborough when every stone of that great building may justly put him in mind of his own great actions and how much he has done to preserve the liberties of a great and free people . . . Though I know dear Lady Duchess is not fond of being at Blenheim, yet I must own I cannot help admiring of it extremely and wondering you don't like it more, but maybe that may come from my never having had any of those uneasinesses that I believe always attend great grandeur . . .

But Marlborough was not to die at Blenheim. It was at Windsor Lodge, leased to Sarah by Queen Anne in happier times, that the family again foregathered for the deathbed scene.

It was June, 1722. Sarah called for prayers and asked Marlborough if he had heard them. He told her yes and he had joined in them. After which he lay quietly in a coma for some hours and died in the dawn of June 16th. He was seventy-two. At his funeral in Westminster Abbey (Blenheim's chapel was unfinished) the Duke of Montagu was chief mourner, with Cadogan and eight Knights of the Garter following the hearse. Marlborough lay in the vault of Henry VII's Chapel for the twenty-two years of Sarah's widowhood. At her death in 1744 his body was transferred to the vault below the chapel at Blenheim where, side by side, they now lie together.

'He had proved himself', wrote Archdeacon Coxe, 'the "good Englishman" he had aspired to be; and History may declare that if he had had more power his country would have had more strength and happiness and

[47]

[48]

Europe a surer progress.'

Lord Bolingbroke, reminded of covetousness, the one weakness Marlborough had shared with his Duchess, said, 'He was so very great a man, I had quite forgotten that fault'.

The Marlborough monument in the chapel at Blenheim Palace

[49]

II

Sarah first Duchess of Marlborough and her Children

——————— 1660–1744 ———————

Sarah, daughter of Richard Jennings and his wife, who had been Frances Thornhurst, daughter of a baronet, was born in a small house in Holywell, St Albans, on May 29th, 1660 and was baptised on the 17th of June. There were family connections with an estate at Sandridge (Water End), north-east of the city, and the beginnings of that, wrote Sarah, 'might have been in William the Conqueror's time, for ought I know'. Her two brothers died in infancy of smallpox, as most infants then did; while of sisters Frances, eight years older than Sarah, preceded her to Court as a Maid of Honour. Frances had the misfortune to marry a Roman Catholic, the Duke of Tyrconnel, and so was to find herself exiled, in poverty, for many years. The other sister Barbara married Edward Griffith and died in 1678. She was twenty-six.

Sarah's mother was as uncommonly plain as she and her sisters were beautiful. Frances and Sarah were both fair, but about Sarah, even as a child, there was a quite extraordinary quality of radiant vitality which captivated everyone she met. As a young woman she was described by a contemporary as 'certainly the fairest thing that ever God made'; and she had but to marry John Churchill for the pair of them to be declared 'handsome to a proverb'. But that was not until she was seventeen and he was twenty-seven.

Sarah claims to have first met Princess Anne, daughter of Charles II's brother James Duke of York, when she (Sarah) was only ten. Anne, five years younger, was instantly charmed. 'There was', writes Sir Winston, 'a romantic, indeed perfervid element in Anne's love for Sarah, to which the elder girl responded warmly several years before she realised the worldly importance of such a relationship.'

'Of Courts I have seen a good many', wrote Sarah much later, 'but I protest I was never pleased but when I was a child, and after I had been a Maid of Honour some time, at fourteen I wished myself out of the Court as much as I had desired to come into it before I knew what it was.'

One recurrent annoyance was the presence at St James's of her watchful mother, who was said to have sought refuge there from her creditors; but she was soon packed off to Holywell, where presumably her debts were settled.

And so for a time the two girls, Sarah and Anne, played happily together, went to the same parties, shared the same friends; but then both grew up and married, Sarah losing her heart completely to John Churchill, Anne dutifully loving Prince George of Denmark, while continuing to love Sarah too. In short, Sarah had changed infinitely more than Anne, who now began to become an embarrassment which, as time went on, tended to increase rather than to diminish. 'It was extremely tedious', Sarah tells us, 'to be so much where there could be no manner of conversation. I knew she loved me and I suffered by fearing I did wrong when I was not with her, for which reason I have gone a thousand times to her when I had rather have been in a dungeon.' And again: 'I used to pass many hours in a day with her and always endeavoured to give her notions . . . of making herself (as Queen) be beloved rather than feared; and I always showed her how easy that was to do where she had so much in her power to do good.'

In 1688, at that time of crisis when Anne fled from the Cockpit in Whitehall to avoid her father, James II, himself about to flee to France, Sarah had been there to help her, as was Henry Compton Bishop of London, who had taken along his stout gardener, George London, later to partner Henry Wise, master-gardener at Blenheim. The flight, said to have been unpremeditated, had in fact been carefully planned. Anne was safely conducted to Nottingham. Her father was heartbroken.

It would be pleasing to be able to record that Anne's elder sister Mary, sharing the throne of England with Dutch William, was grateful to the Marlboroughs for their welcome, and more especially for persuading Anne to let William continue to reign as king should Mary predecease him, which in fact by eight years she did. But on the contrary, the sisters – Mary talkative, Anne reserved – soon fell out; and William did nothing to reconcile them. It was he, as we know, who sent Marlborough to the Tower; and when Anne not only refused to dismiss Sarah but boldly brought her to Court, Mary was enraged and remained so.

Sarah offered to retire but Anne would not hear of it. 'I beg it again', she insisted, 'for Christ Jesus's sake that you would never name it any more to me, for be assured that if you should ever do so cruel a thing as to leave me, from that moment I shall never enjoy one quiet hour. And should you do it without asking my consent (which if I ever give you may I never see the face of heaven), I will shut myself up and never see the world more, but live where I may be forgotten by human kind.' Was ever a queen (or a princess) more emphatic or a subject more desperately loved? In 1694, when Mary lay dying from smallpox Anne, herself ill, sent notes of sympathy, but their quarrel was never made up.

William then, bereft and melancholy on his alien throne, had no alternative but to allow the Marlboroughs to return to Court, although that can hardly have been a cheerful place to be. As we have seen, Marlborough was eventually entrusted with the guardianship of Anne's sickly son, the Duke of Gloucester; but Time soon caught up with young and old, with Gloucester and Blandford and, in 1702, with William himself.

At Anne's accession in 1702 she found, as she said, a war ready made with France. William had deliberately done much towards it; and Louis XIV had lit a fuse by acknowledging the Pretender, on James II's deathbed in 1701, as the rightful claimant to the English throne.

Queen Anne knew nothing of war, but she gathered together her own strongest forces, her most trustworthy friends: Mr and Mrs Freeman (the

Marlboroughs) and Mr Montgomery (Sidney Earl of Godolphin, her Lord Treasurer). With them alone she felt secure from all enemies at home and abroad, including 'the merciless men of both parties' (Whigs and Tories). 'And we three must never part', she solemnly wrote, 'till Death mows us down with his impartial hand.'

Of the favours she delighted to shower upon the Marlboroughs we have already heard; and for the thanksgiving at St Paul's, after the victory at Blenheim in 1704, the Queen and her Mistress of the Robes rode in an open coach together, 'the Duchess of Marlborough', as Evelyn noted, 'in a very plain garment, the Queen full of jewels'.

In our own time we have known cases where a woman's loyalties, with the best will in the world, have been split between a monopolising husband, children (naturally self-centred and demanding) and a career. In Sarah's day there was no shortage of servants who, when she was at Court, could keep an eye on her four daughters: Henrietta, Anne, Elizabeth and Mary. The heir, the Marquis of Blandford, had died from smallpox in Godolphin's house near Newmarket, at the age of seventeen. As for Marlborough, now so often on campaign abroad, he had been, she found, too indulgent with them, and so she had taken their management upon herself. It was not a success.

Meanwhile Queen Anne was complaining of Sarah's long absences from Court. She played endless games of cards, but when Sarah was not with her she felt lifeless. Usually she wrote every day. 'If you do but recollect', she ran on, 'how often last week I sent and wrote to beg for the satisfaction of seeing you . . . but if you would be so kind as you used to be in coming whenever you were at leisure it would make everything easy.' Since the death of her son Gloucester Anne had taken to signing herself 'Your poor unfortunate faithful Morley' – a pathetic adaptation of the Churchills' own motto: 'Faithful but unfortunate'.

And now, as killing as the canker to the rose and at first as negligible, there enters upon the scene a chamberwoman of the Queen's called Abigail Hill. Sarah had never heard of her until someone asked if she knew some cousins of hers were living in want. No indeed; but of course she would investigate and she did; so that quite soon she found herself nursing cousin

[53]

Abigail through smallpox and finding her some menial job at Court. There was also a brother in rags who needed to be clothed and enlisted in Marlborough's army, where he was later to prove a disaster. She then forgot about them. She had a great deal else to do.

On the face of things it might seem surprising that Sarah, who missed little, took so long to realise that Abigail had quietly insinuated herself into Anne's affections and, with Robert Harley (also distantly related to her) and Henry St John, was beginning to plot the Marlboroughs' downfall. Perhaps Sarah had stayed away too long. Abigail's portrait in the National Portrait Gallery has a question-mark beside it in the catalogue; yet the face is so exactly as one imagines it – plain and vulgar, with a dash of guile – it would be disappointing to find that it belonged to someone else.

Sarah was stunned to hear that the Queen herself had not only attended Abigail's wedding to a Mr Masham, but to help celebrate it had called for a round sum from the Privy Purse. Being Sarah she went at once to Anne and taxed her with it, whereupon the Queen looked embarrassed; but as Sir Winston found, 'she had immense powers of reserve and dissimulation'. It was *Cinderella* with a difference. Abigail, Sarah tells us, she had 'taken from a broom'; and although she was later to be ennobled – political chicanery which needed her husband's vote in the House of Lords – even Anne was reluctant to try to turn a bedchamberwoman into a Lady who might in the course of duty have to 'lie upon the floor'; while Masham himself, a natural lackey, was far from convincing in the part of a fairy prince.

The tale so often told since Sarah first wrote it with vitriol in her *Conduct* need not be fully told yet again; but three highly explosive scenes are memorable. The first was when, on their way to St Paul's for the Oudenarde thanksgiving in 1708, Sarah noticed that Anne was not, as for the Blenheim occasion, covered with the jewels she had put out for her; and as they entered the cathedral Sarah had the effrontery, or so Anne said, to tell the Queen to be quiet. This, explained Sarah, was to prevent bystanders from overhearing an unseemly altercation. Afterwards however came recrimination, Sarah accusing Anne of letting Abigail interfere; and Anne of course denying it.

The second scene occurred two months later when Prince George of

Denmark died at Kensington Palace; and it can safely though sadly be said that it showed the Duchess at her worst. Anne, having loved her husband to the last, was devastated and wanted only to be left alone, so that when Sarah burst in, the Queen handed her her watch and said, 'Don't come in to me till the hand comes to this place'; and as Sarah withdrew Anne asked her to send for Abigail. This last request Sarah ignored; nor was Anne allowed to stay beside the deathbed. No, she must leave at once for St James's; and that unwillingly she did, taking marked notice of Lady Masham as she left.

Even then Anne could bring herself to write to Sarah, 'I scratched twice at dear Mrs Freeman's door' – to beg her to ask Lord Godolphin to see that there might be 'a great many yeomen of the guard to carry the Prince's dear body that it may not be let fall, the great stairs being very steep and slippery'. But the most heartless thing of all was when Sarah took it upon herself to remove Prince George's portrait from Anne's bedroom. 'I cannot end this', Anne pleaded in one of her many notes, 'without begging you once more for God's sake to let the dear picture you have of mine be put into my bedchamber, for I cannot be without it any longer.'

Their third and final scene – a gift to the dramatist; and indeed in *Viceroy Sarah* Ginsbury did it full justice – happened in one of those small and dismal closets, which Anne preferred (even at Windsor she lived in a 'small box' of a house she had bought from Godolphin), in Kensington Palace. Sarah had heard, she said, that the Queen had been told she had said things about her which she was no more capable of saying than of killing her own children. Could this possibly be true? Anne refused to answer, but countered with parrot-phrases: 'Whatever you have to say you may put it in writing' and 'You desired no answer and you shall have none.' This was more than Sarah could stand. She broke down and sobbed. But the Queen was obdurate. 'I am confident', said Sarah, 'that your Majesty will suffer for such an instance of inhumanity.' And Anne? 'That will be to myself.' They never met again; nor of course was Anne ever to see Blenheim.

For a time Sarah, encouraged by Arthur Maynwaring of the Kit-Cat Club, who drafted letters for her to send to the Queen, bombarded Anne with apology and self-justification. She received no reply. 'It has always been my observation in disputes', wrote Marlborough from Flanders,

[55]

'especially in those of kindness and friendship, that all reproaches, though ever so reasonable, do serve to no other end but the making the breach wider.' If only she had been half as wise as he was!

As a secret go-between Sarah then turned to one of the Queen's physicians, Dr Hamilton, and went so far as to suggest that some priest of Anne's choosing be called in to arbitrate and help heal the quarrel. At this Anne was scandalised. 'Pray keep her from that!' she cried.

And so with the help of Harley (created Earl of Oxford) and St John (later Viscount Bolingbroke) and their creature Abigail Masham (so still and self-effacing compared with the tempestuous Sarah), the dismissals began. First Marlborough's son-in-law Sunderland (Lady Anne Churchill's husband), whom the Queen had never liked, had to resign as Secretary of State. Next Godolphin, who had lost health and fortune in Anne's service, was sent a note of dismissal by the hand of a servant. Sarah's fall was postponed only because it served Harley's purpose to keep Marlborough at the head of the Grand Alliance until a secret and separate peace had been made with France; but in January 1711 the blow fell, when Marlborough took Sarah's letter of submission and apology to the Queen. He found her icy. She demanded Sarah's gold key of office within three days, and when Marlborough on his knees pleaded for ten days, she made it two. Marlborough, returning defeated to Sarah, who is said to have thrown the key upon the floor, had to be revived with her strongest remedy, Sir Walter Rawleigh's Cordial, which had thirty-two ingredients and called for a strong man to pound and mix them. Sarah's chief office was filled by the Duchess of Somerset, while Abigail became Keeper of the Privy Purse.

Marlborough himself was not dismissed until the following December; after which there followed every kind of treachery, the worst being the desertion of our allies on the field of battle. That a bloodbath was averted was due solely to the perspicacity of Prince Eugene. In Sir Winston's opinion, 'Nothing in the history of civilised peoples has surpassed this black treachery.'

At Blenheim of course all work on the building stopped. Marlborough left the shell in charge of a young clerk-of-the-works called Henry Joynes ('Honest Harry') and the gardens in the care of Tilleman Bobart. The latter

[56]

too was honest enough, but not to be compared with Anne's master-gardener, Henry Wise, who had from the first played a leading part in the laying-out of the park and gardens. What in fact these two men were faced with was the maintenance of buildings and courts covering seven acres, plus an eight-acre kitchen-garden and at least two thousand acres of park. They sensibly went fishing or, while the sun shone ('Qui sait quand reviendra?'), made hay in the gardens. Vanbrugh, with his 'rough, bachelor stuff', moved into the ruins of Woodstock Manor there, from what was left of the roof, to contemplate the bridge and the unfinished mansion beyond.

The Marlboroughs' voluntary exile on the Continent has already been dealt with; and on their return in 1714 one of the first things they did was to hurry to Blenheim. Sarah was enraged to find signs of neglect everywhere and – the most impudent thing of all – Vanbrugh's occupation of the ruins of Woodstock Manor, which she had long since ordered to be demolished. He had even had the nerve to add to the roof a kind of closet, 'as if he had been to study the planets'.

Beyond protection from the weather nothing could be done at Blenheim until 1716 when, in November, Vanbrugh resigned and all his leading masons and craftsmen, including his colleague Hawksmoor, left with him. One of the reasons for the final rift between Sarah and Vanbrugh had nothing to do with Blenheim at all. It concerned the forthcoming marriage between Henrietta Godolphin's daughter Harriet and the Duke of Newcastle, Vanbrugh's friend at the Kit-Cat, for whom he had planned a delightful house called Claremont (since demolished) near Esher in Surrey. 'A matchmaker's', he told Sarah, was 'a damn'd trade', but for the sake of her family he was prepared to exert himself, even though Newcastle, who longed for his posterity to be descended from Marlborough, aired doubts, 'expressed in a very gentle manner', as to Harriet's 'bodily perfections'.

In all honesty Vanbrugh felt bound to admit that Harriet's face was more agreeable than beautiful. Yet, rallying, he assured the Duke he was prepared to pawn all his skill 'that in two years' time no woman in town would be better liked'. In short, thanks to Vanbrugh's enthusiasm, Newcastle's misgivings were overridden. No wonder Vanbrugh was enraged to hear later that Sarah, falling in with a professional matchmaker at Bath, had hired his services and was now giving him the credit (and cash) for having sealed the match. This made such a fool of Vanbrugh at the Kit-Cat that he seemed to feel it as keenly as he did the diatribe against his 'extravagance' at Blenheim, which Sarah had just sent to a mutual friend. He only hoped, he told her, that her 'glassmaker Moor' (James Moore the cabinetmaker, who specialised in pier-glasses) would make 'just such an end of the Duke's building as the Queen's minister Harley did for his victories, for which it was erected'. As for himself, he would never trouble her again 'unless the Duke of Marlborough recovers so far as to shelter me from such intolerable treatment'.

Unluckily for Vanbrugh and for Blenheim, Marlborough never did fully recover; although Sarah, floundering amidst inadequate workmen, recalled Hawksmoor to complete the gallery (now called the Long Library), which he made, as Vanbrugh had intended, 'a noble room of parade'. We may thank Sarah too for the Column of Victory, built by Roger Morris and his patron Lord Herbert; the panegyric facing the palace being by of all people Henry St John, Lord Bolingbroke, who with Harley (Lord Oxford) had contrived Marlborough's downfall. The triumphal arch at Woodstock, by Hawksmoor, is a Roman pastiche which deliberately hides the splendour of the prospect until the visitor has passed through that narrow approach. 'It is not a transition from nothing to something', as Boydell put it, 'but from nothing to everything.'

'If only', sighed Sarah in 1716, 'I could compass a habitation at Woodstock.' About architecture she knew nothing, but that failed to daunt her. She worshipped reason and commonsense and if they could not solve her problems, then nothing in her opinion could. To all but herself her weaknesses were obvious, but one has to admire her courage. She wrote to Henry Wise to find out if there was to have been a way through from the service-courts on east and west to the great forecourt on the north. Wise, who had chosen as his motto 'Be ye wise as serpents and harmless as doves', sent a disingenuous reply, denying all knowledge of such plans: they were the province of Sir John and Mr Hawksmoor.

There was nothing for it but to send for a plan of the main floor, and this she covered with endorsements; and the one that occurred most often was

[58]

'nothing done'. In another of these notes she observes: 'Three or four towers built in this house after the Queen stopped it in 1712, and then there was no one of the staircases finished in the whole house'; nor were there steps to the porticoes on north and south, the Plymouth Moor stone ordered for them having failed to arrive. The chapel was 'three foot high'. Even in the private wing Sarah's Bow Window Room still had no floor; while on every side of the house ground had to be levelled, 'in order to get into it'. The Saloon had one elaborate marble door-case by Gibbons and a chimney-piece in purple marble; the Hall a minstrels' gallery which lay open to the Saloon. West of that the staterooms and the gallery lay unfinished. Sir James Thornhill was painting the ceiling in the Hall, but Sarah fell out with him about fees, so that Laguerre had to be called in to paint the walls and ceiling of the Saloon. In his murals he included himself and Marlborough's chaplain, Dean Jones; and for good measure gave French spies enormous ears.

In three more years the east wing was habitable, but as we know, even by 1722 the chapel was not ready to receive Marlborough's coffin. In Vanbrugh's time Godolphin had had the temerity to change the chapel plan so that the high altar was at the west; and the date on the great monument there by Kent and Rysbrack is 1733, the year that Henrietta Godolphin second Duchess of Marlborough died. Upon the inscription there is no mention of any daughter, although there had been four, the youngest of whom, Mary Duchess of Montagu, outlived her mother.

The marble monument, out of scale with the chapel, is headed with Marlborough's crest as Prince of Mindelheim. Then comes his effigy, in Roman dress, his Duchess gazing up at him adoringly while caressing the infant Charles. His right hand rests on the shoulder of the first Marquis of Blandford; and beneath them History and Fame record his glory, on either side of a sarcophagus which crushes his last enemy, the dragon called Envy.

But there is more than ordinary tragedy here about the children, for there can be no question but that, from their birth, Marlborough adored them. In an early, undated letter addressed to 'my Lady Churchill at the Princess's', he tells her, 'You cannot imagine how pleased I am with the children, for they having nobody but their maid, they are so fond of me that when I am at

[59]

home they will be always with me, a-kissing and hugging me. Their heats are quite gone, so that against your coming home they will be in beauty . . . Miss is pulling me by the arm that she may write to her dear Mama, so that I will say no more, only beg that you will love me always so well as I love you and then we cannot be but happy . . . Lady Anne asks for you very often, so that I think you would do well if you wrote to her to thank her for her kindness in enquiring after your health.' To which, rather shakily, Henrietta adds: 'I kiss your hands, my dear Mama – Hariote.'

Anne constantly asked after them: 'Give me leave to ask', she wrote, 'how all ye great and litle popetts do.' In Closterman's studio she had admired his group of them all, except that he had failed to do justice to Sarah's eyes. Of the young Marquis, an elegant figure in the foreground, Anne tells her, 'Your son danced a minuet last night, which upon my word he performed very well and I do really believe in time he will make a very fine dancer; therefore I hope you will encourage him in it.'

Only fate at its most malignant can shatter such pictures. Blandford was not to be given time to become a very fine dancer, nor a very fine soldier either. On January 2nd, 1703, he wrote to Marlborough, from Godolphin's house near Newmarket, begging him to intercede on his behalf with his mother whom, for no given reason, he had offended; and on the 9th he wrote to her of 'the joy I had when I found I had some hopes of my being friends with my Dear Mama'. On February 20th he was dead.

Sarah owns she thought she owed a great deal of care to the education of her children; but for 'education' there might with more accuracy be substituted the word 'discipline'. As Bishop Hare reminded her, 'One must wink hard and connive at many faults to preserve peace and love in families.' Naturally we find few letters from the children, though among those tedious bundles of Sarah's letters (her own and others) one may chance upon a tear-stained apology from a child who had lost her clogs.

In 1706 Sarah complained about her children to Marlborough, when he was in the act of planning the battle of Ramillies. He replied: 'Hitherto I really have not had time to write to my children; but when I do, be assured that I shall let them know my heart and soul as to their living dutifully and kindly with you; and let me beg, for my sake, my dear soul, that she [sic] will

[60]

Kneller: The Ladies Henrietta and Anne Churchill

[61]

pass by little faults and consider they are very young and that they can't do other than love you with all their hearts; for when they consider how good a mother you have been to them, they must be barbarians if they do not make a kind return.'

Time would show if all four daughters were barbarians or if, as their mother later decided, that applied only to those two who after 1716 survived. The second daughter Anne Spencer, who became Countess of Sutherland, was popular enough with the Kit-Cat to be toasted as 'the little Whig' in a wine-glass engraved with her name. She died in 1716. The third daughter Elizabeth Countess of Bridgwater, said always to have been her father's favourite, died in his absence abroad in 1714.

Kneller: Elizabeth Countess of Bridgwater

[62]

Lady Henrietta Godolphin: the Kneller portrait at Blenheim

The young Godolphins, Henrietta and Francis, had a son they called Willigo who, in August 1711, sent congratulations to his grandfather upon 'that glorious success of passing the Lines', and added: 'I am now at the lodge in the little park (Windsor) and like it very well, the birds are very pretty. . . On Thursday, 2 of August, I presented the Banner [the quit-rent standard for Blenheim] to the Queen and was received but coldly.'

His mother Henrietta, Sarah seems to have found the most wayward from an early age. Her every peccadillo was reported to Marlborough at the battle-front, to which again he with infinite patience would reply: 'I can and do grieve as much as any parent can when a child is unkind. We must hope the best and be always careful not to resent their carriage to such a degree as

[63]

to make the town judge of who is in the right. I think we should do all we can to make our children easy, but it should be in things that are solid and not in trifles that will only show partiality. The quiet of my life depends upon your dear self and children . . . By your saying nothing to me of your going to Woodstock I find your heart is not so much set on that place as I could wish. Vanbrook [sic] writes me that I shall not see him in the Army, believing that I shall approve better of his going into Oxfordshire.'

At twenty-two Henrietta, who had been married to Francis Godolphin for five years, was, or so Sarah reported to her father, keeping bad company. He must write to her, and that he secretly did. She could, he told her, never find any lasting happiness in this world but from the kindness of her husband, so that she ought to omit nothing that might oblige him, and so on . . . While to Sarah he wrote: 'I should hope that if she commits indiscretions it is for want of thinking. I know you are so good and kind to them all that I need not desire you to persist in letting her see her ruin if she should govern herself any other way than you would have her. I know she loves and esteems you.' He could have been wrong.

One wonders at what stage Sarah decided to embark upon a detailed record of her children's misdemeanours. It was to be her Green Book (the Brown Book contained Queen Anne's passionate letters, which after her dismissal she threatened to publish), its full title being *An Account of the Cruel Usage of my Children*. Certainly there was to be no shortage of material, from the time when Mary, the youngest, would 'snap her up' to the death of Marlborough in 1722 when, most naturally, his two surviving daughters were present. But what an extraordinary thing to do! How negative and depressing, how trivial and sad. It did nobody credit and reflected mainly upon herself, for it amounted to nothing more edifying or entertaining than a long tale of self-pity.

In old age Sarah wrote: 'Tis not to be expressed how much I suffered before I could overcome the tenderness I had in my heart for them; but thank God I am now at ease as to that matter, and if I have done anything wrong I am sorry for it . . . and if there is any mother that has had more patience I wish I could see her, for I have yet met with no such person.'

As most of us have found, by an almost unfailing law of Providence it is

The first Duke of Marlborough and his family by Closterman

Lady Diana Spencer, fourth Duchess of Bedford

Kneller (?): Francis second Earl of Godolphin

almost always the more charming and the more delightful friends who are
the first to go, leaving an impoverished world to cope with the sour
delinquents and dismal dullards – in short with what a Duke of
Marlborough once described as 'the kind of people one might not wish to
meet again'. And so it was with John and Sarah's two beloved daughters,
Anne Sunderland and Elizabeth Bridgwater, and the two male heirs, all of
whom had died by 1716, the young wives leaving children to be brought up
by Sarah and her servants; and leaving too Henrietta Godolphin and Mary
Montagu, whose conduct towards their mother – to use another of her
phrases – wanted a name.

[65]

During Sarah's long lifetime she could coax only her few remaining sycophants to read and to be duly shocked by her ridiculous Green Book. Today no one would have patience with such trivial grievances. Their only interest to us lies in the roots or causes of some of those quarrels, which were quite fantastic. For example, before Sarah left London to join Marlborough in their two-year voluntary exile, she called together most of her grandchildren for, of all things, a raffle of diamonds at Marlborough House; but Mary Montagu's children were not invited because, as Sarah put it, she believed Mary and her husband, who owned the site of the British Museum (Montagu House), had already enough diamonds to cover her table. In the Churchill family that was wounding enough to cause lasting coldness. But years later Mary set the seal upon her sins by coveting Rysbrack's model for her brother's (Lord Blandford's) statue upon the monument in Blenheim Chapel. Henrietta Godolphin's affair with Congreve was far more serious; but what seems to have upset Sarah most of all was the behaviour of Henrietta and Mary at their father's bedside at the beginning and at the end of his terminal illness.

The crowded scene at High Lodge in Blenheim Park, after Marlborough's second stroke in 1716, will be remembered. Mary Montagu, though summoned, was ill and unable to come; which was as well since, as Sarah tells us, 'There were but three rooms to lie in, and garrets . . . The very little lodge was prodigious full.' When Henrietta Godolphin arrived she ignored her mother and made straight for Marlborough's bedside. 'She took no more notice of me', Sarah noted, 'than if I had been the nurse to snuff the candles.' Next day, for the patient's benefit, she pretended to be on loving terms with Henrietta and embraced her; but 'she looked', wrote Sarah 'as if she would kill me'. All of which was reported to Francis Godolphin when he too arrived. 'He looked uneasy' but was far too frightened of his wife and mother-in-law to speak.

After Marlborough had begun to recover Sarah – this time to impress the servants – linked arms with Henrietta, who turned to admire herself in a glass. 'You're extreme pretty' was all her mother could then find to say. 'When we returned to London', Sarah concludes, 'we went on in the usual manner – dogged rudeness, and I trying to hide it.'

[66]

Kneller: Mary Duchess of Montagu

At Marlborough's deathbed in June, 1722, the scene, with variations, was repeated at Windsor Lodge. True, there was more room there, but the company was larger because, in addition to all the doctors, nurses and attendants, Mary Montagu was there, and Henrietta had brought along her daughter Harriet Duchess of Newcastle, with four other grandchildren, all kneeling at each side of Marlborough's bed, as though posed on a Tudor tomb. Sarah, feeling as though her own soul was tearing from her body, begged the others to withdraw, which at the third time of asking they did, but waited in the next room until four in the morning. The children of course had left.

After Marlborough's funeral, for which Sarah queried the bill, it was the

[67]

talk of London that Sarah had ill-treated her daughters while their father was dying. This was the final blow. She wrote them both off and decided never to see them again. Marlborough's chaplain, Dean Jones (he who could play cards and make Marlborough laugh) she dismissed; whereupon Henrietta sent him £100, which sent him into transports of gratitude for her 'most condescending sweetness, her most emphatical goodness'. Unluckily, as often happened, his letter was delivered to the dowager, who thought it amounted to 'something like blasphemy in comparing her [Henrietta] to God'.

Meanwhile Henrietta, now second Duchess of Marlborough in her own right, although with no intention of occupying Blenheim, had allowed her emphatical goodness to care for Congreve at Bath, where, at fifty-three, he was taking the waters for gout. 'These waters', wrote John Macky, 'have a wonderful influence on barren ladies who often prove with child even in their husband's absence.' In 1723, nearly twenty years after her last pregnancy, Henrietta, who was forty-one, gave birth to a daughter Mary. 'She is as much embarrassd by the loss of her big belly', wrote Lady Mary Wortley Montagu, 'as ever a dairymaid was with getting one.' If there had been any doubt about paternity it was in time dispelled by the wills of both Congreve and Henrietta, who contrived to leave all they could in cash, jewels and plate to Mary, who by then had married Thomas Osborne, fourth Duke of Leeds.

Francis Godolphin behaved impeccably. Writing to his own daughter Harriet he told her: 'You will, I dare say, my dear child, be glad to hear that your Mama is very well, after having been brought to bed about two hours ago of a little girl, who is likewise in a prosperous way.'

In 1728, while again in Bath with Henrietta and John Gay, who wrote *The Beggars' Opera*, Congreve's coach overturned, inflicting internal injuries from which in the following January he died. To Henrietta, already immensely rich, he left £10,000; and to his former mistress Anne Bracegirdle £200; but all had been carefully planned. Henrietta would leave everything, including silver engraved with Congreve's arms, to Mary (affectionately known as Minos); while as for Mrs Bracegirdle, she too had no need of more money.

[68]

Kneller: William Congreve

[69]

In Westminster Abbey, south of the west door, Henrietta raised a monument designed by Francis Bird to show Congreve in the pose Kneller had chosen for his Kit-Cat portrait. The inscription reads: 'Set up by Henrietta Duchess of Marlborough as a mark of how dearly she remembered the happiness and honour she enjoyed in the friendship of so worthy and honest a man.' 'Happiness perhaps', was Sarah's comment, 'but not honour.' But for some time she had been referring to her daughter as 'Congreve's moll'.

There then ensued the pantomime (not funny to Henrietta – and what did her husband make of it?) when the bereaved Duchess had an effigy – some say of wax, others of ivory – made to resemble Congreve, which she fed at table. It had a bandaged leg and could nod when spoken to. The figure was eventually dropped and broken by a servant who was carrying it downstairs. After which, Henrietta had to make do with living acquaintances, among them Bononcini who had composed the funeral anthem for Marlborough; and Vanbrugh to whom she confided her fear that 'Covetousness having happened to appear so very odious in some other people, she was sometimes frightened lest she should have seeds in her blood that might spring up some time or other'. She herself was generous in her patronage of the arts, particularly music.

When she died in 1733,* having it was said, like Vanbrugh, been forbidden even to enter the park at Blenheim, she left directions in her will that she was to be buried in Westminster Abbey 'in the very same place with the Rt Hon. Sidney late Earl of Godolphin deceased; and it is my desire and express will', she added, 'that my body be not at any time hereafter or on any pretence whatsoever carried to Blenham [sic]'.

With Sarah still in sole charge of finishing Blenheim, there was no risk of her successor's directions being set aside. On the contrary, the dowager saw to it that, as far as she was able to effect it, all traces of her daughter's liaison with Congreve were destroyed.

But the ultimate in absurdity – the quarrel with Mary Montagu, the only

---

* On the death of Henrietta in 1733 the Sunderland earldom became one of the secondary titles of the Dukes of Marlborough.

[70]

surviving daughter, about the chapel monument at Blenheim – had still to be squeezed into Sarah's Green Book, which surely must already have been bursting its covers. 'She went to see the tomb for Blenheim at Mr Rysbrack's', Sarah explained. 'They always make a model in clay to make that in stone by and what is done first in clay is often more like than that in marble. She liked that extremely of Lord Blandford and got Mr R to tell her she should have it, which I suppose he was not unwilling to gratify her in as she would pay him for it . . . But when I saw that of my son, it was so extreme like that I was fond of it and desired him to bake it and send it to me, which he did . . . When she heard I had got Lord Blandford's model she was in a most violent rage and said it was only out of crossness to her that I had taken it, tho' I never had heard the least word of her having a mind to it till some time after I had it . . . But now I have taken my resolution unalterable that I never will have anything more to say to her.'

In May, 1732, Sarah told Sir Philip Yorke, 'The chapel is finished and more than half the tomb there ready to set up . . . The rest of it is finished decently, substantially and very plain. And considering how many wonderful figures and whirligigs I have seen architects finish a chapel withal that are of no manner of use but to laugh at, I must confess I cannot help thinking that what I have designed for this chapel may as reasonably be called finishing of it as the pews and pulpit.' In fact, with a bottomless purse and in an age of peerless craftsmanship, she missed an opportunity which must for ever be regretted.

After Marlborough's death Sarah lived for twenty-two years, dying at Marlborough House in 1744 at the then exceptional age of eighty-four. In that long and vexatious widowhood she had the care of a group of motherless grandchildren, a duty to be performed in her own fashion. Towards the end she had outlived most of her friends and enemies and had grown weary of herself. Much of her time was spent in litigation, in buying estates (she left more than thirty), in 'labouring like a packhorse to save the Duke of Marlborough [Charles Spencer] from the cheats', in revising and dictating her *Conduct* and in making twenty-six drafts of her will, which in its final form provided handsomely for her family, for Lord Chesterfield and William Pitt, for her servants including chairmen who had carried her

[71]

for the past twenty-five years, and for her last companion, Grace Ridley, daughter of a vicar in the Woodstock diocese. Her own funeral, as she directed, was to be 'only decent and without plumes or escutcheons'.

The Grandchildren

For John and Sarah in their relatively long lives no year was more hapless than 1716; for on April 15th their second daughter Anne Countess of Sunderland died (she was thirty-two), and in May Marlborough suffered his first cerebral stroke. Compared with this, Sarah's parting with the architect of Blenheim was merely by the way.

Even as a girl Anne was said to have had a much needed softening influence on her mother who, when Anne died, said she had been all that was good and all that was charming. In childhood she had shown her father's tenderness and could never bear to be in her mother's bad books: that ominous Green Book of Sarah's. 'What have I done', scrawls the infant Anne, 'that you think so ill of poor me that loves you so passionately?'; sleepless and tearful she had grieved for a fortnight. And in another undated note to her mother she says: 'I have one of my dear Mama's colds, with very great pleasure, for it was a great uneasiness to me to hear you say you thought it a sign your constitution was broke, for I hope it looks more now like being natural. I am sure whatever it is I shall like being as you are; and indeed I should have more ease in enduring anything than I can express if it could take off any pain from my dearest Mama that I adore more than I can ever show.'

Anne's own children – Robert, Charles, John, Anne and Diana – she loved devotedly and, with what would seem to be a premonition of death, wrote movingly as to their care to her husband:

> As to the children, pray get my mother, the Duchess of Marlborough, to take care of the girls; and if I leave my boys too little to go to school (to be left to servants is very bad for children, and a man can't take care of little children as a woman can), for the love that she has for me and the duty I have ever showed her, I hope she will do it, and be ever kind to you who was dearer to me than my life . . . Pray let Mr Flournoys get some goodnatured man for Lord Spencer's governor, who may be fit to go abroad with him . . . and don't be careless of the dear children as when you relied upon me to take care of them. But let them be your care though you should marry, for your wife may wrong them when you don't mind [notice] it. We must all die, but 'tis hard to part with one so much beloved and in whom there was so much happiness as you, my dearest, ever were to me.

Her letter brought tears, and Sarah wrote to the widower:

> You may be very sure that to my life's end I shall observe very religiously all that my poor dear child desired. I was pleased to find that my own inclinations had led me to resolve upon doing everything that she mentions before I knew it was her request, except taking Lady Anne, which I did not offer, thinking that since you take Lady Frances* home, who is eighteen years old, she would be better with you than me, as long as you live, with the servants that her dear mother chose to put about her . . . But I will be of all the use that I can be to her in everything that she wants me; and if I should happen to live longer than you, though so much older, I will then take as much care of her as if she were my own child. I

---

* Lady Frances Spencer was the third Earl of Sunderland's daughter by his first wife Lady Arabella Cavendish. Lady Frances married Henry Howard Earl of Carlisle. Lady Anne Egerton was the daughter of Elizabeth Countess of Bridgwater, who had died in 1714. Lady Diana (Di) Spencer, Anne Countess of Sunderland's second daughter, was Sarah's favourite granddaughter.

have resolved to take poor Lady Anne Egerton, who I believe is very ill looked after. She went yesterday to Ashridge, but I will send for her to St Albans as soon you will let me have dear Lady Di; and while the weather is hot I will keep them two and Lady Harriet with a little family of servants to look after them and be there as much as I can; but the Duke of Marlborough will be running up and down to several places this summer, where one can't carry children; and I don't think his health so good as to trust him by himself.

Sarah must only just have had time to make all these arrangements at Holywell before Marlborough fell dangerously ill on May 28th. The children then had willy-nilly to be left to that 'little family of servants' while their grandfather recovered enough to be taken to Bath. Motherless and grandmotherless though they were, no doubt the children having each other, a large garden and a stream to play with, managed to enjoy themselves. Robert, Anne's eldest son, was now fifteen, his brother Charles ten, John nine and their sister Diana eight.

With Henrietta Godolphin's children – Willigo, Harriet and Mary – we are less directly concerned, since their mother lived until 1733; and Harriet's match with the Duke of Newcastle was, as we know, being arranged in that fateful year 1716. Willigo (Lord Ryalton), the same who as a youth was coldly received by Queen Anne at Windsor, was at his aunt's death seventeen; and we hear little of him until, with Lord (Robert) Spencer and a Mr Mann, who had been 'a sort of a playfellow at Cambridge', he visits the Netherlands and is shown over the house — 'very pretty and handsome' – in Antwerp where his grandparents had stayed. The town of Angers however, as he wrote to his grandmother, was not to be recommended to 'any person who desired to live as he should do and at the same time not lock himself quite up from company, for all the gentlemen there are the heartiest drinkers and the most entirely given up to it that ever I saw in my life.' Robert Spencer he found 'extremely kind and goodnatured, which you know he has by inheritance from his mother'; while as to their 'governor' Mann, 'There is not an honester breathes on this earth; and I am sure what faults there were in his behaviour were owing

[75]

purely and unavoidably to a scholar's education, which hindered him from knowing enough the rules of politeness and behaviour.'

Sarah, never one to be hoodwinked by disingenuous letters, had her suspicions of Mr Mann, even though – or perhaps because – she had known him as tutor to her own son the late Lord Blandford. She had had enough worry when in 1717 the Spencers' father, Lord Sunderland, had married again, this time to Judith Tichborne, 'a lady of great fortune and of Irish extraction'. Sarah had strongly disapproved. The girl was so much younger than he was, it was as though Sunderland had 'come out of his library to play with puss'. They had had three children who had all predeceased him when in April 1722 he suddenly died. He had lost thousands in the collapse of the South Sea Bubble, so that part of the great library he had collected had to go to Blenheim in discharge of a £10,000 debt. His son Robert, the new earl, was quickly recalled from the Continent and remained in England for his grandfather's death two months later.

Willigo Blandford failed to arrive. Nine months after Marlborough's death he wrote to his grandmother: 'I have hardly courage to write to you after so long a silence . . . The true reason was my not knowing how to return so speedily from my travels as you seemed then to desire.' She had seen to it that by Marlborough's will Blandford should have £3,000 a year until Blenheim was finished; then £8,000 a year, rising to £20,000 a year on Sarah's death: 'the kindest and greatest thing that ever was done for any young man'.

In 1724, in a letter from Paris, Mann tells Sarah that Willigo Blandford seems to have no ambition to sit in the House of Lords, 'nor any inclination to make a figure in the world'. Both he and Willigo send advice upon 'the obelisk' (Column of Victory), triumphal arch and chapel monument for Blenheim. Looking-glasses in the Versailles tradition are carefully despatched to Sarah, with four and a half reams of 'the best gilt paper'. ('I love paper that is thick', she had written, 'and I think the French paper is smarter and better than any I see in England.') Would she care for a large painting of Abraham and Agar by Pietro da Cortona? 'May you long maintain', they add, 'that vigorous health of body that carried you from Blenheim to London in a day without inconvenience.'

Writing, still from Paris, to his mother, Willigo tells her, 'The Italian singers are all in raptures with your Grace's bounty to Bononcini. As a lover of the art I think myself obliged to return your Grace my hearty thanks for this encouragement of Italian music.' But did he or could he read the immensely long letters he received from his grandmother? In one of them she says, 'Concerning your mother living with [on such terms with] me as she has done for many years, I am her mother and never yet was the aggressor, but she is in so ill hands that she finds new ways every day of surprising the world with her behaviour or rage against me, which is much increased since the death of her father.'

And now it was Willigo's turn to surprise the world with his behaviour. In August 1728, writing from Charenton, he tells Sarah he has decided to marry a Dutch burgomaster's daughter: 'as good a gentlewoman and related to as considerable families as any that are in Holland'. Sarah was stunned. It would certainly break her heart, she told him, to see the Duke of Marlborough's heir married to 'such a woman unknown to all the world but low people, and one who could not possibly make a figure as all your friends would wish your wife should do . . .' and so on and so on. Why, he had not even consulted his father! His mother too was offended. Sarah advised him to come over and try to make it up with both. She herself could do nothing to help in that direction, Henrietta having just told her daughter Harriet Newcastle to pay her grandmother no respect. Blandford might stay at Marlborough House or at any of Sarah's country houses, three of them fully furnished.

It seemed an excellent plan, but Willigo had already asked his sister to intercede for him with their parents. They had both of them however proved implacable. 'My father upbraids me', he told Sarah, 'for what he calls indecent omissions towards my mother and has told my sister 'tis a proposal he can never come into'. Although Sarah would have nothing to do with Henrietta, she still urged Willigo to see his father who surely must have too much sense and good nature to refuse to see his only son 'just because he has the misfortune of having a mad woman to his wife . . . Your father certainly loves you', Sarah assured him, 'but he loves quiet too much, which is the true reason for many misfortunes which have happened . . .'

[77]

But none of these kind intentions was to have good effect. Even to his sister, the Duchess of Newcastle, Willigo had become 'Lord Worthless' and, from his shocking manners during his visit to England, he had upset everyone except, surprisingly, Sarah herself, who had teased him but 'kept her good humour all day'. But 'Sure', adds his sister, 'there never was such a creature born!'

On July 25th, 1729, in Utrecht, Willigo Marquis of Blandford married Maria de Yonge. Francis Godolphin, writing to Sarah of his son's 'weak, improper, ill-judged step', added, 'As he has baked, so he must brew'. But he was not to brew for long. Two years after his marriage, while drinking heartily at Balliol, he collapsed and died. Sarah, arriving too late at Oxford, to stay in the Judges' Lodgings with his sister, Lady Diana Spencer, said, 'I would have given half my estate to save him. I hope the Devil is picking that man's bones who taught him to drink.' And then, turning to her granddaughter, 'Where is my basket, Di? Did I not charge you to bring it?' Di ran to the coach and brought it. For two hours Sarah discussed the case with the doctors, and sympathised with the widow who had since arrived. Sarah then left for Blenheim.

Lady Blandford sought maintenance on the grounds of being a poverty-stricken widow, although she had in fact £3,000 a year, mainly from the rentals of Holdenbury, a large estate Sarah had bought within sight of Althorp. In her will Henrietta second Duchess of Marlborough, who died in 1733, directed that on no account must her daughter Mary leave anything to 'the widow of the late Marquis of Blandford or to any of her family or relations'. But the widow had in the meantime married again, the bridegroom being a widower, Sir William Wyndham, who promptly sued the Marlborough Trust for a better settlement. Sarah consoled herself with the thought that her grandsons, Charles and John Spencer, had had a lucky escape, whether Sir William won his case or not, because if their cousin Willigo Blandford had had a son, that would have meant 'a sort of Regency for the use of a Dutch family'.

Taken all in all it had been a squalid affair from which it is refreshing to turn at last to someone Sarah wholeheartedly approved of, her favourite granddaughter, Lady Diana Spencer, known as Di (an abbreviation which she herself favoured). She may have inherited subservience from her mother Lady Anne Churchill, who had died when Diana was eight years old. One of her earliest letters was addressed to Sarah as 'Her Royal Highness the Princess of Mindelheim at her Villa near Windsor'. 'Dear Mama', she begins, 'I love you better than anybody in the world and shall always do so, for if I did not I should be very ungrateful. I hope both Papa Duke and you are very well, for I am sure nobody wishes them so well as your most dutyful daughter . . . I have so many obligations to my dear Grandmama that I don't know which way to show my thankfulness and express my gratitude.' The confusion between 'Mama' and 'Grandmama' may well have arisen from the recent death of her mother. However it was, in Sarah's sharp eyes, she could do no wrong. She nicknamed her Cordelia and gave her lessons in history, although they got no further than the death of Charles II ('Some suspect he was poisoned').

Later she built and rebuilt a house for her at Wimbledon and was determined to furnish it. She was equally determined to have 'no one thing carved, my taste having always been to have things plain and clean, from a piece of wainscot to a lady's face'.

When, indecently soon after Marlborough's death, Sarah, still desirable at sixty-three and Europe's richest widow, was being pursued by dukes and earls (one of them a religious maniac with a troupe of daughters), the most ardent and persistent of them all was 'the Sovereign', that proud Duke of Somerset, now a widower, who at sixty-five was still having the roads cleared for him before bowling over from Petworth to Blenheim in his coach-and-six. And there is a charming scene where, although Sarah has gently refused him, he still calls and on this occasion steals a prayer from Lady Di and, for one so pompous, quite skittishly owns to it – 'that I may not lie under your Ladyship's youthful censure that an old man is a heathen and do want a prayer and all other good things, when I stole yours the other night off from your Mama Duchess's table. I confess I did want that very prayer, I do admit it.' Whereupon Di forgivingly copied it for him and, at his bidding, closed with 'Diana' instead of 'Amen'.

Even so, life for a young woman in the constant company of her grandmother wherever she might choose to go, can hardly have been fun.

[79]

At Tunbridge Wells in 1730 her sister Harriet Newcastle noticed that Sarah 'kept altogether in one room upon the Walks, where she plays at hazard from morning till night'. At seventy Sarah had to be carried everywhere in some form of sedan-chair. 'I hear', added Harriet, 'she says I maintain myself much better than that great lady the Duchess of Montagu, for that I curtsey when I happen to meet her . . . I am very sorry for poor Lady Di, who I doubt has but a dull time of it.'

It must have been a wrench indeed for Sarah to have to part with her; yet of course Di had to marry, but who in the world could be worthy of such a girl? There were suitors a-plenty – Lord Middleton and the Earl of Chesterfield among them – but Sarah aimed much higher – at in fact George II's son, 'Poor Fred' the Prince of Wales; and it might too easily have happened but for Robert Walpole's intervention at the eleventh hour.

'See how the Fates their gifts allot' – In 1733 we find Lady Diana blissfully installed as a duchess at Woburn; 'for indeed, my dear Grandmama', she writes, 'if possible the Duke of Bedford is more kind to me every day than other, which happiness I can never forget I owe to you and I beg you to believe that I am with the greatest gratitude imaginable your most obliged and most dutiful daughter.

Diana Bedford'

And so for some months all went cheerfully. Sarah was pleased with her son-in-law and began, when she heard of promising symptoms, to look forward to having a great-grandchild. ('I have an extreme good nursery for dear Lady Di', wrote her mother-in-law from Woburn.) But with a swelling in Di's neck anxiety set in. Harriet Newcastle, when this trouble had occurred before, made light of it. It was nothing, she said, and Di herself 'handsome as an angel' (as Sarah had said of Marlborough); but Sarah was not so easily reassured. She wrote to Di's doctor and sent Marlborough's campaigning tent for the patient to lie in. But in September, in her twenty-sixth year, Diana Duchess of Bedford died. It had almost certainly been some form of tuberculosis. As she lay dying, even her desperate husband lost favour, preventing his mother-in-law, Sarah, as he did, from rushing into the sickroom, armed with every ultimate remedy, among them no doubt Sir Walter Rawleigh's Cordial. 'Your Grace knew very well', she

[80]

wrote afterwards, 'that I must have more experience than anybody about her. It would be too much to repeat the monstrous usage I received . . . I sat silently in outward rooms, bathed in tears.'

Whom was she left with? Harriet Newcastle, too apt to side with her impossible mother Henrietta; Mary Montagu – like her sister, barred from Blenheim – and Mary's daughter Bella, now married to the inebriate Duke of Manchester; her sister being named after her mother and married to the fourth Earl of Cardigan. Bella, *en deuxième noce*, was to marry Earl Beaulieu, and it was for her that Sarah had styled herself the best upholsterer in England.

As for that other Mary of Henrietta's, fathered by Congreve and now Duchess of Leeds, she could hardly be counted as one of the family, although she seemed to be popular with everyone else. As a child of twelve she wrote frequently – sometimes in French – to her sister Harriet Newcastle. 'I can assure you', she told her in 1735, 'that I can now play the ninth sonata in Corelli not only well but quite in good time.' Nor would Sarah have welcomed further trouble with the Bridgwater family ever since the Earl had stormed into Marlborough House at night and kidnapped his daughter Anne Egerton, whom he married to the third Duke of Bedford.

No, Sarah must concentrate on her two Spencer grandsons, Charles and his younger brother John who, in spite of setbacks, was to become her 'Torrismond',* her beloved Johnny. He reminded her of his mother Anne, who had died when Charles was ten and John a year younger.

By Sarah's reckoning, 'about a dozen' heirs to the Marlborough dukedom had succumbed to smallpox or, in Willigo's case, to drink. Without a fight the Churchill lion had been beaten by the Spencer unicorn (or rather, the griffin), since those were their two family crests. The transfusion of rich and ancient blood would seem all to the good. For one thing it brought a passion for the arts, which John and Sarah had never known. John might and in fact did send from abroad vast tapestries and paintings for Blenheim; while Sarah sang satirical ballads and bought a chamber-organ which played eight tunes; but the Spencers, like the

* From Dryden's *The Spanish Friar*

Herberts, were and have remained natural connoisseurs. Their one damaging weakness was their inborn addiction to gambling – known to Sarah as 'play'. With Sarah herself of course it was a different matter, for she was astute enough not only to play profitably at hazard, but even to cream £100,000 from the South Sea Bubble while Sunderland, a typical Spencer, hung on until it burst. And now it made Sarah weep to see how at some simple game of chance Sunderland's son Charles clumsily mis-handled his cards.

The only thing to do was to pack the brothers off to the Continent with a guardian she could trust, and for this responsible job she chose one who had been her own page, Captain Humphrey Fish. At first, in 1723, Charles had stayed in Geneva with Mann and Willigo; but when Willigo went to Utrecht, Charles stayed boarded with a Swiss tutor, Gallatin, to be joined there in 1725 by his brother John and Humphrey Fish.

It was not long before Sarah came to deplore what she was hearing of her grandsons' occupations. 'Drawing', she told Fish, 'may be useful and is a pretty entertainment, but as to architecture I think it will be of no use to Charles or John, no more than music, which are all things proper for people that have time upon their hands and like passing it in idleness rather than in what will be profitable.'

But Humphrey Fish stuck up for them. 'They understand French very well and speak it and write it very fluently . . . Mr Charles has very little curiosity and looks upon all travelling as a very insipid entertainment and thinks of Italy with great dread . . . but Mr John is far from being in the same case.' However, Charles had now 'given his voice strongly for Paris'.

'You tell me', Sarah replied, 'that the expense at Paris will scarce be less than £200 a month. That is more than the Duke of Marlborough and I spent when we were abroad with more than twenty horses and a house full of servants . . . I have been told lately by a great traveller that there are fixed prices for seeing the greatest curiosities and that six people may see them for eighteenpence and an opera for three halfpence'. Far too much, she noticed, was being spent on clothes; and worst of all, she suspected 'play'. Very well, she must solemnly warn them that if they gambled, except in her company, she would never allow them a shilling, 'either living or dying, tho' I am

[82]

tenderly theirs'. Up till now, she concluded, she had managed to love them both.

But then, as too often for Sarah, came disappointment. She had been looking forward to Charles's visiting her at Windsor Lodge and to hearing him prattle away in French with Di. When he arrived he looked sickly and when he spoke, even in English, it was 'through his teeth' so that it was hard to tell whether he was saying yes or no. 'I think it is very indifferent', wrote Sarah disgustedly, 'what language he talks in.' It so happened that she had at the time a Frenchman staying with her, she told Fish, who was perfectly bilingual. 'His name', she added casually, 'is Voltaire.'

She hoped to heaven that Charles's mumble had not infected John, whom she had always liked 'for his spirit and quickness and good nature'. She had not long to wait to hear how competently John Spencer could deal with an emergency. Fish suddenly died in Paris; and the lone grandson had everything to deal with. He had the body embalmed, the burial service read and was now awaiting orders as to the coffin's being sent to England. Sarah, sad enough about 'poor ffyshe', was deeply concerned in case her 'Dear Dear Johnny' should be contaminated. 'No words can express', she wrote, 'how dear you are to me and I shall be in torture till I see you.'

When at length John joined Charles in England they both saddened their grandmother further by their lunatic extravagance. Having vowed never to soil their hands with silver, they scattered largesse in gold to chairmen who fought for their custom. Short of death, nothing could have upset Sarah more than to see Marlborough's hoarded fortune so ruinously dissipated:

For man walketh in a vain shadow
and disquieteth himself in vain: he heapeth up riches
and cannot tell who shall gather them.*

She did all she could to keep them short of cash, but there is no armour against folly; and it was rumoured that Charles had resorted to money-lenders on the likelihood of Sarah's not having long to live.

---

*   Psalm 39, verse 7

[83]

There could hardly have been a worse moment for Charles to announce that he had decided to marry Elizabeth Trevor, the daughter of a man who in 1713, with Masham and ten others, had by Harley's trickery been raised to the peerage solely for the purpose of forcing through the Treaty of Utrecht. Sarah was outraged. In typical phraseology she wrote that, bad as the world was, there were 'still men that have honour enough not to have liked to have married the granddaughter of a remarkable prosecutor of their own grandfather, who gave him such a title and such an estate . . . I believe her grandfather', she later added for good measure, 'was not a gentleman'.

And the she-devil who had begun it all, Sarah was convinced, was Anne Sunderland's daughter, now Lady Bateman, across whose portrait Sarah had scrawled: 'She is blacker within'; for it was she who had introduced the couple and encouraged the match. For the moment all Sarah could think of was to threaten to cut Charles out of her will. Charles was furious. The match, he assured her, was of his own choosing and was no concern of Lady Bateman's. 'As for your putting me out of your will', he added, 'it is some time since I either expected or desired to be in it. I have nothing more to add but to assure your Grace that this is the last time I shall ever trouble you by letter or conversation.'

Sarah's strange attempt at retaliation was to offer John Spencer £400,000 for ceasing to communicate with Charles; but John happened to love his brother and was not to be bribed. Frustration ate into Sarah's soul. As she saw her, Elizabeth Trevor looked almost as bad as a burgomaster's daughter; and although the word 'snobbery' had yet to come into common use, Sarah was unquestionably cursed with that kind of pride.

The astonishing thing (at least to Sarah) was that the marriage proved a success. It was a love match which lasted. Charles was given the Garter and made Lord Steward of the Household; while in the army (although Sarah had strictly banned his enlistment) he was steadily promoted to the rank of General and, like his grandfather, became Master General of the Ordnance. However, he was not of such stuff as history is made of. He was strangely inarticulate and continued to mumble even in the House of Lords.

Although with the death of his aunt Henrietta Godolphin, Charles had become third Duke of Marlborough, it was out of the question for him and his growing family to live at Blenheim. He was, as we know, estranged from Sarah who, in her brave but parsimonious way, was trying to 'compass a habitation' in what she herself thought of as 'a wild and unmerciful house'. Not long before Di's death she had told her: 'I am going to Rysbrack to make a bargain with him for a fine statue of Queen Anne, which I will put up in the Bow Window Room* at Blenheim, with a proper inscription. It will be a very fine thing and though but one figure will cost me £300. I have a satisfaction in showing this respect to her because her kindness to me was real, and what happened afterwards was compassed by the contrivance of such as are in power now' – meaning Sir Robert Walpole and King George II. For the inscription she drafted two versions: one for the public, the other for her own satisfaction. In the latter she owned that, while the Queen had been no fool, 'nobody can maintain that she was wise, nor entertaining in conversation . . . She was ignorant in everything but what the parsons taught her as a child'. Rysbrack was commissioned too for busts of Marlborough and Sunderland and for the overpowering monument, designed by Kent, in the chapel.

In Blenheim Park, having called in Colonel Armstrong, once Marlborough's Chief Engineer, to canalise the river Glyme and to make formal pools on each side of Vanbrugh's bridge, Sarah directed him to design a cascade for the Woodstock side of the great arch; all of which is now beneath Brown's lake. Her final memorial to Marlborough – the Column of Victory – gave her more trouble than anything else at Blenheim. Hawksmoor took infinite pains to design an obelisk, but all his projects were discarded in favour of the stylito statue on its 130 foot Doric column, built by Roger Morris, the protégé of Lord Herbert (later Earl of Pembroke).

In 1738, having been ousted by Sarah from the Little Lodge in Windsor Park, Charles Marlborough moved temporarily into a folly called Monkey Island, near Bray-on-Thames. He had the whole place renovated, with monkeys painted upon the ceiling, at a total cost of £8,000. It was and is

---

* This is confusing, since the western gallery or Long Library has a bow or apse, as has the eastern sitting-room in the private wing. The statue was originally in the central apse of the Long Library. It now stands at the southern end of that apartment, with a brief inscription.

delightful; but with babies arriving – Diana in 1734, Elizabeth in 1737, George the heir in 1739, Charles 1740 and Robert in 1747 – the island was obviously going to be too small; and so in 1738 the Duke, looking ahead, bought Langley, the Buckinghamshire house Abigail had retired to and where she had died in 1734. Charles bought it from the widower, had it rebuilt and enriched the park with a large lake and woodland. His family lived there for fifty years.

Before moving to Bray and then to Langley Charles had, with Roger Morris as architect, added much to Althorp, making that place, in Sarah's opinion, 'infinitely worse than it was before he did it'. For Althorp's owner, John Spencer, Sarah had arranged a marriage with Lady Georgina Carteret; so that in 1742 we have a delightful letter from grandmother to grandson in which she tells him: 'I saw Mrs Spencer and your children. They are both of 'em charming and they talk enough and I find they are mighty fond of coming to me, for I play at drafts with 'em and they both beat me shamefully. I believe really they like to come to me extremely, tho' I heard they had been told I intended to give them a present; upon which they pressed Grace [Ridley] mightily to know what it was; and after she had acquainted me with their curiosity I asked 'em whether they would have a kiss or gold and they both cried out very eagerly "Money!"'

Sarah had then two more years to live, John Spencer only four. Like his father he died suddenly. He was thirty-seven and had only two years in which to enjoy Sarah's fortune. However, he left an heir from whom the present Earl Spencer is directly descended.

Charles's wife Elizabeth, though looking stolid enough in her portrait at Blenheim, by Van Loo, suffered acute depression every time her soldier husband was sent abroad. In 1741 he wrote to her at Bath: 'I left your boys well at Langley this morning. Adieu, my dearest, consider that giving way to low spirits is preventing all the good of the Bath waters. If you won't keep up your spirits for your own sake, I yet hope you will for him whose happiness depends on yours.'

And in the following year: 'Forgive me, my dearest, for saying there is a most unreasonable expression in your letter – that there is a possibility of your never enjoying a happy security. I can't deny but that there is a possibility of the world's being destroyed, but for God's sake, my dear, don't afflict yourself for possibilities'.

Two years before he died Charles commissioned Thomas Hudson to paint on one huge canvas which now hangs beside the main staircase at Blenheim Palace, his whole family including of course his heir who, in the left foreground, holds a formidable-looking cricket bat. In the background Blenheim looks silvery, almost ghostly; and it had in fact formed only a backcloth to most of this third Duke's life. 'After this', runs a note in the British Library, 'Mr Hudson left off painting'. He died in 1779.

In May 1758 (the year of his death) we find Charles, again on campaign and again imploring his much loved wife to keep up her sinking spirits: 'You can have no cause for concern', he assures her, 'but that of my being absent, which I hope will soon be removed for the rest of our lives'. 'As for money', he writes more lightly in June, 'I want none for I don't know what to do with it. Every time I open my box I see a purse of guineas that I am quite tired of and am tempted to throw it overboard. I would give it all for a dozen of clean shirts, as we can't spare any water on board to wash. Blandford and I are in perfect health but rather dirty'. And finally, on October 6th: 'Blandford and I are both very well and I repeat a truth you don't doubt of – that nobody ever did or ought to love a wife by half so much as I do you.' His last present to her was his own ring – 'rather too large for a lady's hand, yet you must keep it for my sake'. His heir was with him when he died of dysentery.

The widow Elizabeth died in 1761, leaving three sons and two daughters. Subconsciously echoing Sarah she directed that her funeral expenses should be 'no greater than common decency may call for'.

[87]

George fourth Duke of Marlborough
——— 1739–1817 ———

When his father died in 1758 George, the heir, became fourth Duke of Marlborough at the age of nineteen. His brothers, Charles and Robert, were eighteen and eleven. His two sisters had married young and unhappily: Betty, in 1756, to Henry Earl of Pembroke, and Diana, the following year, to Frederick Viscount Bolingbroke.

Luckily, although as Horace Walpole had said of the third Duke, he had had 'a vast landed estate and wanted a guinea', he had, thanks to the Marlborough Trust devised by Sarah and Francis Godolphin, managed to leave his family a good deal better-off than they had been in his lifetime; and by their nature they might seem to have deserved it. 'Sweetness of disposition', comments Dr Rowse, 'was a marked characteristic with all these children.'

Nor had the widow before she died failed to protect her sons by finding wise tutors for them. The first, Jacob Bryant, was a Fellow of King's College, Cambridge; and of his successors John Moore was one day to become Archbishop of Canterbury, while the less fortunate Archdeacon Coxe was landed with two all-but-impossible tasks: first, controlling Lord Blandford (fifth-Duke-to-be), and secondly, putting the Marlborough muniments into some sort of order. He did his best and wrote a quite

[88]

helpful biography of the first Duke; but he must have been thankful to leave for Wilton and so to abandon his intractable struggles.

In 1762 George fourth Duke of Marlborough married Lady Caroline Russell, only daughter by his second wife of John fourth Duke of Bedford. They had three sons and five daughters, the heir, born in 1766, inevitably taking the name George – George III having come to the throne in 1760. No Christian name, surely, was ever less inspired; yet six of our kings (not to mention princes) have borne it; while to date four Dukes of Marlborough have been christened George, which all helps to confuse the historian and his readers.

Langley had still to be finished; but now at last it was time for Blenheim to come into its own. Sarah had in her own fashion done her duty by it before leaving – 'hoping never to see it more' – for Windsor Lodge and Marlborough House. If she thought Charles would move in and care for it, she was to be disappointed. His heart was at Langley.

In 1760 Horace Walpole visited Blenheim and was shown 'all Vanbrugh's quarries . . . and all the old flock chairs, wainscot tables and gowns and petticoats of Queen Anne that old Sarah could crowd amongst the blocks of marble. It looks like the palace of an auctioneer who has been chosen King of Poland.'

It is hard to imagine that the state garden on the south, with its fountains and bastions, its arabesques in dwarf-box and its innumerable 'clipped greens' had been kept in good order. We hear nothing of it; and even on the north, where one might have expected the formal pools and canals to have cared for themselves, we see from an oil painting of about 1750, at Blenheim, that although Armstrong's cascade still foams beneath Vanbrugh's bridge, the canals have reverted to the mazy motion of the original Glyme, with swans upon it, while in the foreground deer crop the unmown grass. Two years after Sarah's death Charles third Duke, writing from Langley, asked a Dr Stephens for £400, which he understood was owing to him 'for keeping Blenheim in repair'. But even then it might hardly have paid for mending the statue of Pallas, by Gibbons, which fell from the north front.

In the fourth Duke's time – and he reigned at Blenheim for nearly sixty

[89]

years – all this was to be altered. Thanks to Pope, Kent, Lord Burlington and others fashion in landscaping had completely changed; and while Nature had subtly to be controlled, formality was out and was to be tolerated, if at all, only as the immediate setting of a symmetrical and so to that extent formal house.

The fourth Duke, as we see from his portraits at Blenheim by Romney and Reynolds, was handsome with a distinguished presence. He was in fact a Fellow of the Royal Society, with a lifelong interest in astronomy, and altogether a man of intelligence and culture.

Certainly the Duke was both sensible and fortunate when, for his architect, he called in Sir William Chambers (1723–96), who was to be responsible for Somerset House in its present form. As both of them realised, Vanbrugh was to be respected in that he had deliberately given Blenheim, as he had written of another of his houses, 'something of the castle air'; and that to soften that citadel look could be ruinous. All then that Chambers suffered himself to do was to titivate the forbidding eastern gate (Vanbrugh's cistern-tower, since rechristened Flagstaff Lodge) with laurels and lion heads, topped off with four of Gibbons's urns, annexed from the north front. The inscription there, in pounds, shillings and pence, is said to have been added much later by the ninth Duke. For the fourth Duke's agent Thomas Walker, Chambers designed Hensington House, Woodstock (built 1769 and since demolished).

Chambers showed further respect to Vanbrugh by adding little to the interior of the palace: a noble state-bed, since cast aside; and Marlborough's private room, the Cabinet in the south-east tower, which Chambers refurbished with pier-glasses and with gilded pelmets, all enriched with red damask to set off a collection of priceless paintings by Rubens and others.

To the grounds Chambers added the faultless New Bridge at Bladon; and with the help of John Yenn designed three classical temples in honour of Flora, of Diana and (the Temple of Health) of the temporary recovery of the Duke's close friend and ally King George III, from his attack of insanity in 1789. Chambers added too to the walled kitchen-garden a Tuscan gateway, and designed a town hall for Woodstock, its ground floor originally arcaded as an open market. In London he made modest

[90]

improvements to Marlborough House, but at Blenheim he left minor works such as chimney-pieces to his protégés, Yenn and Hakewill. The latter painted the ceiling of the Bow Window Room with Pompeian arabesques in the manner of Kent, which have long since been covered over. In 1786 John Yenn went so far as to design a memorial at Rosamond's Well, but that, like much else for Blenheim, was never executed.

Of infinitely more lasting importance was the fourth Duke's gigantic (one could almost say Vanbrughian) commission to Lancelot Brown in 1764, to re-landscape the entire park. It would of course be misleading, as his learned biographer Dorothy Stroud has made clear, to think of Capability Brown as some kind of conjuror, since he was in fact an architect and a hydrographer as well as an original genius in the intricate art of landscape-gardening. Even so, as one studies that well-known and altogether unusual portrait of him, one cannot help feeling that if at that moment he were not tongue-in-cheek, then at least some private joke (had he got away with murder?) is at the back of his quick and amiable mind. The fourth Duke gave him a trial run in the park at Langley: a very small-scale model for the capabilities of Blenheim, but evidently impressive and sufficiently encouraging for his Grace to take, as it were, the bigger splash.

With hindsight Brown's task at Blenheim may look simple. All he had to do, some might think, was to slice through two causeways, one leading from the old manor to Woodstock, the other to Oxford, and so to let the Glyme course through the foot of Vanbrugh's bridge and so form a second lake which, discharging itself over a cascade into calm waters, would eventually fall into the Evenlode, a tributary of the Thames. In the event it was far more complicated, calling first for a very substantial dam to prevent pent-up waters from engulfing Bladon; and there was also some anxiety as to whether Vanbrugh's bridge could withstand a lesser but still substantial inrush.

With computers and other modern equipment there would doubtless have been no problem. As it was, both Duke and landscapist must surely have held their breath. To a miracle, but a well-thought-out one, it worked; so that, in Sir Sacheverell Sitwell's phrase, 'The lake at Blenheim is the one

[91]

great argument of the landscape-gardener. There is nothing finer in Europe.' Brown's Great Cascade too is, for its modest height, impressive and ingeniously contrived. In full spate its roar may be heard minutes before one sees it.

Except for the elm-avenues on north and east, it looks as though Brown was given a free hand to surround the two-thousand-acre park with deciduous trees, while planting cedars where they would show to most advantage. For the rest, he punctuated the park with clumps and spinneys. But those of course were for posterity, and no one could foresee the ravages of freak storms and of beetle-borne disease which have since meant planting and replanting all over again.

Brown completely grassed over the three-acre forecourt on the north as well as, on the south, the state garden, fountains, bastions and all. That is now one vast cricket-pitch, with ha-has.

Over a chimney-piece at Chartwell, where Sir Winston's eyes must often have strayed while he revised his definitive biography of Marlborough, one sees inset a delightful oil painting of the launching on Blenheim lake in 1787 of a gondola christened *The Sovereign* – 'a magnificent pleasure-boat'. It is by an unknown painter who puts one less in mind of Canaletto than of Watteau. In the foreground the men and women in eighteenth-century dress are, one might think, about to embark for Cytherea. They are out for pleasure of a celestial kind, drifting in a world more than halfway to heaven.

Much of this knowledge we owe to that saintly man the Reverend William Fordyce Mavor, schoolmaster, rector and mayor of Woodstock for ten years. From his *New Description of Blenheim* (1787) it soon becomes obvious that he has given his heart to the place and to everything and everyone about it, not excepting its owners, with whom he is on the friendliest but of course the most respectful terms. He was tutor to Lord Blandford (no easy task); and upon everything that happens at Blenheim – the launching of a gondola, even the acquisition of more land – he writes an ode. True, his style is obsequious, but that was in tradition with the times. The historian's one objection is that he tells us so little of important events – such as the making of the lake and the rebuilding of High Lodge – while 'turning all to prettiness and favour'.*

One of Mavor's odes is entitled: 'On Converting the Greenhouse into a Private Theatre'; and in prose he volunteers to tell us that Vanbrugh's eastern orangery has been 'fitted up in a style of peculiar elegance and with appendages correspondent to the munificence and fortune of the owner'. There was room for an audience of more than two hundred, with boxes each side of the stage. In the summer of 1788 the Duchess commissioned scene-painting to include a backdrop 'with a view of a garden through an arch'. It cost £10. The theatre's motto was 'Laugh where you may, be candid where you can'. Admission was by invitation, 'persons of quality' attending the last performance when actors and actresses had learned their parts.

Just after Christmas, 1789, the last plays – *The Deaf Lover* and *Cross Purposes* – were performed.* The girls had grown up and were about to marry. Would that one might picture them enjoying their own homes, but Mavor shatters that picture. To his greenhouse ode, reprinted in 1817, he adds the epilogue that 'Ladies Caroline, Elizabeth and Charlotte Spencer, who performed in the drama – not one of them lives to read these recording lines'. Happier far to remember their childhood when charades were a palace pastime, and Reynolds painted them. In those days, as in more recent times, children romped through the empty staterooms and the public were asked to keep to the times when those rooms were shown, 'because the little Ladys are continually in those Appartments'.

The great Reynolds, dated 1778, in Blenheim's Red Drawing-room, shows the whole family posing for posterity, the little ladies – Elizabeth, Caroline, Charlotte and Anne – enacting a scene with a mask as though to frighten the youngest, who was four and had told Reynolds, 'I won't be

---

* The fourth Duke's theatre is now once more an orangery. In the depths of Vanbrugh's bridge a large, windowless apartment has plastered walls and something in the nature of a proscenium arch.

---

* 'The *chef d'oeuvre* of Brown was the improvements at Blenheim. He had the noblest field to display his talents on and he did not labour in vain. But though he traced the outline with effect, the correct taste of the noble possessor of this magnificent place at that period enabled him to give it many additional touches and to improve its drapery.' Mavor: *New Description of Blenheim* (1787)

painted!' Everything has been thought of: handsome Duke with Garter, gazing at his feeble-faced heir who clings to the Marlborough gems, one of which his father holds in his left hand. In the background twisted columns flank a coffered arch; while in the top right-hand corner a statue of Marlborough stands with winged Victory at his fingertips, as on the Column of Victory. But as its central figure the Duchess Caroline steals the picture, her right hand resting lightly upon the Duke's forearm. For good measure Reynolds has thrown in a couple of Blenheim spaniels and a timorous whippet. The story goes that while painting the picture Reynolds scattered snuff, whereupon the Duchess sent for a footman to sweep it up. 'Go away', said Reynolds, 'the dust you make will do more harm to my picture than my snuff to your carpet.'

It was courageous indeed of Sargent to attempt to 'answer' Reynolds, in the same room, with the ninth Duke and Duchess and their two sons. He was perhaps the last painter, British or American, to attempt so vast a painting in the grand manner; and he succeeded.

In public and political affairs the fourth Duke was outstanding. He was still under thirty when made Lord Privy Seal, and in Fox's administration he was Home Secretary (1806–7). He became President of the Royal Institution and for forty years was a trustee of the British Museum. The Sunderland Library, then said to be still the finest in Europe, he moved back to Althorp from Blenheim.

To maintain all this, it was said, called for the fortune of a sovereign prince; and though the Duke, unlike his heir, was no spendthrift, he clearly believed in providing himself and his family with the stately background he thought their due. Brown's works alone, superb as they were, had in ten years (1764–74) cost him well over £16,000, and the estate itself had been greatly enlarged by the addition of Cornbury (once Lord Clarendon's) in Wychwood Forest, Dornford and Hordley. True, Woodstock town hall had cost less than £500, but for the making of the Oxford to Banbury canal he had subscribed £10,000.

At Blenheim there were now eight children to be cared for (each birth lavishly celebrated); and even when the staff had been reduced from eighty-eight to seventy-five (187 rooms were then in use), their pay totalled seven hundred and eighty-five pounds, nine shillings and tuppence three-farthings. The clerk of the kitchen had £100 a year, the chaplain ten guineas. The Duke began to worry. In 1766 he had written, 'I don't know what we shall do for money to pay the quarter's bills.' Visits to Brighton and to Bath too, with staff, coaches, horses, provisions and luggage could be expensive.

When charades and play-acting had been the rage two of the most enthusiastic actors were Lord Charles Spencer and young Professor Nares (ordained in 1792) who often rode over from Merton and, after seven years of courtship, asked the Duke for the hand of his daughter Lady Charlotte, then twenty-seven. Nares, though his love was warmly returned, was refused. In April 1797 they eloped and were married at Henley. Charlotte's parents were so upset that, though the Duke allowed her £400 a year, she and her husband were forbidden the house. They settled happily in Kent, where Nares had a living, and had a daughter, but never saw Blenheim again.

The Duke's troubles increased. Lord Robert's bankruptcy in 1780 had made him realise the necessity for further retrenchment at Blenheim. He might even have to give up his favourite hobby of collecting carved jewels and cameos. In one of the southern towers he had set up a small observatory and now spent more and more time there. He would consult too his wise and most reverend friend John Moore, who replied: 'If that word "Fuss" were struck out of the language, or rather the thing itself turned out of the doors at Blenheim, I do think it would be the pleasantest place and the possessors of Blenheim would be the happiest persons in the world.'

Have all archbishops been blessed with so much sound sense? He wrote again, urging their Graces 'not to be afraid of society. At present the Duke uses himself to look too much at difficulties in everything that comes in the shape of employment, and I much fear that both your Graces would look upon it as a distress if four or five of the best friends you have in the world should be announced to you unexpectedly any day in the week. While this is the case you will never enjoy society as other people do.'

Imagine, then, the dismay at Blenheim when in the summer of 1786 the Marlboroughs learned that they were to be honoured with a royal visit.

[95]

True, George III was, as near as kings can be, a personal friend, but this, for a semi-recluse, must amount to a state visit. Moore once again did his utmost to reassure his friends: 'Nobody has so fine a family in so fine a place to show, and my lord Duke will be amply repaid for all his misgivings . . . by the reflection that what is done is right . . . and I am sure you will all think it right when over.' At every moment one expects him to quote:

> Ye fearful saints, fresh courage take,
> The clouds ye so much dread
> Are big with mercy and shall break
> In blessings on your head.

In the event of course all went royally.

Considering the shortness of the notice [the Duchess told Moore afterwards] it all went off very well. They stayed here from eleven till six. We had breakfast for them in the Library and, after they returned from seeing the park, some cold meats and fruit. Lord and Lady Harcourt told us we were to sit as lord and lady of the bedchamber all the time they stayed here; and poor Lord Harcourt seemed quite happy to rest himself; the Duke found him sitting down behind every door where he could be concealed from royal eyes. We were just an hour going over the principal floor, as they stopped and examined *everything in every room*; and we never sat down during that hour nor indeed very little but while we were in the carriages; which fatigued me more than anything else. Lord Harcourt told the Duke that he had been full-dressed in a bag and sword every morning since Saturday; but the Duke could not follow his example in that, as he had no dress-coat or sword in the country. He desires me to tell you he had no misgivings. All the apprehensions were on my side. Nobody could do the thing better or more thoroughly than he did.

Dr Mavor quickly composed an ode beginning:

[96]

The fourth Duke of Marlborough and his family by Reynolds

The ninth Duke of Marlborough and his family by Sargent

Dread Sovereign, hail! An humble bard
His loyal gratulation pays.
Ah! How unequal are his lays
To win a Monarch's great regard.

The King's comment on Blenheim – 'We have nothing equal to this' –
has been much quoted; and his thank-you present, a ten-foot telescope by
Herschel, was delivered by the astronomer himself. From recent biographies it now appears that George III, in spite of losing us America, was not
as weak as former historians had led us to suppose; but no one has claimed
that, like the fourth Duke of Marlborough, he was the cultured epitome of
the Age of Elegance. Strangely, though, contemporaries as they were, they
did, towards the turn of the century, appear to share what psychiatrists now
call the Victoria syndrome: an escapism worthy of a hermit with, on the
luckless King's part, bouts of insanity.* But while the Duke would shut
himself into a closet 'as if he had been to study the planets' (which he had),
the King, as we know, pursued Lady Pembroke and Fanny Burney and, at
his most violent, had to be restrained with a strait-jacket.

One must be thankful that England had become civilised enough for the
whole nation to sympathise and to rejoice when he had a remission.
Certainly it showed goodwill flavoured with optimism for the fourth Duke
to commission the Temple of Health in Blenheim Park to commemorate the
King's recovery in 1789; for decline had set in both at Windsor and at
Blenheim where the Duke and Duchess were 'not at home' even to the most
distinguished visitors.

In 1788 the Duke sold Langley; and in 1789 he showed some interest in
the removal of Blenheim's dairy to the menagerie, near Park Farm, in the
park. He was concerned however about a steady supply of butter and cream.
'At Marlborough House', he observed, 'we are forced to use the cream from
Syon because it is better than London cream, but it is very different from
the cream we have at Blenheim.' He still kept 'twenty couple of hounds,
with a lady to boil the dogs' meat'.

* At one time it was thought that George III's complaint was porphyria, but that
theory has since been abandoned.

[97]

In July, 1802 Lord Nelson with Sir William and Lady Hamilton called at Blenheim. There was a long pause before a footman hurried out to tell them that a cold collation would be served to them in the park. This was haughtily refused. However, as might be expected, Lady Hamilton 'with a spirit, energy and shrewdness of observation characteristic of her superior mind', (I quote the Reverend Edward Marshall), rose to the occasion and declared that if Marlborough's services had been rewarded with Blenheim, that was because a woman had then reigned, 'and women have great souls'. For her part, had she, Lady Hamilton, been Queen at the time of the battle of Aboukir, Nelson should have had 'such a principality that Blenheim Park would have been only as a kitchen-garden to it' – a remark which, we are assured, reduced Nelson to tears.

The Duke became more and more reserved and silent until one unfortunate day when he was told of yet another importunate visitor, the celebrated Madame de Staël, whom Byron had called 'frightful as a precipice'. The Duke was appalled and shouted 'Take me away! Take me away!' They did.

When in October 1811 the Duchess was gravely ill, an express message was sent to Whiteknights at Reading to summon the estranged heir to her bedside. She would see him, she said, on condition that he made no attempt to trouble his father. And indeed, when Blandford arrived that evening he found a message from his father to say that he felt 'too nervous' to see him, but that he considered this the beginning of a reconciliation. Lord Blandford was then conducted to his mother, who shook hands and told him he must seek his father's forgiveness, not hers. 'She wished him only to acknowledge that she had ever stood his friend', which he readily did. 'She then talked calmly about his children, hoping he would breed them up well; and that she should like to live a little longer, but the medical gentlemen knew best. On the whole Lord Blandford was affected with the interview.'

'On his retirement', the account in the British Library continues, 'Lord Blandford was given a cold collation and received a message from his father that he wished to see him. He later described this interview as one scene of sobbing by the Duke whilst he was on his knees before him.'

On November 24th the Duchess was pronounced out of imminent

danger. The Duke went to her bedside, felt her cold hand and burst into tears. She died before the end of the year. The Duke outlived her by six lonely years.

And so now, whether subconsciously or knowingly, every visitor who catches his breath with wonder as he enters Blenheim Park from Woodstock, whether poor pedestrian, or rich man in his Rolls passing as it were through the eye of a needle, pays tribute to the memory of the fourth Duke and to that of Brown whom he commissioned to transform the neglected landscape he had inherited into one of the most romantic prospects in England.

George fifth Duke of Marlborough
——— 1766–1840 ———

George sixth Duke of Marlborough
——— 1793–1857 ———

After the long reign of the distinguished and personable fourth Duke of Marlborough there was, by a strange but all too frequent trick of genetics, bound to be an anti-climax when his heir, George fifth Duke, succeeded in 1817 as owner and master of Blenheim. (Marlborough House had reverted to the Crown on the death of his father.)

It was not that the young man was a hopeless delinquent, nor even, like Willigo, an alcoholic. On the contrary, as bibliophile and botanist, he came up to professional standards. He was simply and sadly weak and perilously so when it came to living within what most people would then have called ample means. True, there had been extravagance, but towards the end the fourth Duke had been wise and retiring enough to curb his own spending; and if his heir had been half as wise as himself he could have managed quite comfortably without ruining the estate. As it was, his first tutor Dr Coxe had had to admit defeat and leave Blenheim. George was beyond his control.

Long before his succession he had, as Lord Blandford, had the bad luck to be involved in a scandal for which, as Dr Rowse has observed, he was not to blame. Among a gaggle of mothers anxious for him to marry one of their daughters, a Mrs Gunning, encouraged by the old Duchess of Bedford, proved the most determined. And while it was true that Blandford had written affectionately to Miss Gunnilda Gunning, he had made it clear, so he said, that there could be no question of marriage. Mrs Gunning having, as some hinted, forged more compromising letters from the Marquis, then wrote what Sarah would have called a narrative, running to nearly two hundred and fifty pages, in which Gunnilda was referred to as 'her glorious darling'. For gossipmongers no doubt this helped to shorten long winter evenings, but for the rest it was no more than a nine-day farce.

Like Sarah's mother, Blandford sought refuge from moneylenders by lodging in St James's, where disapproving parents gave him a mean allowance. In fairness to them however it has to be owned that of all the Churchills and Spencers he was the most thriftless and the most extravagant. In his coach he had shown Captain Gronow fifty thousand-pound notes which were all borrowed money. 'You see, Gronow', he explained, 'how the immense fortune of my family will be frittered away; but I can't help it, I must live. My father inherited £500,000 in ready money and £70,000 a year in land; and in all probability when it comes to my turn to live at Blenheim I shall have nothing left but the annuity of £5,000 a year on the Post Office.'*

In 1791, almost secretly in Lord Dashwood's house, he was married to Susan, daughter of the seventh Earl of Galloway. For Blenheim he still had twenty-six years to wait, but that was no bar to his having a country seat at Reading called Whiteknights (its site now occupied by a redbrick university), which he kept up 'with a splendour worthy of a royal residence'. Conservatories, shrubberies and flowerbeds called for the labours of more than twenty gardeners. His enthusiasm for rare plants ran away with him; while for books and manuscripts he outdid Sunderland by acquiring the Valdarfar Boccaccio and the Bedford Missal.

---

* The pension, granted to the first duke in perpetuity, was commuted in 1884 by a payment of £107,780.

His life was a fantastic farrago of luxury and squalor. When at long last, in 1817, he succeeded to the dukedom, the celebrations at Blenheim must have cost a fortune in themselves. These were some of the arrangements:

> The stable people to be stationed on the steps when the company arrive . . . The lamps round the court, steps and portico to be lighted by nine . . . The other servants to be ranged in the Hall to announce the company and conduct them through the Bow Window Room to the Grand Cabinet. The double doors to be opened as far as the diningroom . . .

> Dinner was to be served precisely at half-past five; and directly it was over, the rooms were to be lighted, one servant attending all evening to the lamps and another to the candles.

> The band to play in the Hall while the company arrive, then in the Diningroom as they pass to the Saloon. They will afterwards return to the Hall and during dessert play at the door leading to the Saloon. When the ladies retire they will cease and be ready to recommence in the Library when the gentlemen go to the Drawingroom. A person will attend to give them refreshments in the Colonnade, but *on no account whatever* must anything be taken into the Library.

After such frolics one of the Duke's more sensible acts was to apply for official approval to add to the surname of Spencer that of Churchill, 'in order to perpetuate in his family a surname to which his illustrious ancestor John first Duke of Marlborough had added such imperishable lustre'. This was granted.

Luckily for Blenheim the fifth Duke had no plans for laying 'the improver's desolating hand' upon its approaches. He had taste enough to see that the scene set by his father and Lancelot Brown was idyllic and could never be surpassed. Besides, this Duke was a botanist and must have realised that the immediate environment of Vanbrugh's colosseum was no place to show off what the architect had scathingly called 'a parcel of foolish plants'.

Certainly he would create new gardens, but they would be a coach-ride west of the house, some near Brown's cascade, some to surround the suitably named Temple of Flora; and for those gardens he would order thousands of those exotics – the hardier the better – now pouring in from China and from the New World. There would be a Chinese Garden, a New Holland or Botany Bay Garden, a Dahlia Garden, a Terrace Garden and of course a Rose Garden. All would be encompassed by individual borders, some composed of dwarf oaks.

Brown's Great Cascade called for treatment on a grand scale; and so, near the head of it, boulders were brought to make one of the first rock-gardens in England, the largest monolith of all crowning a Druid's Temple: 'an altar formed by an immense tablet of rock supported by huge pillars of unhewn stone, overgrown with moss'. Not far from it, in odd contrast, stood the Swiss Cottage 'for the watchman of the Private Gardens'; and near the foot of the cascade, on both banks of the Glyme, exotics flowered against a background of shrubs, swamp-cypress and cedars. But this was by no means all in what was known as the Valley of Streams. There was an island with rustic bridges and a Shepherd's Cot. There were a Garden of Springs, a Lion Fountain, a Trysting Tree, a Grotto, and for good measure Bernini's *modello* for his river-gods fountain in Rome, given long ago to the first Duke and now 'flung together in rude pomp'. On the west of this valley the ground rose steeply and there, amid twisting paths in the *Flora Petraea*, guests suddenly found their way blocked by yet another gigantic boulder. This in fact was the Duke's idea of a joke. In large gardens it had become fashionable to conjure up moods of rapture or, in the manner of Salvator Rosa, of something between 'a perceptible thrill of terror' and delight. This, then, was the Duke's cue to step forward and touch a hidden spring which caused the rock to swivel and so to clear the way. The lodge nearest this place is still called Spring Lock and the casual visitor wonders why.

Within the palace we hear of elaborate redecoration on the west. Beneath the Long Library, where Vanbrugh had intended a grotto, the new owners furnished one of what are now called the Arcade Rooms* with:

* 'Now fitted up with the contents of the old China Gallery'. Mavor: *New Description of Blenheim* (13th edition, 1835)

Waterloo blue puckered drapery, ornamented at intervals with black rosettes, and a large rosette of the same material in the centre of the ceiling, from which all the ribs of the drapery diverge. This room looks immediately on to the Arcade Flower Garden and a pavilion of an octagon form composed of various coloured woods with their natural bark. This is supported by columns of yew with a carved colonnade around it. Two other apartments are now added, one a withdrawing room fitted up entirely with a Japan wainscotting round a painted representation of a Tiger Hunt in India . . . The Refectory is in imitation of an Italian diningroom of *verd d'antique* and Sienna marble, with corresponding columns and doorcases. The doors are of polished Blenheim oak and with acacia also grown in Blenheim Park.

In Lady Mary Ann Sturt, wife of a Dorsetshire MP, the Duke had long since found a mistress, who had borne him a daughter Georgiana. 'Suffer this innocent babe', he had begged her, 'to cement our union, so that it may know no end. Love the little Georgiana for the sake of your George, of your Blandford, of your faithful husband.' But in spite of all this, the cement failed to last. In 1801 Lady Mary sued him for £20,000 and was awarded £100.

All that his Duchess Susan has left us is a large, bound portfolio of flower paintings. It was not unusual at that time for more or less talented women with time on their hands to take to painting and needlework; but these water-colours by the fifth Duchess are outstandingly beautiful. She must indeed have loved flowers as did her spendthrift husband. In 1793 they had a son – inevitably George – who became sixth Duke in 1840; but long before that the bailiffs had moved in. The Boccaccio, which had cost the fifth Duke £2,260, went to his cousin Earl Spencer for £875; and his whole library (not the Sunderland) fetched less than £14,500. Whiteknights had to go to Sir Charles Cockerell, one of the Duke's creditors. The gardens alone had cost nearly £50,000, plus a further £10,000 still owed for plants.

In 1824 Mrs Arbuthnot, visiting Blenheim in the company of Wellington, found it 'a disgrace to the illustrious name of Churchill'. The Duke was overloaded with debt and, in her view, very little better than a common swindler. 'It has required all the authority of a Court of Chancery', she added, 'to prevent his cutting down all the trees in the park . . . He did melt and sell the gold plate given the Great Duke by the Elector of Bavaria, substituting ormolu ones to deceive the trustees.'* The fourth Duke had left directions that the Marlborough Gems were to be kept locked in a vault. 'It was fortunate for the family', comments Dr Rowse, 'that the Blenheim estate and the heirlooms were strictly entailed or they would surely have gone the way of the rest'. When in 1835 Queen Adelaide and her sister called at Blenheim the Duchess was absent.

Five years later the fifth Duke died, leaving in his will dated 1838 'all and singular my goods chattels and effects unto Matilda Glover now living in my family at Blenheim and I do hereby nominate constitute and appoint the said Matilda Glover to be the sole executrix of this my will'. Of Matilda Glover we would know nothing but for a book called *Oxford Common Room* by V.H.H. Green (Arnold, 1957), in which its author prints a statement made in 1823 by a Mr Richardson of Combe, a village bordering the park:

> There was an old woman and three young ones lived at the Home Lodge a good while, and the Duke there or at Blenheim every night. We heard the Marquis fetched his brother away, and the women are gone all but one and she lives at the Home Lodge. The Duke has given Miss Glover a pony and gig, and Miss takes her eldest daughter there every morning and fetches them [sic] at night. The woman and Miss seem very comfortable companions. Both the misses and the Duke are at the Home Lodge most nights to a late hour, playing on music and they say she is their singer . . . We hear she is in the family way and Miss Glover is quite forward in the same way.

Towards the end he had lived 'in utter retirement at one corner of his magnificent palace'. His Duchess, who had a grace-and-favour apartment

---

* Mrs Arbuthnot, was almost certainly misinformed. The gold plate was given to the first Duchess by Sophia Electress of Hanover and bore her arms. Of that service only one plate now remains.

at Hampton Court, died a year later. There was no mention of her in his will.

George Spencer-Churchill sixth Duke of Marlborough succeeded in 1840 and married three times. His first wife Jane, daughter of the eighth Earl of Galloway, had been born at Blenheim in 1798 and died in 1844; his second, Charlotte daughter of Viscount Ashbrook, died in 1850; his third, Jane daughter of the Hon. Edward Stewart, outlived him by forty years, dying in 1897, the year the tenth Duke of Marlborough was born.

While his father was Marquis of Blandford, his own title was Lord Sunderland (shortened to 'Sunny'). In the family tradition he went to Eton, where he made an impression with his remarkably good looks. At twenty-three he became involved in the sort of farce dramatised by Vanbrugh. Here again matchmakers had been busy until Sunderland, with his officer-brother officiating, found himself being married to a girl of sixteen in her mother's presence (a Hogarthian scene). When in 1840 Sunderland became Duke the girl went to live privately with her so-called husband; but after a year of this they travelled separately to Scotland, herself as 'Mrs Lawson' with a child called Susan and a servant. It was an impossible situation which ended with a 'settlement' of £400 a year.

In 1829 and 1830 the sixth Duke, then Lord Blandford, had spoken frequently in the House of Lords. For the subject of his maiden speech he chose, of all things, spring-guns. He had, he said, made use of them for the protection of his own property and 'considered the objections urged against them to arise from a kind of morbid sensibility'. Would he, one wonders, have said the same of man-traps? But his own strongest objection was to Roman Catholic Emancipation, and his outbursts on that topic must have cost him much thought and time. Far more sensible was his advocacy for the abolition of rotten boroughs.

He was Lord-Lieutenant and High Steward of Oxfordshire from 1842 until his death in 1857, when he was sixty-three and had for several years been confined to a wheeled chair. When fit he had been keen on yachting, fishing and shooting; and we know that he remained on good terms with his children. His funeral expenses, he directed, were not to exceed £100.

For the rest, he left instructions that at his death all his personal papers were to be destroyed, and so they were. His third widow, to whom he left nothing, was dutiful enough to respect his silence for forty years. On the whole he has failed to endear himself to posterity.

In the muniment room at Blenheim he left no trace, but in the Long Library his marginal notes and expostulations in the last (posthumous) edition of Dr. Mavor's *New Description of Blenheim* show at least that he had a mind of his own. Beside the assertion that 'when men begin to reason they cease to feel' he has written 'Nonsense'; where Mavor has suggested that Raphael has given the Ansidei Madonna a less weak and 'effeminate' expression than usual the Duke has added an exclamation-mark; while the mere mention of a bust by Bacon of Antonina, daughter of Francis Lord Le Despencer, he has obliterated. An explanatory note in another hand tells us:

The great rubbing-out at page 60 was to efface the name of Antonina Lee, the same who made herself so notorious with Lockhart Gordon. Her bust, beautifully executed, found its way to Blenheim . . . Mr King, rector of West Wycombe, told me that Mrs Lee called, requesting him to allow her to put up her father's bust in West Wycombe church on the hill, which her father had built. Mr King assented and upon his return after a short absence was surprised to discover that Mrs Lee had inserted her own bust as well as her father's in the niches she had scooped out of the wall. Mr King told Mrs Lee that he could not suffer the bust of a person still alive to be introduced into the church. She immediately replied that he should not have her father's bust except he took hers. The controversy ended by her filling up both the niches and removing both the busts. Her bust was afterwards placed in (the Bow Window Room) at Blenheim.

During all this time one has to imagine a steady influx of visitors. Before the palace was half built they could not wait to look into the unglazed rooms; and young Joynes was accused by the first Duchess of showing the shell of the house for money. In Mavor's twelfth edition he noted that 'within the last fifty years the improvements of the park and gardens and the expansion of the water have cost little less than £200,000'. People – among them Dr Johnson and Boswell – flocked to see all these wonders, but when they found that to see the palace they must pay ten shillings, whether alone or with five others, they complained that the charge was exorbitant. A writer in the *Illustrated London News*, while owning that the public had no right to demand admission to any man's private house and grounds, suggested that if admission were granted, then it should be on the most liberal principles, 'binding closer the ties of respect uniting the upper and lower classes'. A reply from Blenheim assured the public that the maximum charge was five shillings, that six persons were as many as one man could watch and that for three days in the week no ticket was necessary – 'a privilege which is a great tax upon the Marlborough family'.

There then followed correspondence in *The Times*, in which Lord Alfred Cecil joined. In the last of these rather pompous letters the anonymous writer who had started the rumpus concluded it by holding up to the sixth Duke the examples of 'noblemen who zealously endeavour to elevate the tastes of the humbler classes by lectures, by libraries, by social gatherings, inviting them to visit their domains and encouraging their rustic sports; weaning them from the brawls of the beershop and making them enjoy, in the company of their wives, their families and their neighbours, social intercourse and innocent recreation in the open air . . . Show faith', he implored the Duke, 'and your faith will be justified'. It was a nauseating letter. However, soon afterwards it was proclaimed that from then onwards Blenheim might be visited for one shilling; while as to the gardens, the Duke assured the editor of *The Times* that the head-gardener had permission 'for his own and his men's attendance upon the visitors to require the sum of tuppence per head and no more'. The millennium had arrived.

VI

John Winston seventh Duke of Marlborough
──────────── 1822–1883 ────────────

George Charles eighth Duke of Marlborough
──────────── 1844–1892 ────────────

In 1857, when John Winston Spencer-Churchill succeeded as seventh Duke of Marlborough (his reign lasted twenty-six years), Blenheim found itself landed with an owner whom even the zealous Churchill-protagonist Dr Rowse has called 'a complete, full-blown, Victorian prig'.

For this late flowering of self-righteousness his ancestors on the whole could not, as we have seen, be held responsible; nor was his wife Frances, daughter of the Marquis of Londonderry, less formidable nor less sparing to those she considered below the mark.

Photography, then beginning to reveal not only features but character, has not been kind to this virtuous couple: the tightly corseted Duchess wears a no–nonsense expression which helps us to believe Lady Randolph's assertion that the whole household trembled at the rustle of her silk dress; while the Duke's full, greying dundrearies do little to soften the severity of his face. About the eyes there is a faint hint of kindliness, but the eyes themselves look tired and disillusioned.

[109]

Perhaps his conscience was his worst enemy for it drove him in politics to tilt at windmills which though obsolete were not then ready to topple and now with hindsight seem unworthy of his strife. Chief of these windmills was church-reform (since run to madness); but marrying a dead wife's sister (he was against it) ran it a close second; and education a third.

In common with more recent reformers such as George Lansbury and Sir Stafford Cripps the seventh Duke sincerely believed that with free education, higher pay and more religion (C. of E.) England would become a truly Christian country with every Englishman as considerate as himself. For how should a public-spirited duke know anything of greed and envy, of 'much wants more' and of 'more means worse'? Though not rich as dukes went, he was privileged in an age of privilege, with Victoria on the throne and all the riches of India to back us.

With what he must have considered the best will in the world his attitude was one of *de haut en bas*, as for example towards Sabbath Day Observance. How shocking it was that 'from six to ten on Sundays the public houses were filled with persons carousing and reducing themselves to the level of beasts'. And as for education, while still Lord Blandford in 1850 he had opposed an Education Bill on the grounds that 'you will have taught the people to desire great things without giving them instruction which from God's Word teaches them to be loyal and contented subjects'. As Caliban protested, 'You taught me language, and my profit on't is I know how to curse.'

It was not altogether to be wondered at that such parents bred rebellious sons: George Charles the heir and his brother (five years younger) Randolph; nor that for some years Blenheim became an irreproachably respectable and dismally boring place. Deans and bishops were asked to dine, while the Duchess sat 'evidently racking her brains for some subject for conversation'.

Lady Randolph tells us:

The Duke and Duchess lived in a most dignified and indeed somewhat formal style. At luncheon rows of entrée dishes adorned the table, joints beneath massive silver covers being placed before the Duke and

Duchess, who each carved for the whole company, and as this included governesses, tutors and children, it was no sinecure. Before leaving the diningroom the children filled small baskets with food for poor cottagers or any who might be sick or sorry in Woodstock. These they distributed in the course of their afternoon walks.

When the house was full for a shooting-party, even breakfast was made a ceremonial meal . . . The ladies would be dressed in long velvet or silk trains. Dinner of course was always a full-dress affair; and after it they might play a mild game of whist, with many a covert glance at the clock, since no one dared suggest bed before eleven. Then, after lighting candles, house-guests would in turn kiss their host and hostess before retiring to their rooms.

Lady Randolph found it necessary to invent her own kind of entertainment even if it meant mingling with paying visitors and eavesdropping on their comments. It was an American who, standing in front of one of the family portraits, she heard exclaim: 'My, but what poppy eyes these Churchills have!' This applied to Lord Randolph in later life; but as a man of twenty-four, desperately in love with Jennie Jerome, to whom he proposed within days of their first meeting at Cowes in the Isle of Wight, he was, like most of his family, good-looking.

But their courtship went anything but smoothly because although his love was fervently returned there were on both sides strongminded parents, slow to give consent and when they did, added, on the Marlboroughs' part, that the engagement must be a long one. Jennie was only nineteen and her father, the sporting Leonard, would have preferred an American; while the Duke thought Leonard Jerome sounded vulgar and not sufficiently rich. He had in fact made and lost two fortunes and was in the process of making a third in New York, while his wife Clara lived in Paris with her three daughters, all with strong minds of their own.

It would have been helpful if Lord Randolph's brother, Lord Blandford, had supported him; but he himself had made a disastrous marriage to the Duke of Abercorn's daughter Bertha, one of those tiresome Victorians who found practical jokes amusing. Blandford's humour, though coarse enough

[111]

in its way, ran in different channels and he soon came to detest her. As a feeble rhymester he sent Randolph an *Elegy on Marriage* in which one stanza runs:

I know a youth who scarce a year ago
Rushed into the wedded lock,
Who all his worldly goods would now forego
To take his feet from out the stocks.

It was his version of Mr Punch's advice to those about to marry: 'Don't'. In the meantime Randolph was assuring Jennie: 'Dearest I love you better than anything on earth and shall *never* love another.' He was even prepared to resort to a kind of blackmail should his parents withhold their consent. They were, as he well knew, counting upon his defeating a neighbour to represent Woodstock at the next election; Woodstock being, in Sarah's view and it would seem in theirs, the Marlboroughs' birthright. Well now, what if he refused to stand or, at the eleventh hour, backed out? The plan was, to say the best of it, childish and was never attempted. Blandford was elected and his brother Randolph married Jennie Jerome in the British Embassy in Paris on April 15th, 1874.

The bride first saw Blenheim in fine weather the following May. As their carriage was pulled by the tenants through Hawksmoor's triumphal arch and so into the park, Randolph said, 'This is the finest view in England'. Jennie was determined to get on with her mother-in-law, of whom at first she wrote: 'a very remarkable and intelligent woman with a warm heart, particularly for members of her family; which made up for any over-masterfulness of which she might have been accused' – a charitable view, to be modified later.

It was on November 30th, 1874 that Winston Leonard Spencer-Churchill was prematurely born at Blenheim, where Lord and Lady Randolph happened to be paying one of their frequent visits from their comparatively small house in London.

One might think that such an occurrence, with a number of witnesses, might accurately have been set on record. Yet the late Sir Shane Leslie, whose aunt was present at the birth, assured me that Lady Randolph had been watching the dancers in the Long Library that evening, at a St Andrew's Eve ball, when she suddenly became aware that the birth was imminent; whereupon she was 'hastened' into the nearest room (once the first Duke's chaplain's but used for the ball as a cloakroom) where, without delay and without even a bed to lie on, she gave birth to this sandy-haired child.

But Sir Shane was wrong and it was Sir Winston's son Randolph who proved him so by discovering a letter from Lord Randolph Churchill which made it clear that Jennie had had a fall while out with the guns in the park; and 'a rather imprudent and rough drive in a pony-carriage brought on the pains on Saturday night'. Labour lasted eight hours but there were no complications. As Mr Randolph Churchill pointed out, Victorians would never have danced on a Sunday – and why celebrate St Andrew's Eve in England anyway?

Two footnotes to that great event are irresistible. One is when the tenth Duke of Marlborough, seeking elucidation, was told by Sir Winston: 'Although present upon that occasion I have no clear recollection of the events leading up to it'. The other was told to me by his son Randolph. Again the tenth Duke asked Sir Winston if he would have any objection to the guides telling the public that he had been born in the Coral Rooms, opposite the Dean Jones Room, since the latter was, after the war, so neglected that it would take months to restore it. Sir Winston was displeased. 'You cannot attempt to hoodwink the British public', he answered, 'and if you do, I shall expose you.' It is only fair to add that otherwise they were always on the friendliest of terms.

But that is romping ahead from Victoria to Elizabeth, or rather, to the tenth Duke's godfather, Albert Edward Prince of Wales who, in contrast to his great but censorious mother, set the tone for lavish living among those who could or hoped they could afford it. The seventh Duke became Lord-Lieutenant of Oxfordshire and, rather surprisingly, began to entertain on a scale grand enough even for Blenheim. On more than one occasion Prince Edward stayed in the palace and attended what amounted to state dinners in the Saloon, with dancing afterwards in the Long Library. The servants of course were in livery, the women guests impressively bejewelled. The Prince danced every dance and on one occasion was still dancing the Cotillion at four in the morning.

On his next visit the Prince found the first and second staterooms refurnished in his honour; his own apartments redecorated in white and gold. There was a ball of course, pronounced by the local press 'the most brilliant spectacle in the county for a century'.

The Duchess was far from pleased when, at the wedding of the Prince to Princess Alexandra at Windsor in 1862, the Disraelis were invited but the Marlboroughs were not. After the reception the Prince had had at Blenheim this, she thought, was shameful. And so it was.

The Duke might be a little mollified by being made Lord Steward of the Household and, in Disraeli's Ministry, Lord President of the Council; but with two sons and six daughters, 'faring sumptuously every day', and an income of some £40,000 a year (even in those days a bagatelle compared with other dukes' revenues), he found himself in the 1870s heading for the same sort of disaster as had overtaken his grandfather the fifth Duke. In 1875 he sold the Marlborough Gems, that world-famous collection – 739 jewels and cameos in red morocco cases – to which the fourth Duke had devoted intense study and many an hour of his long life. Agnew, bidding for a Mr Bromilow, bought the collection outright for thirty-five thousand guineas.

The Prince of Wales with his Marlborough House set continued, to his mother's dismay, to lead the fashion in extravagance and loose living. He made it smart to be 'fast', always provided that no breath of scandal should reach the public press. With £112,000 voted him by the Commons and another £100,000 from India he was now off to that country to shoot elephants and tigers and in general to amuse himself. With him went a number of personal friends including Lord Aylesford, known as Sporting Joe. None of which would have mattered at Blenheim had not the heir, Lord Blandford, eloped with Lord Aylesford's wife Edith. When news of this reached Nepal, the Prince declared Blandford the greatest blackguard alive. Aylesford made for his home near Coventry, but his wife and Blandford had decided to leave for the Continent, where they stayed for

[114]

some years and had a child.

Such flagrant behaviour could not, as of course it would today, be brushed under the carpet. On the contrary, everyone from Victoria and Alexandra down became involved because – and this was the worst of all – mud had been flung at the Prince of Wales and, since Edith Aylesford had shown his letters to Blandford, who had passed them on to his brother Randolph, rightly or wrongly some of that mud had stuck. Randolph, hotheadedly loyal to his brother, wrote rashly to everyone, with the result that he and Jennie were ostracised by the Prince and his set for nearly five years. Blandford, divorced by Bertha in 1883, the year his father died, never married Edith Aylesford, although she was by then a widow.

The appalled reaction of the parents, when the scandal was at its height, may be imagined. Disraeli, who had been ennobled as Lord Beaconsfield, tactfully advised the Duke to go to Ireland as Viceroy; and to this with some reluctance, bearing in mind how much it would cost him and his household transported from Blenheim, including two unmarried daughters, he agreed. Randolph and Jennie went with them and of course took Winston, then in 1876 a stout two-year-old with reddish sausage-curls, three of which are still to be seen at Blenheim. Winston, who had an enviable trick-memory, for ever remembered his father unveiling a statue; while as to his parents, they seemed always to be hunting, his mother 'a fairy princess, a radiant being possessed of limitless riches and power'.

There was no doubt about Jennie's popularity in Ireland; and Randolph hurled himself into Irish politics, seemingly without a care in the world. In 1880 Jack Churchill, Winston's beloved brother, was born; and in the same year, when Gladstone for the second time became Prime Minister, the Duke automatically resigned and the whole family returned to England.

Lord Randolph, as a back-bencher in opposition, felt much at home and embarked upon what everyone took to be a brilliant political career. For this reason among others he and his family usually lived in London, which suited them much better than Blenheim.

The fact is I *loathe* living here [confessed Jennie on Blenheim-headed paper]. It is not on account of its dullness, *that* I don't mind, but it is gall

[115]

and wormwood to me to accept anything [from] or to be living on anyone I hate. It is no use disguising it, the Duchess hates me simply for what I am – perhaps a little prettier and more attractive than her daughters. Everything I do or say or wear is found fault with. We are always studiously polite to each other, but it is rather like a volcano, ready to burst out at any moment.

Winston's Nanny Everest, whom he deeply loved, was convinced that the stone walls of Blenheim were as unhealthy for him (he had had pneumonia) as Sarah had believed they were for her gout. She preferred to see him there as seldom as possible. Certainly in its owners' absence Blenheim had been neglected. On his return the seventh Duke found everything clamouring for attention and as usual there was no ready money to pay for it. But he had an idea – the worst for Blenheim he had ever had. The Lord Chancellor was a personal friend. Surely with his help there should be no difficulty in overriding those Acts whereby, thanks mainly to Sarah, the Marlborough heirlooms were protected. Why, selling his share of the Sunderland Library alone might bring enough to relieve his immediate embarrassment. It was. In 1880 the Blenheim Settled Estates Act overruled the entail on the grounds that the library was deteriorating. Lord Randolph, an admirer of Gibbon and Horace, strongly objected and so fell out with his brother. He was brushed aside. It took two auction-sales, each lasting ten days, to disperse, in December 1881 and July 1882, one of the world's great libraries. The total takings were £56,581 6s., the cost today of one semi-detached suburban villa. By ridding himself of that heirloom and so paving the way for even more disastrous sales by his successor, the seventh and eighth Dukes must go down to history as Philistines on a ducal scale.

Ironically enough, the seventh Duke was granted £2,000 towards turning the Long Library back into a picture gallery, which from the beginning had been Vanbrugh's intention. Thanks to that room's proportions (183 feet long) and to Hawksmoor's enrichments, it is still 'a noble room of parade', though lacking the Van Dyck of Charles I (now in the National Gallery) and many another superb painting chosen and sent home by the first Duke of Marlborough.

The summer of 1883 found the seventh Duke still obsessed with the unforgivable sin of marrying one's widow's sister. At sixty-one he seemed cursed with a one-track mind that led nowhere, unless to Woodstock, where he had helped to instigate the narrow-gauge railway, with the *Fair Rosamond* as its engine, which ran to and from Oxford. One scarcely need add that in a diesel-mad world that charming piece of nonsense has long since been obliterated.

His last speech in the Lords, in June 1883 (did anyone except Lord Hugh Cecil listen?), still harped upon the same tedious subject. On July 5th he had a heart-attack and died. After lying in state at Blenheim his coffin was lowered into the chapel vault in the presence of Lord Randolph and of his heir. His statue by Sir Joseph Boehm was added later.

In his will he left his Duchess the house in Berkeley Square, £2,000 a year and all her jewellery 'except the three large diamonds set now in her necklace and which have been substituted for diamonds formerly set in the sword of John Duke of Marlborough'. All six daughters, including the four married ones (one of them the Duchess of Roxburgh) were well provided for. It was the will of a conscientious man who in his lifetime had been known as the *good* duke. But to his dying day he remained the 'complete, full-blown Victorian prig'; an example not to be followed by his successor.

'It is very melancholy here', wrote Lord Randolph from Blenheim, 'sad recollections at every moment. Nothing can be nicer than Blandford to everyone.' But that mood was not to last. With his Blenheim Settled Estates Act of 1880 the seventh Duke had left the way wide open for his feckless heir, who cared far more about farms than about art, or indeed about his posterity, to sell all the treasures and heirlooms he could lay hands on: paintings, porcelain, furniture – what was the use of them? Let them all go. He could do with the cash for barns and hothouses, not to mention more personal and private needs.

At this Lord Randolph exploded. It had been hard enough watching the dispersal of the library; but now the famous Van Dycks and the equally famous Rubens, classics by Rembrandt, Gainsborough, Claude and Poussin – and of course Raphael's Madonna – and a great deal more. Must

Eighth Duke of Marlborough and family. In background part of Blenheim's east front

he stand by and see his home stripped, while paintings chosen by his ancestors, the first and fourth Dukes, went under the hammer? So often in the past, to his own cost, he had stood by his brother, but now frustration and fury made a breach never to be healed.

The National Gallery gave £70,000 for the Ansidei Madonna, from the Green Drawing-room, and £17,500 for Van Dyck's equestrian Charles I which had hung where the organ now is, at the northern end of the Long Library.* In 1763 the fourth Duke had paid four guineas for it to be 'new strained, repaired, cleaned and varnished'. But the sales of paintings alone continued for days at Christies in 1886. Millais was able to snap up Van Dyck's *Time Clipping the Wings of Cupid* for £241 10s. The names of the Italian painters alone are enough to make the mouth water, if not the eyes: Carracci, Giordano, Ricci, Bassano, Carlo Dolci, Titian. At one time a small gallery (in the orangery?) had been reserved for a set of Titians painted on leather and given to the first Duke by Amadeus of Savoy, but those had been destroyed by fire. Their authenticity was doubtful, and in Consuelo's day – or rather, her mother-in-law's – they were considered unfit to be seen by feminine eyes.

Next followed the sales of porcelain, of which a so-called valetudinarian called Spalding, a traveller in the Far East, had given his large collection to the Fourth Duke, on three conditions: (i) that a gallery to house it was to be built in Blenheim Park (with a storey added it has long been the home of the Duke's land-agent); (ii) Spalding was to be curator-in-charge for his lifetime; and (iii) no piece from that collection was ever to leave Blenheim. How much of the porcelain sold by the eighth Duke was Spalding's we are never likely to know. Certainly case after case of Blanc de Chine and Famille Vert is left for the public still to admire today; not forgetting the Meissen and Sèvres in the China Cabinet.

With masterly understatement *The Times* referred scathingly to 'owners who are not enthusiastic lovers of art'. At Blenheim, with its Rubens Room and its Van Dyck Room, the walls must have looked bare indeed until tapestries, presumably stored, replaced the paintings; and perhaps they

---

* Van Dyck's Charles I was at one time at Marlborough House.

escaped only because no one else had room for them. As it is, the most famous of them – the battle of Blenheim scene – has to run round two walls, as it did years ago in the Bow Window Room.

Luckily all of Marlborough's campaigning silver and gold, and Sarah's sets of silver candlesticks, with seals and snuffboxes galore – a hoard worthy of Ali Baba – were safely at Althorp, Sarah having willed them to Johnny Spencer. Even so, I remember Sir Winston's aside to the tenth Duke: 'H'm, the Spencers have had a lot from here. However, you still have a nice lot left.'

'Malignant Fate sat by and smiled', for when all this plundering had been done by the eighth Duke, in the name of Mammon, it was soon found to have been totally needless; for Jerome, Jennie's father, had found him his perfect second bride in Lily Hammersley, daughter of Commodore Cicero Price of the American navy and an heiress who preferred not to be called Lilian because it rhymed with (only one?) million. In 1888 the Duke hurried to New York and within a month they were married.

At Blenheim Lily could see at once that the place needed a few deft feminine touches – an organ here, a boathouse there; and of course electricity and central heating everywhere. There was only one bathroom and one temperamental telephone. The new Duchess was kind and sentimental – 'So may thy craft glide gently on as years roll down the stream' she had inscribed on the boathouse – and at the same time showed a tough American streak which let her enjoy rising to any challenge on the Blenheim scale. Most of the treasures were gone – she had never known them – but she would enrich the house her own way. The Willis organ alone, at first in the western apse of the Long Library, was surely compensation enough for the loss of one Van Dyck?

But could the Duke throw off his melancholy and revel in all these glories as she did? Unhappily not. Together they listened to Mr Perkins of Birmingham, the all-but-resident organist, and seemed content. Yet tucked away at the side of the organ an unsigned inscription reads: 'C.W. Perkins. How often has thy genius beguiled my sad heart.' And when the Duke died, as he did of heart-failure in 1892 (he was forty-eight), a scrap torn from *The Times* was found among his papers. On it he had written the inscription still to be seen on the front of the organ:

In memory of happy days
and as a tribute to this glorious home
we leave thy voice
to speak within these walls
in years to come
when ours are still

LM and MM
1891

In his will the eighth Duke provided for Lily, who married Lord William Beresford (later Marquis of Waterford) and settled near Dorking. The marriage was a happy one. The Duke made no mention of Lady Aylesford or of her son, but – a surprise-package this – left 'twenty thousand pounds absolutely to Lady Colin Campbell as a proof of my friendship and esteem'. £5,000 was left in trust to be invested so that in twenty-one years' time there should be enough to repair the walls of the palace and the roof; although today it might scarcely account for one finial. £3,000 was left for the repair of Bladon Church, which is now being restored. Finally he tacked on a curious clause:

I dislike particularly the exclusiveness of family pride and I wish not to be buried in the family vault in Blenheim Chapel but in any suitable place that may be convenient in which others of my own generation and surroundings are equally able with myself to find a resting place together.

The Duke's democratic wish was granted, so that for the first time that corner beside Bladon Church tower which faces the south front of Blenheim was dug to make way for the mortal remains of a Spencer-Churchill. In time, in that same corner, room would have to be found for Lord and Lady Randolph and for their son Jack, who died in 1947.

[121]

Problems arose when Consuelo Vanderbilt, ninth (dowager) Duchess, living in America as Madame Balsan, directed in her will that she too must be buried there, as in 1964 she was; since by that time it was known that a plot had been reserved by Sir Winston Churchill for himself and his wife. However, all these difficulties were overcome; and there, within sight of Blenheim, they do indeed find a resting place together.

When his brother died, Lord Randolph had but three more years to live. His spectacular success in politics, between 1884 and 1886, has too exhaustively been dealt with by his son and others to need repetition here. At his zenith he was Leader of the House of Commons and Chancellor of the Exchequer, in which post 'those damned dots' in the Budget proved as bewildering as they did to his son Winston when his turn came to fill the same high office.

Randolph himself had presentiments of his downfall. 'I shall lead the Opposition for five years', he predicted; 'then I shall be Prime Minister for five years. Then I shall die.' But for his impetuousness and for his bad luck in contracting a then incurable disease, he could have been Prime Minister indeed. Lord Rosebery found him 'one of the most remarkable men, with perhaps the most remarkable career, of my time'. In Parliament, in India, at Blenheim where with Jennie and his mother he founded the Primrose League, he worked incessantly. Even Queen Victoria was impressed, though she thought he looked very ill. Her son had forgiven him. At one stage he admitted, 'I am very near the end of my tether. In the last five years I have lived twenty. I have fought Society. I have fought Mr Gladstone at the head of a great majority. I have fought the Front Opposition Bench. Now I am fighting Lord Salisbury . . .'

In 1886, without consulting anyone – Queen, Prime Minister, wife – he suddenly resigned. 'What a fool Lord Salisbury was', he said afterwards, 'to let me go so easily.' But on Randolph's part it had meant not only political suicide but a blow at his own Party, which was unpardonable.

Far more saddening for Jennie was her conviction that her marriage was foundering and that Randolph had fallen for another woman. First she unburdened herself to Randolph's sister, Lady Cornelia Guest, who could only gossip. In desperation Jennie then confided in of all people the dowager Duchess. She proved kind and sympathetic but as all the world knew, she doted upon Randolph, and now she could not but think that Jennie might be wrong, either in her suspicions or even in her own conduct. Jennie's own mother, and Randolph, seemed always to be abroad. She had no one to turn to.

In January 1895 Lord Randolph died from general paralysis of the insane and was buried at Bladon. 'I see, as all the public saw, many faults', wrote Lord Rosebery, 'but I remember what the public could not know, the generous, lovable nature of the man . . . I grieve, as all must grieve, that that daring and gifted spirit should have been extinguished at an age when its work should only just have begun.' He was forty-six.

His widow Jennie married a second and a third time. Her second marriage was to a man she found 'a perfect darling', George Cornwallis-West; although in her book of that name our one-time neighbour, the late Eileen Quelch, made him sound insufferable. In 1912 he fell for Mrs Patrick Campbell and was divorced. He died in 1951. Jennie's third marriage was to Montagu Porch, who outlived her by many years (she died in 1921) and died in 1965. Her beauty had not been wasted.

VII

Charles Richard John
ninth Duke of Marlborough
——— 1871–1934 ———

At the time of his accession in 1892 Charles ninth Duke of Marlborough cabled from America to his Blenheim agent, a Mr Angus: HAVE THE LAKE DREDGED. With the help of steam-engines his order was obeyed, at a cost of £1664. Nowadays of course, after a dry summer when the Glyme flows sluggishly, the cost would be astronomical.

But from the first it was obvious that this Duke, a short, moustached man, not in the least like any of his predecessors, was devoted to his Oxfordshire home; and so he was to remain for the rest of his life.

Born in Simla on November 13th, 1871 he had, he said later, been bullied by his father. He went to Winchester and to Trinity College, Cambridge. In 1895 he married Consuelo, daughter of William Vanderbilt; and so, financially speaking, the future of Blenheim, despoiled as it had been and then partially rescued by another American, Lily Hammersley, was now assured.

It sounds straightforward enough, but in the background, on the far side of the Atlantic, Consuelo's mother had exerted so much pressure that, in effect, the daughter was compelled to throw over the American to whom, at the age of seventeen, she had secretly been engaged, for the honour of becoming an English duchess.

We have still to hear the Duke's side of the story, and perhaps we never shall. His son, when questioned, would only say, 'Everyone was doing it. Everyone just then was marrying an American heiress' – by which I took him to mean every duke – and so in his father's case there was nothing singular about it. One simply followed the fashion. But this of course was an over-simplification. The Duke, at twenty-four, had been much run after, and who was to say that his heart was still whole? In fact it was not and nor was Consuelo's. Each was in love with another, and within a month of marriage each had told the other so.

Mrs Vanderbilt, after divorcing her husband, had threatened heart-attacks and had firmly confined her daughter to the house. Charles's first duty, as he saw it, was to Blenheim which, if fit to be seen by his bride, must swiftly if partially be restored. And so Consuelo's first meeting with his family was in London where at the station she was welcomed by her mother-in-law, the Duke's two unmarried sisters Lilian and Norah, a cousin (Ivor Guest), an aunt (Lady Sarah Wilson), Lady Randolph with her son Winston, and several more. 'I felt the scrutiny of many eyes', she wrote later, 'and hoped that my hat was becoming and that my furs were fine enough to win their approval . . . The sight of these strangers, Marl-borough's family, brought the loneliness of my position sharply into focus . . . I was glad to turn to Winston, a redheaded boy a few years older than I was. He struck me as ardent and vital . . . He was the next heir to the dukedom . . . His mother was beautiful with a vital gaiety that made her the life and soul of any party.'*

So far so good. The first major jolt came when Consuelo was confronted with the dowager duchess. 'Your first duty', she told her coldly, 'is to have a child and it must be a son, because it would be intolerable to have that little upstart Winston become Duke. Are you in the family way?' As yet she was not.

At Blenheim, in cold weather, Consuelo arrived for the first time in sables. There were no cars and so from Oxford they took the single-track

* Consuelo Balsan (née Vanderbilt): *The Glitter and the Gold*.

[125]

railway (a special train pulled by the *Fair Rosamond*) to Woodstock, where they were welcomed by the mayor and corporation. As with Jennie, so with Consuelo, the carriage was dragged through the park by loyal staff and tenants; and of course there were speeches and addresses, flags and bouquets which all but overwhelmed her. She was thankful to be able to relax in a hot bath before dressing for dinner.

But her trials were far from over.

How I learned to dread and hate those dinners, [she wrote in her autobiography *The Glitter and the Gold*] 'how ominous and wearisome they loomed at the end of a long day. They were served with all the accustomed ceremony, but once a course had been passed, the servants retired to the hall; the door was closed and only a ring of the bell, placed before Marlborough, summoned them. He had a way of piling food on his plate; the next move was to push the plate away, together with knives, forks, spoons and glasses – all this in considered gestures which took a long time; then he backed his chair away from the table, crossed one leg over the other and endlessly twirled the ring on his little finger. While accomplishing these gestures he was absorbed in thought and quite oblivious of any reactions I might have. After a quarter of an hour he would suddenly return to earth or perhaps I should say to food and begin to eat very slowly, usually complaining that the food was cold. And how could it be otherwise? As a rule neither of us spoke a word. In desperation I took to knitting, while the butler read detective-stories in the hall.

One might reasonably guess that the thoughts in which the Duke was absorbed concerned Blenheim: so much to be done within and without and who was to do it? Still, at least he now had the funds and besides that, he and he alone could read Vanbrugh's mind and so knew just what was called for, and that on a gigantic scale. What was that ridiculous verse from *The Mikado*?

My brain it teems
With endless schemes

Both good and new
For Titipu . . .

That was it and no time was to be lost. He must get hold of that fellow in
Paris – and he had made a note of the name: Achille Duchêne. Let him be
wired for. He had done marvels restoring formal gardens in France and was
an architect too. Why not see if he had it in him, under iron supervision of
course, to give Blenheim the setting it would have had if Sarah had allowed
Vanbrugh his way?

Almost it might seem as an afterthought, on September 18th, 1897, an
heir was born at Spencer House, St James's, and was christened in the
Chapel Royal. The names chosen were John (after the first Duke), Albert
Edward (after the Prince, his godfather, who was present) and William
(after William Vanderbilt). 'We vainly tried', wrote his mother, 'to eschew
the Albert . . . but in spite of all these names he was called Blandford, for it
was the custom in the family to name the heir by his title.' Winston
Churchill, writing from India, felt in a quandary: 'My dear – I hesitate how
to begin . . . "Sunny" though melodious sounds childish, "Marlborough"
is very formal, "Duke" impossible between relations; and I don't suppose
you answer to either "Charles" or "Richard". If I must reflect, let it be
"Sunny". But you must perceive in all this a strong case for the abolition of
the House of Lords and all titles.' At Blenheim flags were run up and
cannons fired from the roof. Nor was the heir to be denied a medal bearing
his date of birth and the profiles of his parents. A second son, Ivor Charles,
was born on the 14th of the following October.

In the meanwhile work had begun on the main front of the palace where,
with Duchêne's help, the three-acre forecourt was restored to its original
form, with terraces, and granite-setts from France, so that no newcomer
would ever guess how Brown had grassed it over. And even before that had
been finished, the Duke was replanting the two-mile avenue north of
Vanbrugh's bridge with elms, since most of the original trees had, after two
centuries, died. 'In the year 2000', he predicted, 'this avenue will form a
remarkable feature in the park . . . but any man who cuts down the trees for
the purpose of selling the timber will be a scoundrel and deserve the worst

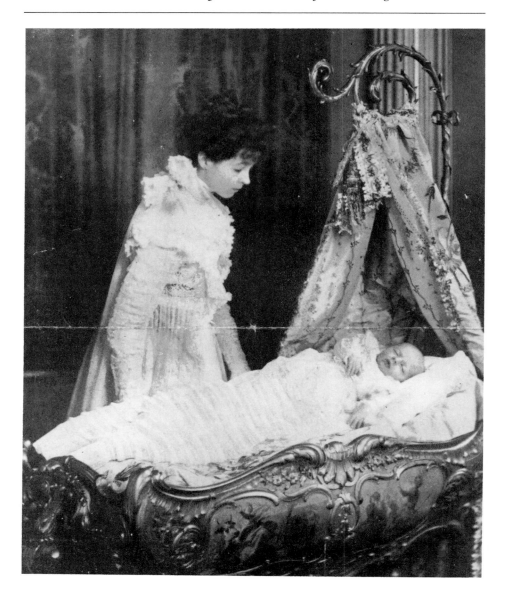

Consuelo ninth Duchess of Marlborough with the tenth Duke (then Marquis of Blandford) in his Italian cradle at Blenheim

[128]

Charles ninth Duke of Marlborough with his younger son Lord Ivor on his knee. The heir, Lord Blandford, stands on the Duke's right.

fate that could befall him'. He was not of course to know that the scoundrel was to be a beetle: Dutch elm disease; and that his grandson would need to replant the whole avenue with lime trees. In the very middle of it the ninth Duke embedded a square block of stone, which he reckoned would stop any madman from speeding down the avenue from the Ditchley Gate to the palace.

One good idea can lead to another. Halfway down the eastern approach from Woodstock he would have a hump (now known as a sleeping policeman), again to slow down ill-mannered motorists. It was a little distressing that one of his first visitors, after this innovation, Lady Ottoline Morrell in her chauffeur-driven landau, should be found senseless on arrival at the north portico. However, she was tough enough to revive quickly, after being carried in and given brandy; and the hump was done away with.

[129]

For the Duke at least, if not for his Duchess, these years at Blenheim must have been some of the happiest in a not altogether happy life. A fig for politics. In Lord Salisbury's last government (1899–1902) he had been Paymaster-General; and in Balfour's administration (1903–5) he was Under-Secretary for the Colonies. In 1900 he had been honoured with the Garter and now in 1905 he would get that American, Sargent, to paint him in Garter robes. The huge painting of himself, his swan-necked Duchess (her robe copied from Mrs Killigrew's: a Van Dyck in the same Red Drawing-room), faces the equally vast Reynolds of the fourth Duke and family, on the opposite wall. Blenheim spaniels appear in both paintings; and Sargent has included a quit-rent standard and a bust of the first Duke. The young heir stands between his parents, himself angelically dressed in yellow silk. Like any other boy of eight he loathed that silk suit and kept fooling around in Sargent's studio until he broke a leg and, to his father's annoyance, held up the sittings. In her autobiography his mother described him as 'audacious and wilful, forever rebelling against authority', in contrast to his brother Ivor who was 'gentle and sensitive . . . with a studious trend'.

At Blenheim there were balls or shooting-parties or, for royalty, both. Gerald Horne, then a hall-boy, remembered:

The Duke and Duchess entertained very lavishly. Wonderful weekend parties they gave, with tea in the boathouse, and the Blue Hungarian Band from London to play at dinner, not to mention Mr Perkins's organ-playing afterwards.

But the greatest occasion of all during my time at Blenheim was the visit of the late King Edward, then Prince of Wales, and the Princess. The Princess Victoria was also of the party, as were Prince and Princess Charles of Denmark, and they all stayed several days for the shooting. Altogether there were thirty-six guests and on the evening of their arrival we had first a torchlight procession (and very pretty it looked crossing the lake by the old stone bridge) and then a banquet.

Some of us were allowed to go up on the balcony and to look down into the front hall where at one long table they were dining; and of course I

Autumn, 1896: the royal shooting-party outside High Lodge in Blenheim Park
Left to right, back row: Earl of Gosford, Lady Emily Kingscote, Hon. Sidney Greville, Mr
George Nathaniel Curzon, General Ellis, Countess of Gosford, Arthur Balfour, Mrs
William Grenfell, Sir Samuel Scott, Marquis of Londonderry, Lady Helen Stewart, Lady
Lilian Spencer-Churchill, Mr William Grenfell, Prince Charles of Denmark, Viscount
Curzon.
Middle row: Earl of Chesterfield, Lady Randolph Churchill, Consuelo Duchess of
Marlborough, HRH the Princess of Wales, Mr H. Chaplin, HRH the Prince of Wales
(later King Edward VII), Mrs George Nathaniel Curzon, the Marchioness of London-
derry, Princess Victoria, Princess Charles of Denmark.
Front row: Lady Sophie Scott, the Duke of Marlborough, Viscountess Curzon

went up and looked down and there it was, all gleaming with wealth. I
think the first thing that struck me was the flashing headgear of the
ladies. The Blue Hungarian was playing and there was the Prince himself
looking really royal and magnificent in military uniform. The table was
laid of course with the silver-gilt service, the old silver Duke (a massive
centrepiece showing Marlborough on his horse, writing the famous
despatch to his Duchess after his greatest victory), busy writing as usual
in the very middle of it all; and the royal footmen waiting side by side
with our own.

Shooting-parties at Blenheim were elaborate affairs, and sure enough next day this royal party was no exception. Sixteen to twenty keepers were always kept; and the food, sent out in padded baskets, was reheated on a stove when it reached a lodge or a luncheon tent. To prevent accidents all the beaters were dressed in white smocks and red tam-o'-shanters. The keepers were very smart in Irish green velvet for their coats and vests with brass buttons, brown breeches and leggings and black billycock hats. The head keeper was distinguished by a hat like Mr Churchill's. It was at Blenheim that we once had the record shoot of the world, five guns shooting 7,500 rabbits in one day. One of the guns that day was the Duke, another Prince Duleepsinhji, a frequent visitor, as was also Mr Churchill with his mother, but he usually went out riding.

In 1896, soon after the royal visitors had left, the Duke riding escort beside them, fire broke out in the roof of the Saloon, but the resident brigade, with its antiquated pump, prevented it from spreading.*

To sit in a leather-hooded chair in the Great Hall and help open the doors, and to stand behind her chair at table (himself in yellow or scarlet turban, tunic, skirt and sash), the Duchess kept a Mohammedan page-boy (Mike, the servants called him), whom she had brought from Egypt. Impressive in public, he was what in Oxfordshire is known as a nineter, and a natural fighter with fists, feet and knife. While he still fitted his gorgeous uniform his barbarity was tolerated. But he grew up, with all that that implies, and so had to be packed off to Egypt where, years later, he popped up as a local guide to a party from Blenheim.

'Sweet days of wild delight!' For the Duke this was Gracious Living indeed – 'keeping up one's position', as he put it – but for Consuelo it meant a vast amount of organising (precedence alone was a headache); and once the guests had gone, boredom and loneliness set in again. When she woke of a morning her first sight was that of a Vanbrugh chimneypiece in white marble across which the eighth Duke had written: 'Dust. Ashes. Nothing.'

---

* 'They've had fires at Blenheim they don't know they've had', an old Woodstock sweep, small enough to climb up inside Vanbrugh's chimney-stacks, told me years ago.   D.B.G.

The gatekeeper, with Blenheim spaniels, at Flagstaff Lodge in the time of the ninth Duke of Marlborough

While another bedroom still bore the ducal graffito: 'They say. What say they? Let them say.'

The Duke remained preoccupied. The staterooms west of the Saloon had been refurnished with French chairs and Boulle cabinets for the royal visit of 1896; but in the Duke's opinion they still cried out for gilded *boiseries* in the manner of Versailles. 'When I was young and uninformed', he was later to tell Duchêne, 'I put French decoration into the three staterooms here.' (Twenty craftsmen from Paris were at work there for at least six months.) 'The rooms', the Duke added, 'have English proportions . . . and

[133]

the result is that the French decoration is quite out of scale and leaves a very unpleasant impression on those who possess trained eyes.' To which may be added that an expert from the Victoria & Albert Museum, on a recent visit to Blenheim, pronounced the *boiseries* magnificent and observed that some of them had been faithfully copied from those once in Louis XIV's bedchamber at Versailles, since demolished.

The Long Library was refurnished with richly bound books, which a guide used to tell visitors were taken from their cases and dusted once a year. Edwardian taste, running to such horrors as potted palms, still prevailed, but Consuelo was not to be blamed for that. Far more beautiful was her own portrait, painted by Carolus-Duran just before her marriage, which hung and still hangs over the chimneypiece in the first stateroom. 'My mother', she wrote, 'wished my portrait to bear comparison with those of preceding duchesses who had been painted by Gainsborough, Reynolds, Romney and Lawrence. In that proud and lovely line I still stand over the mantelpiece of one of the staterooms . . . with a slightly disdainful and remote look as if very far away in thought.'

Little was done in the way of comfort; although it is difficult if not impossible to believe that Blenheim still had but one bathroom. Even in Sarah's day a plunge-pool of sorts with hot water existed in the undercroft beneath her bedroom and could be reached, with assistance, by way of 'my Lady Dutchess's back stairs'.

But the Duke's ultimate goal all along had been to give the palace the formal setting he was convinced it deserved; and to that end, in 1908, having dealt with the north, he made a fresh start on the east front with a sunk, formal garden, protected on the north by Vanbrugh's orangery and on the west by his range of private apartments. With the help of Duchêne, arabesques in dwarf box, on a ground of hand-crushed brick, were plotted as a *jardin d'honneur*, with statues and of course orange trees in tubs; the whole surrounded by what Wise would have called clipped greens: mostly box and yew. Flowers looked well enough when massed in large earthenware wine-jars; but the main idea was to look down from the Bow Window Room and its neighbours to such a vista as might have graced Villandry, and with nothing to check the eye as it rested on the cedar and the croquet-lawn beyond.

Even so, as the Duke realised, that garden still needed a centrepiece, as his banqueting table called for the silver Duke. And then by inspiration (always a strong point) he remembered Waldo Story, that American sculptor he and Consuelo had befriended in Rome. And so he it was who made the central fountain there of Venus and her gilded mermaids and dolphins, with Venus herself holding aloft a ducal coronet through which a spray-fountain plays, to fall into the lily-pool below. As though this were not enough, hidden in the wainscot beside an eastern window was a button which, when secretly pressed by the Duke, would make the fountain play. It was a still better idea than the spring-lock boulder, or the sleeping policeman.

As for the ingenious sculptor, his daughter Mrs Stewart told me: 'My father was American, but educated at Eton and Oxford. He lived in Rome and from there all his works were shipped to England. A personal friend of the Duchess Consuelo, he made a charming bust of her [there are in fact two still at Blenheim], for which she posed in Rome. He sculpted not only the fountain but a statue of John Duke of Marlborough for Clevedon [Cliveden?], Lord Randolph Churchill's statue in the House of Commons, the Portal Monument in Winchester Cathedral and other works including a bust of the ninth Duke.' He died in 1918 and was buried in the Protestant Cemetery in Rome.

'The mornings began with prayers in the Chapel', Consuelo remembered, 'after which breakfast was served . . . At the toll of the chapel bell housemaids would drop their dusters, footmen their trays, housemen their pails, carpenters their ladders, electricians their tools, kitchenmaids their pans, laundrymaids their linen, and all rush to reach the chapel in time'.

She felt sorriest for those servants who slept in what were called the Housemaids' Heights in a tower where there was no running water; 'but since housemaids had so lived for nearly two centuries, I was not allowed to improve their lot'. Like Jennie before her she soon discovered the time-honoured custom of distributing left-overs to poor villagers. This she viewed with mixed feelings. 'With a complete lack of fastidiousness', she wrote, 'meat, vegetables and puddings were mixed in the same tin'. But she

Blenheim Palace: the Venus fountain outside the Bow Window Room

[136]

could easily settle that. 'I sorted the various viands into different tins, to the surprise and delight of the recipients'.

In the 'domain towns' (the villages surrounding Blenheim Park) Consuelo came to be adored. Naturally, when the coach-and-four was heard in the distance cottagers popped in for a spotless apron, to pop out in time to drop a curtsey as the ducal equipage passed; but personal visits by the beautiful American Duchess of course made red-letter days. As an old Long Hanborough woman told me: 'I had a dream last night. I dreamt our Duchess visited me, and do you know what she said? She said mine was the cleanest cottage she had ever been in'. Such visits and such dreams were treasured in a way which nowadays might easily be despised; yet treasured they were and they made for happiness and self-respect.

There were times however when, in her husband's view, Consuelo's role as Lady Bountiful bordered upon presumption. A case in point was when, to relieve unemployment (the perennial problem) she took on a gang of men to repair the main drives in the park. This, she found, was trespassing upon the Duke's preserves. For his part he seemed inclined to accept local loyalty as a matter of course. It was understood that, for his breakfast every morning, a little girl from one of his Bladon farms at Folly Bridge (at least two miles from the palace) would bring in a basket two brown, new-laid eggs. Years later, when that girl had grown up and was running the same farm, she received a postcard from Nice. On one side a brown photograph showed the Boulevard des Anglais. On the other the Duke had written: 'Pray press on with the haymaking while this glorious weather lasts.' It need scarcely be added that when the postcard reached Bladon, it was teeming with rain.

In *The Glitter and the Gold* Consuelo has left for posterity a wonderfully detailed contrast of the lives, public and private, then led by the aristocracy. On grand occasions – and they were many – precedence seemed almost as important in the servants' hall as it was in the Saloon; and for an American this took some mastering. Contrast stepped in when she showed distinguished guests to their rooms and found 'a washstand with its pitchers and basins prominently displayed against the heroic form of a dying horse [in tapestry] . . . The round bathtub placed before the fire with its accompanying impedimenta . . . made me shudder'. The housemaids were obliged to prepare some thirty baths a day. But no fault could be found with the dinner-table, tricked out with malmaisons and orchids, nor with the food and wines, nor with Mr Perkins-at-the-organ afterwards.

One has only to glance at the visitors' book for these early nineteen-hundreds to see that Society flocked to Blenheim. Edward and Alexandra had given the lead and so of course the rest followed:

My name is George Nathaniel Curzon,
I am a most superior person;
My face is pink, my hair is sleek,
I dine at Blenheim once a week.

The London season was equally glamorous and on the whole, for Blenheim's hostess, more carefree; though there were anxious moments when, for example, she was received by Queen Victoria (but that was at Windsor) and again when, at the postponed coronation of Edward and Alexandra, she helped to hold the canopy over the Queen, while the Duke acted as Lord High Steward. There was Ascot, there was a kind of state visit to Russia, there was Sandringham; there were more royal visits to Blenheim, both British and German. 'Alexandra made us laugh', wrote Consuelo, 'telling us how she had to use a ladder to get into my bed, which was on a dais, and how she kept falling over the white bearskins that were strewn on the floor.' Nevertheless Consuelo found that visit 'a tiring and anxious experience'. In four days she had had to wear sixteen dresses, not to mention jewels including pearls that had belonged to Catherine of Russia.

When you have nothing else to wear
But cloth of gold and satins rare,
For cloth of gold you cease to care,
Up goes the price of shoddy.

In winter Marlborough was forever shooting, until they took a small house in Leicestershire where, naturally, he was forever hunting. 'From my window', Consuelo remembered, 'I overlooked a pond in which a former butler had drowned himself. As one gloomy day succeeded another I began to feel a deep sympathy for him.' Soon after Ivor's birth Consuelo made a brave effort to take up hunting but, shocking as it was in that county, she found she preferred reading.

Back at Blenheim Consuelo found she was expected to organise an important house-party, but this time with a difference. The guest of honour was the Crown Prince of Germany, whose father had visited Blenheim the year before and had been much impressed. Another guest, whom Marlborough had met and taken to just after the birth of his heir, was Gladys Deacon. Her family, though no Vanderbilts, were rich and, in American terms, old-established. In Society, in Paris as in New York, she was already a familiar figure; and now she was dining at Blenheim, but not like Curzon once a week – she had been asked to stay for six months. In the Duke she had – to quote her biographer, Hugo Vickers – come face to face with the man of her American dreams; while on their side the Duke and Duchess were both enchanted.

'Gladys Deacon', wrote Consuelo, 'was a beautiful girl endowed with a brilliant intellect. Possessed of exceptional powers of conversation, she could enlarge upon any subject in an interesting and amusing manner. I was soon subjugated by the charm of her companionship and we began a friendship which ended only years later.'

At Blenheim the Crown Prince of Germany, tall and slight with charming manners but a foolish expression, fell for the dazzlingly blue eyes of Miss Deacon, whose own expression had been likened to that of the sphinx. She enjoyed flirting with him and gave him a bracelet; whereupon he gallantly gave her the ring his mother had put on his finger at his Confirmation. After writing in the visitors' book 'I felt very much at home here', he insisted upon driving the Marlborough coach-and-four to Oxford. Consuelo, though nervous herself, sat next to the Prince in order to seize the reins in an emergency. Gladys was sandwiched in the back seat between Marlborough and Metternich; and the Crown Prince kept turning round to gaze at her, to the alarm of the other passengers and the near apoplexy of the ambassador.

[139]

In Germany the brief flirtation was taken more seriously than it was over here. Gladys's bracelet was returned, but on her part the ring was sent back reluctantly, with a murmur of 'childish nonsense'; and although she was soon paying a return visit to Berlin with Consuelo, the Kaiser saw to it that his son was banished from the city during their stay and that they were attended by a eunuch. Gladys liked Germans but Consuelo detested them. The Crown Prince, forbidden to attend Edward VII's coronation, toed the line and in 1905 married a German princess.

After a brilliant season in London Society with the Marlboroughs, Gladys returned to Paris; but she was disappointed to hear that Charles and Consuelo were off to the Delhi Durbar, and said so. When they returned, the Duke made a point of visiting Gladys Deacon in Paris. Of course she was delighted, and doubly flattered when the Duke of Norfolk arrived too – he was a widower – with the intention of finding himself a second wife. In spite of all this, however, Gladys remained single for nearly twenty years. Much of her time was spent shuttling between London, Paris and Blenheim.

In 1904 with her mother, now Mrs Baldwin, and her sister Audrey, Gladys Deacon moved into the Palazzo Borghese in Rome; but Audrey soon became ill and died in a nursing home in Florence. At that time Gladys would certainly seem to have encouraged a wide variety of suitors, from the Duke of Marlborough and Lord Brooke to Bernard Berenson and Prince Doria Pamphili.

For some years Consuelo had been miserable with her gloomy and neglectful husband. The ugly word incompatibility can cover a multitude of sins and scenes – and of maddening habits – of which only the two partners directly concerned can know. Consuelo was an American not only of startling beauty and wit but also of spirit. Gossips insisted that she had been unfaithful with an unnamed prince. Lord Hugh Cecil, that paragon of self-righteousness, wrote, 'Whatever Sunny's wife may have done, at any rate he is to blame, as himself unfaithful.'

With hindsight it is easy to see such a marriage as one doomed from the start, founded as it was without love but upon cash on one side and compulsion on the other. (When Charles first proposed, Consuelo burst into tears.)

Just as no one living today on inflated wages and with more luxury than their parents dreamed of could imagine what it can be like to manage on a pittance and on rationed food and clothing (not to mention bombs); so now we find the starchiness of the Edwardians almost beyond belief. After Victoria there had of course, with her son's mistresses and so on, to be some relaxation, but public scandal was still taboo – and that included divorce.

In October 1906 Charles and Consuelo agreed to separate, and in the following January their separation became legal. As though to set the seal upon their discomfort, King Edward and Queen Alexandra 'made it clear that any question of divorce between the Marlboroughs would be met with distinct disapproval'. Mrs Whitehouse, thou shouldst have been living at this hour! The glasshouse from which Edward hurled this stone had not yet become manifestly transparent.

Roosevelt, then President, wrote to Whitelaw Reid: 'I thoroughly dislike these international marriages; but the lowest note of infamy is reached by such a creature as this Marlborough, who proposing to divorce the woman when *he* at least cannot afford to throw any stone at her, nevertheless proposes to keep and live on the money she brought him. Come, my dear sir, surely you don't object to my considering the Duke of Marlborough a cad!'

'It is an awful business', wrote Winston Churchill. He had always been fond of them both; but Gladys had no admiration for him. Writing later she said, 'He was incapable of love. He was in love with his own image – his reflection in the mirror . . . He was entirely out for Winston.'

Those whom Love had not blinded might by this time have levelled the same criticism at Gladys and her reflection in the looking-glass which, thanks to rash experiments to make her profile more Grecian, had not improved. The slight dent between her perfect nose and forehead had always worried her; but the art of face-lifting was still at a far from professional stage and, as one easily sees now, she would have done far better to have left her almost perfect face alone.

However, for the time being at least, Marlborough was able to ignore it. He commissioned Boldini to paint her portrait in Paris, and grew impatient

[141]

at her long absence in wartime (1916), when she had taken a house in Savile Row and he was, at least nominally, a General Staff Officer with the temporary rank of Lieutenant-Colonel. It was perhaps typical of Gladys that her war-charities included the Horses' Relief Society. She became a naturalised British citizen in 1915. In the Duke's notes to her at this time one looks in vain for affection; but he sent lots of orchids and sometimes game. In London they dined together; and when Charles visited his sons at Eton, he would meet Gladys surreptitiously in the Long Walk.

His feelings against Consuelo were bitter and lasting. 'Now I do not often complain', he told Gladys, 'but few men have been plagued by such a woman as C. Truly her life is spent in doing harm to the family whose name she bears.' Ignoring the fact that the name she had been born with was Vanderbilt, and that he had profited by it, it would seem that his bitterest resentments were on two counts: first, that with her war-charities (a good deal more practical than Gladys's) she continued to act the part of Lady Bountiful, against a background of an uncharitable duke; and secondly, that she backed Lord Lansdowne for the Lord-Lieutenantship of Oxfordshire, an honour upon which he had set his heart. Still, he was not without influence. He rallied support from his cousin Winston, and his friend F.E. Smith (Lord Birkenhead), from Bonar Law, Sir Edward Carson and Lord Beaverbrook. Who could withstand such a team? The Lieutenantship was his.

It was not until 1917 that Charles could be persuaded to take office as Secretary to the Board of Agriculture. At Blenheim he had already gone through the motions of Planting for Victory by introducing cabbages into flowerbeds and having some of the south lawn dug up to make room for potatoes. 'The national food problem may not have been greatly lessened by these practices', commented *The Times*, 'but it was a patriotic gesture.'

The Winston Churchill exhibition at Blenheim contains a curious relic from the first World War. It is a large and jagged piece of shrapnel bearing two undated inscriptions. One of them reads: 'This fragment of a 30 lb shrapnel shell fell between us and might have separated us for ever, but is now a token of union' (between Winston Churchill and his cousin Charles ninth Duke). The other reads simply: 'M.M. from W.S.C.' 'Why "M.M."

[142]

when your father's name was Charles?' I asked the tenth Duke. 'But don't you see?' he said, ' "M.M." stood for "Marlborough Marlborough". You'll notice the same thing (the eighth Duke's cypher) on the front of the organ.'*

Although the zeppelin raids on London were as nothing compared with the blitzes, V1s and V2s of the last war, they were quite frightening enough. Long before the war had started, the Duke had commissioned Duchêne to demolish a chapel at the corner of Curzon Street and Shepherd Market and to replace it with a mansion to be called Sunderland House. After their separation, Consuelo made it her headquarters (they had equal custody of their sons); and from there she would organise her manifold works for charity including what was mysteriously called 'a conference of sweated women'. In 1917 the basement, perhaps like the chapel before it, proved the salvation of her neighbours, one of whom wrote from Curzon Street: 'Your Grace, I feel I cannot help letting you know that your kindness in opening the basement of Sunderland House saved our lives last night. We sheltered there and during our absence our drawing-room windows were shattered and a very large piece of shell-casing came into the room which we had left only ten minutes before. Pray believe I am very grateful.'

When in 1918 the Armistice was declared, Consuelo, from the LCC building, watched the march past with a thankful heart. Both her sons – Blandford in France with the Life Guards, his brother Ivor (medically unfit for the army) at War Office Headquarters – had come through the war unscathed. As for herself, after months of committee-work on the London County Council, she was so exhausted that, on doctor's orders, she joined her mother on the French Riviera, where she had bought a villa at Eze-sur-Mer. But she was back in good time for the wedding of Blandford to Mary Cadogan, daughter of Viscount Chelsea, at St Margaret's, Westminster. 'A fashionable wedding', she wrote, 'it was graced by the royal family's presence. It was also my valediction, for steps had already been taken to secure my divorce.'

---

* I am grateful to Mr Harold Fawcus, Blenheim's Education Officer, for suggesting that 'M.M.' may have stood for Prince of Mindelheim: the title awarded the first Duke and his successors by the Emperor of the Holy Roman Empire.

But divorce was still difficult and in this case both parties, with the utmost distaste, had to act the charade of 'being seen to cohabit', which they did for just over a fortnight at a small manor-house in the north wolds called Crowhurst. Formal letters passed between them; but even then the Law insisted upon Charles's spending a night with an unnamed woman, which he did, booking in at Claridges under the name of Spencer. It was a farce fit for fools, the most foolish of all being the Law, as it then was, itself.

'Thank Heavens it is all over', wrote Marlborough, 'the last blow that woman could strike over a period of some twenty years has now fallen. Dear me, what a wrecking existence she would have imposed on anyone with whom she was associated.' Yet Consuelo's subsequent marriage in London, in 1921, to Jacques Balsan proved happy and lasting for both of them; whereas Marlborough's marriage in Paris to Gladys Deacon, in the same year, led to total disaster.

While Consuelo had been still a débutante in Paris in the 1890s – *La belle Mlle. Vanderbilt au long cou* – Balsan had fallen in love with her at a *bal blanc* and had told his mother next day, 'I met last night the girl I would like to marry'. He had to wait twenty-seven years, during which he distinguished himself as a dare-devil pilot and was awarded the Légion d'Honneur (an honour later to be conferred upon his wife).

In spite of all obstacles, legal and ecclesiastical, Consuelo married Jacques Balsan in the Chapel Royal on July 4th, 1921. A civil ceremony followed. Yet even after that she found that in France the marriage of a Catholic to a divorcée could not be recognised unless her marriage had been annulled by the Roman Catholic Church. Moreover Balsan's family as devout Roman Catholics could not receive her. The only way round it, she was told, was to prove that her mother had forced her to marry Marlborough against her wishes, which in fact she had. For Consuelo's mother this of course was embarrassing, but she loved her daughter enough, on this second occasion, not to stand in the way of her long-postponed happiness. Consuelo had then to appear before an English tribunal of Roman Catholic priests, an ordeal she could hardly have faced without the loyal support of her one-time governess, Miss Harper, whose testimony helped to persuade the Rota to grant the annulment in February,

[144]

1927. Consuelo was then remarried to Jacques, according to the rites of the Roman Catholic Church, and was allowed to join the family circle.

In New York the annulment created a storm, particularly in church circles. 'The plea of duress', protested Bishop Manning, 'after a quarter of a century of married life and the birth of two children would not be entertained by any civil court.' And he was backed by another priest who wrote, 'If being tied together by marriage vows . . . if living together and having children could not make a marriage real, then it is fair to ask, what could make a marriage real?' To which Bishop Dunn replied, 'If mere cohabitation of itself or even the birth of children constitutes a marriage . . . then there are many people now married who do not know it.'

As for Marlborough, he made it clear that it had not been himself who had sought the annulment; and indeed it worried him until he was assured that the two children resulting from the union would not lose their legitimacy. It was bad enough that he had been refused Communion by the Church of England; so bad indeed that, after preparation by Father Martindale, he became converted to Roman Catholicism and went to Rome to be blessed by the Pope. His own marriage to Gladys Deacon, at the British Consulate in Paris in April, 1921 (a civil ceremony, to be followed by a religious one at her cousin's home) had produced its own obstacles. An American pastor and an English priest had both refused to marry them; but finally the rector of the Presbyterian church in Paris agreed to conduct the religious service and did so. Presents poured in. Gladys had asked for of all things feathered fans, and eighteen in various colours arrived. The scene was crowded with what Sarah would have called persons of quality from both sides of the Channel.

Meanwhile Consuelo was writing of 'the profound goodness and kindness' of her second husband, whose appreciation of great art echoed her own. Together they bought Renoir's *La Baigneuse* for their salon – and in 1946 gave the 115,000 dollars it then sold for to provide food for French children. 'Our cosmopolitan parties', she remembered, 'were gay, and how gratifying it was to have a guest admire a recent acquisition.' Even though strict Catholics might still prove stand-offish, the cream of French Society did not. Nor was Consuelo neglecting her passion for good works, for she

[145]

now founded and financed a hospital for the *bourgeois*, who then had none.

No Churchill except the bridegroom himself had been at Gladys's wedding; but her guests – Princess George of Greece, the Princesse de Polignac, Anatole France, Marshal Foch and so on – could hardly be said to have lacked distinction. The couple were as usual pestered by the Press. 'We are awfully poor', Marlborough told a reporter, 'but what would the miners think of wedding-presents costing £50,000? You can say I gave the bride a motor-car.'

Among old friends introduced by Gladys to Charles was Marcel Proust, who was promptly invited to Blenheim; but frail as he was and with but a year to live, he had to decline. Epstein however accepted and it was to him that she later admitted she had married a house, not a man. With his bronze bust of the Duke, still to be seen in Blenheim's hall, Epstein took infinite trouble. Argument as to what he should wear seemed endless; and that was followed by whether or not Epstein should include the hands. Gladys insisted that he should. He had already sculpted Gladys once and now made a second bust of her: 'a particularly remarkable head', Hugo Vickers comments, 'because she allowed herself to be depicted with the ravages of the paraffin-wax in full evidence . . . It was a head she much liked.'

At Blenheim Epstein, having sculptured not only the duke and his bride but the Duke's brother Ivor, asked to see the chapel but, as he told the Duke, he found no evidence of Christian worship there. 'The Marlboroughs are worshipped here', was the Duke's reply. Epstein left, as he said, 'out of spirits and out of pocket'.

Gladys did her utmost to enliven what Sarah had called that wild, unmerciful house, by inviting guests likely to appeal more strongly to a Spencer than to a Churchill. Lytton Strachey was enchanted with the place:

> I wish it were mine. It is enormous, but one would not feel it too big. The grounds are beautiful too, and there is a bridge over a lake which positively gives one an erection. Most of the guests played tennis all day and bridge all night so that, apart from eating and drinking, they might as well have been at Putney.

[146]

Gladys had three miscarriages and felt not only ill but, like Consuelo, lonely and bored. 'Most interesting to me', she wrote, 'is Sunny's rudeness to me. Not very marked in public yet – but that will come. I am glad because I am sick of life here. Convention and the commonplace and selfishness alone voice themselves over us. *Quelle vie*! But we will separate perhaps before long and I will then go away for good and ever.'

Blandford only tolerated her, while his father had recalled Duchêne to finish the eastern garden and to discuss ambitious plans for a *parterre d'eau* to replace what she called the crooked lawn on the west. Very well, she too would create a garden, but one of a very different kind, and as far from the palace as possible. And so in an old bull-nosed Morris – one day, with children aboard, the brakes failed and they ended up in the mud of the lake – she would drive herself down to the western extremity of the lake where, just above his Great Cascade, Brown had made on a steep slope that Salvator Rosa background for the spring-lock boulder, the winding paths and the Druid's Temple which had so much pleased the fifth Duke and his privileged guests.

There she would be joined by a gardener's boy, a strong lad called Bert Timms, who lived at Hanborough and made nothing of moving rocks and slabs of stone to the positions plotted for them. She is said to have specialised in saxifrages and in yellow primulas which, when massed, looked well, reflected in the Glyme below them. When from distant Blenheim the luncheon bell rang out, she ignored it, preferring to picnic at the Druid's Temple (little more than a flat-topped cromlech) with her gardener friend. When she found that he was a non-smoker she brought a large box of chocolates and urged him to help himself. One morning he told her his orders for that afternoon were to help clip the yews bordering the east garden. 'Just savage them', she said, 'make as much mess of them as you like.'

After her third miscarriage, in 1925, she found the rock-garden too much for her, and took instead to the breeding of Blenheim spaniels. She had been told by her doctor that another miscarriage might be fatal. The dogs were kept at first in the gardeners' bothies, near the kitchen-garden, but later had their own two rooms in the palace. The Duke approved and had a favourite

[147]

spaniel of his own called Snowflake. Later however he complained that they soiled the carpets, smelled and were allowed too much freedom; all of which she denied. At one stage several died of distemper and were buried, with small headstones, on the slope between the Druid's Temple and the Glyme.

Lady Lee of Fareham, visiting Blenheim with her husband at that time reported: 'Gladys is very executive and more than a match for the Duke whom A (Lord Lee) has always thought a very poor creature.'

There was a curious moment when to mark some occasion – it may have been Easter – the ninth Duke had his grandchildren line up in the hall. They had been given to understand that they were to receive a special present and naturally they were excited. The Duke made no appearance but sent his butler with a silver salver upon which, though barely visible, were four small eggs. (Lord Charles had not then been born.) 'With his Grace's compliments', said the butler, solemnly handing each child one hard–boiled plover's–egg. Since the children were of Churchill breed there were of course no tears; but one of them at least, as many years later she told me, could never forget her disappointment.

In 1925 the Duke, disappointed in both his marriages, might like at least three of his ancestors have given way to melancholy and retired in seclusion to a corner of the palace. Instead he roused himself to begin, with Duchêne, the formalising of Blenheim's setting on the west. What Gladys called a crooked lawn was in fact a shrubbery with a rustic rotunda, a slope of grass and a winding path down which 'Sunny' and his brother Ivor would run to the lake to bathe. Above the boathouse there were cedars and they found it one of the few secret places they could call their own. Blenheim otherwise was too public. Even in prams or push–chairs the children might be stared at by strangers.

But now, at forty-six, the ninth Duke, no longer 'young and uninformed', felt confident that he and he alone knew what had been in Vanbrugh's mind for that all-important slope between the house and the valley. It never seemed to occur to him that, with the grotto Vanbrugh had planned to build beneath the Long Library, he might, as at Saint-Cloud, have contrived with baroque rusticity a long cascade all the way down to the river or canal below; or just possibly a more formal water-ladder as one may

[148]

still see and marvel at at Chatsworth.

Nevertheless, looking down upon those lovely terraces today, or wandering among their fountain-basins, one is astonished at the confidence and courage of that small man, not greatly gifted, prepared not merely to compete with Versailles, but to patronise it. 'You have stood with me at Versailles', he reminded Duchêne, 'and pointed out that the Grand Canal is too narrow . . . I do hope the line of vision [at Blenheim] has been taken with care'. It had been, but this did little to subdue loud arguments between two strong-minded men. Workmen on the site had to pretend not to notice as Marlborough and Duchêne stormed at each other in French, the Duke stressing his points with savage thrusts of his stick.

'The problem for Monsieur Duchêne', the Duke insisted, 'is to make a liaison . . . between the façade of Vanbrugh and the water line of the lake made by Brown. To reconcile these conflicting ideas is difficult. The difficulty is not diminished when you remember that the façade of the house is limited and the line of the lake is limitless. As an example, if you turn your back to the lake and look at the façade, your parterre, basin etc. is in scale to the façade; but if you look at the same parterre from the rotunda to the lake, it is out of scale with the panorama.'

But then, characteristically, he adds: 'I cannot close these remarks without a philosophic reflection. Whether you modify your plans and your decoration or whether you do not, try to inspire in them a feeling of joyousness, for joy means the birth of everything: of spirit, of hope and aspiration. With that tinge of melancholy in your temperament you are inclined to be sombre and therefore severe. Vanbrugh had faults but *panache*. Monsieur Duchêne is faultless, but he must also remember to be human.'

And this from a duke who was said never to smile! There seemed little to choose between the pot and the kettle. But Duchêne rashly decided to adopt a patronising tone. He replied: 'Je suis très content de voir tout l'intérêt que vous prenez vous-même au travail que nous avons entrepris et il me semble que c'est moi-même qui suis le propriétaire qui fait exécuter les travaux!' But that was going too far. 'You are the Architect, I am the Duke', he was brusquely reminded. 'You must be sure that your measurements are correct.' And again: 'Of course I hold you responsible that these *vasques* [large clam-shells forming cascades between the two terraces] will look all right, that they will be in proper proportion and that you will not ask me to have them altered a year hence because you do not like them. I hold you entirely responsible for the artistic merit of these *vasques*.'

As the great work went on there were obstacles and annoyances great and small, from geological fissures big enough to swallow a horse and cart to loud whistles from the machine that was doing the digging. When the Duke complained, the contractors were a little hurt. 'We proposed to use a steam-navvy', they reminded him, 'for excavation and your Grace agreed to this, though it was pointed out that the navvy would make some noise and would occasionally whistle'.

But there were to be compensations. 'It is certainly a stroke of genius on your part', the Duke conceded to Duchêne, 'bringing the water line up to the first terrace [as seen from the Long Library]. I certainly should not have thought of this idea myself and I doubt any English architect would have.' At the same time he could not resist a caution: 'I do not want you in building your terraces to spoil the effect of Brown's lake. You have won your victory: you have made the water *baigner* the first terrace; do not lose the spoils of your victory. This victory would be lost if you left the north wing of the first terrace the height as shown on the plan . . .'

Ambitious as the scheme looks today, although of course on a far smaller scale than at Versailles, it was to have been a good deal more so with a third terrace leading almost to the brink of the lake. This however proved impracticable and perhaps dangerous. The Duke found, in looking at old documents, 'that the bed of the river runs at the water's edge. The depth is considerable and I fear the earth would slide into the middle of the lake.'

With two great terraces, then, connected by a wall of *vasques* and caryatids (for one of which Bert Timms posed), the Duke had to be content. But next came the all-important question of decoration. Recalling his enrichment of the staterooms the Duke wrote to Duchêne: 'I do not wish to make this mistake a second time . . . We must be very careful not to decorate in the French style' – advice which a French architect may reasonably have felt some reluctance to adopt. And indeed at first, as we see from his own

[150]

sketch with its 'perpendicular trees', as the Duke scathingly called them, he could not bring himself to accept an alternative. But across Duchêne's impressive drawing (though one hopes the architect never saw it) the Duke wrote in bold capitals:

IF YOU STUDY THIS PICTURE AND COMPARE IT WITH THE FINISHED WORK ON THE TERRACES YOU WILL REALISE THE IMMENSE INFLUENCE I HAD OVER THE ARCHITECT IN MAKING THE EFFECT OF THE TERRACE CLASSICAL IN APPEARANCE, AND HOW I SUCCEEDED IN DESTROYING THE FRENCH MIDDLE CLASS VIEW OF A FORMAL GARDEN.

MARLBOROUGH

Yet on the whole, surprisingly, the Duke and his French architect were well matched, the patron knowing precisely the effect he wanted, and his assistant, while no sycophant, respecting his intelligence, grasping his meaning, interpreting it – if sometimes into too literal French – and carrying it out.

I frankly admit to you [wrote Marlborough in 1927] that I want you to work later on more in the spirit of Bernini than of Mansard or Le Nôtre . . . The value of the obelisks is this, that they give an architectural transition between a lateral line of stone and the perpendicular effect of the trees. Pray therefore do not despise them. I think we can get a magnificent effect, something like the Trevi Fountain or the Fontana Hispana in Rome.

At long last Bernini's *modello* for his glorious rivergods fountain in the Piazza Navona in Rome, given to the first Duke by the Papal Nuncio, approved by Gibbons and 'flung together in rude pomp' by the fifth Duke, was to be given a place of honour on the second terrace. Experts sped to Italy to check each stone and to measure proportions, while others at Blenheim raised a red porphyry obelisk to 'answer' the Bernini model.

At this stage the Duke would stand for hours, gazing at the terraces which he had begun to fear he might not live to see completed. 'I have placed two big lead statues on the second terrace', he told Duchêne, 'at the two angles where the roads meet, which is just above the steps. In my judgment they look well. I have also placed provisionally the six columns in marble. I am having made in England six statues of Victory . . . These columns really replace the perpendicular trees which you put in your original plan. Sir Edwin Lutyens is coming to see the work in four days' time.'

But later, in 1928, there is more than a hint of petulance:

> After so many years it is tiring that I cannot make you realise that movement is essential in any decoration which you desire to employ on the terraces . . . The drawing of the console you have sent me is in the style of Gabrielle and I fear is not in harmony with the baroque of Vanbrugh.
>
> I have been turning poetry into prose these last twelve weeks. It had to be one or the other. There was no room for compromise. I have therefore removed the cedar tree which was near the chapel. I have planted two large trees on the two angles of the terraces . . . I have planted the walls of the first terrace with magnolias. The walls are now covered. I have gained twenty years. I hope the trees live . . .

But if the Duke could be dictatorial, as we see he could, he could be magnanimous when the long struggle ended in victory. 'Pray tell Monsieur Duchêne', he wrote in 1929, 'that the ensemble of the terraces is magnificent and in my judgment far superior to the work done by Le Nôtre at Versailles. The proportion of the house, the terrace and the lake is perfect.'

Duchêne of course was pleased, but pleaded that the water – the very life of the whole scheme – should be kept ever in motion: 'N'oubliez pas qu'il est absolument nécessaire que notre parterre d'eau *vive*, c'est-à-dire qu'il y ait des effets d'eau; ce genre de parterre ne peut pas *vivre au repos*, si je puis m'expresser ainsi; sans cela, cela aura toujours l'air d'un parterre où il y aurait eu des inondations et les bassins deviendraient des flauqes d'eau sans intérêt'.

The Duke replied:

The ninth Duke's Water Terraces: the Sphinx bearing the features of Gladys Duchess of Marlborough.

I shall not contradict you. Bear in mind however that the situation is grandiose. Limpidity of water is pleasing and possesses a romance. You have got this effect in the basins and in the large area of water contained by the lake. Be careful not to destroy this major emotion which Nature has granted to you for the sake of what may possibly be a vulgar display of waterworks which can be seen at any exhibition or public park. Turn all these matters over in your mind when you are at rest in the evening, for it is only by thought, constant thought and mature reflection that artists have left their great works for the enjoyment of posterity.

How stupendous had been the labour! Yet a still greater work – the restoration of the state- or military-garden on the south – still waited to be restored. Without that the palace still had but three-quarters of its formal setting. Did Marlborough contemplate it? There is some evidence that he did; or at least that knowledgeable friends urged him to it. In a letter dated 29th January, 1932 Mr (now Sir) Sacheverell Sitwell wrote:

> My dear Duke,
>   As your long labour on the terraces is nearly at an end, I feel I must write and tell you how fine their effect is upon someone who has not seen them growing every day under his eyes . . .
>   I have a longing one day to row across the lake to the beautiful plantation that lies opposite it, and to see what Blenheim and the terraces look like from there. If a generation preceding yours plundered the house of a great number of its treasures of art, you have certainly repaired the damage in another way by completing the garden. But I am convinced that when it is finished you will feel the need of something else to do, and I am sure that the parterre on the great [south] front ought to be re-created – or at any rate laid down in some sort of patterning that would avoid all the expense of cutting and trimming incessantly . . .

To which Sir Sacheverell has more recently added: 'It seems to me that I remember telling the Duke that he must restore the Great Parterre at Blenheim, and that I remember him shrugging his shoulders and smiling. In fact he agreed but knew it was impossible.' Had Sir George Sitwell owned Blenheim instead of Renishaw one can imagine him taking that vast garden in his stride, with a great deal of what he called 'lifting and dragging' by teams of strong men. Yet the cost of upkeep alone now scarcely bears thinking of.

Strolling through those terraces today, with the fountains playing, one sees several inscriptions, perhaps the most prominent: CAROLUS DUX ORNAVIT MCMXXV; and on the porphyry obelisk: TO THE GENIUS OF THE ARCHITECT – BY THE KNOWLEDGE OF THE DUKE – CAROLO DUCI FILII AMANTISSIMI; and on the south wall of the chapel: ACHILLE DUCHÊNE

ARCHITECT, TO WHOSE GENIUS POSTERITY ENJOYS THE BEAUTY OF THESE
TERRACES.

And the Duke himself?

For various reasons I have not had the heart or courage to write an
account of the six years of labour and study that I devoted to
superintending the work on these terraces. Perhaps I will write one day.
But let not the reader assume that this work was simple, that any architect
could have done it. The result is the combination of brains, knowledge of
technique and culture of two men working in harmony. These two men
have left the park – East and West fronts of Blenheim – in perfect
architectural design: a worthy frame to the Palace.   M.M. 1933.

As Sir Winston Churchill said of his cousin, he had sacrificed much – too
much – for Blenheim; 'and at his death it passed from his care in a finer state
than ever'.

One imagines Gladys at this time bored beyond words, as she too often
was; but then she would perk up again – her resilience was astonishing – and
decide to show some interest in the terraces (her features, in their time of
perfection, grace the twin sphinxes by Ward Willis (1930) near the Bernini
Fountain); and to have her eyes painted in triplicate (the Duke's ditto), on a
huge scale, upon the coffered ceiling of the north portico. Her eyes, as we
know, were of a startling blue, and while Colin Gill was copying them, she
climbed his ladders and left him with a scarf which matched them. In
Sargent's paintings of the ninth Duke he shows him too with blue eyes. Yet
as one looks up today, within that portico, one sees, staring down at every
visitor, three blue eyes and three brown ones! Once again, this is the kind of
mystery which happens only at Blenheim: the riddle of the sphinx.

It is almost as hard to imagine what the Duke himself thought; but as Sir
Shane Leslie observed, since Marlborough's conversion, or even for some
time before it, there had seemed something of the mystic about him; while
Gladys was apt to indulge in sensationalism. One evening at dinner she
casually put a revolver on the table. 'And so what do you mean to do with
that?' a guest asked. 'Oh, I don't know', she said, 'I might just shoot

[155]

Marlborough with it.'

At Blenheim on November 13th, 1930 Gladys threw what her biographer calls 'the final festivity before the collapse'. It was supposed to celebrate Marlborough's sixtieth birthday, when in fact he had just turned fifty-nine. The guests included the Earl and Countess of Carnarvon, Lord Berners, Sir Frederick and Lady Keeble, Mr and Mrs John Masefield, Colonel and Mrs Maurice Wingfield, Frank Pakenham (now Lord Longford) and Lord David Cecil. The Duke, with the Garter superimposed upon a golden coat, waltzed so giddily that his partner fainted.

> The courtyard at the front of the palace was filled with glittering fairylights . . . a bonfire 100 feet high had taken three weeks to build . . . There was a torchlight procession and dancing in the open air . . . Winston Churchill and the new Lord Birkenhead, smoking enormous cigars, surveyed the scene from the side . . . while Sunny and Gladys watched from the steps . . . It was the last public occasion where they shared any happiness, for by June 1931 their marriage had deteriorated to a state of hostility, pending the declaration of open warfare.*

The ninth Duke, having finished his masterpiece – the formal gardens – and seen the shipwreck of two marriages, now took an interest in racehorses and in other more or less frivolous entertainments in London; but already he was terminally ill and may have known it.

In 1931, at a reception at 7 Carlton House Terrace (then the Marlboroughs' London house), about a week before the wedding of Winston Churchill's daughter Diana (1904–63. After a divorce she married Duncan Sandys), Gladys begged her husband not to shout, since he could be overheard by the servants. He ignored her. 'Can you not show some consideration for me?' she asked. To which he answered: 'I have no consideration for you and never had'; which hurt her so much that she burst into tears and left the room. Once again however her resilience served her enough to suggest a ball for her birthday, at the London house. 'No you

---

* Vickers: *Gladys Duchess of Marlborough* (Weidenfeld, 1979) pp. 223–4

don't', said the Duke, 'I forbid you to come to my house and if you do I will have you thrown out by my servants.' 'I was dumb with astonishment', declared Gladys, 'and seeing he was getting into his stride . . . for one of his screaming demoniacal furies, I ended the conversation and went out.' It was hopeless. He would live his own chosen life, the Duke told her, and never wanted to see her again.

Rodin had given her a statuette of a boy, which she put on view in the First Stateroom – and was disgusted when no one praised it. Unquestionably she and the Duke had different tastes, different interests and different circles of friends; and after marriage the chasm yawned between them.

Gladys retired to Blenheim, where she tried to console herself with her dogs. Marlborough came seldom, stayed usually at The Bear in Woodstock, and on January 3rd, after an unedifying scene at Blenheim, he left for London and took most of the servants with him. At Newmarket races, happening to meet the wife of an M.F.H., who had known him and Gladys for several years, he told her that 'during the last two or three years he had found life with his wife impossible, that she was going mad and would certainly be locked up within a year.'

Their friend laughed and told him Gladys was 'an extremely intelligent woman'. The Duke countered this by saying that she carried a revolver and might shoot him, and that his doctors had told him he must not see her again. 'I again laughed at the absurdity of this statement', countered Mrs G. 'He told me he had thirty servants who would say that she was an impossible person to live with. I told him I was surprised that he should ask the servants such a question. He said they were the people that knew as they were always there, and added that for the last six months the Duchess had gone about spreading terrible stories about him . . .'

But the Duke was in earnest and his next step was to send a private investigator to Blenheim to question such staff as Gladys still had about her. But no, not one of them had noticed the slightest evidence of insanity or of drug-taking. As far as they could tell, she was as normal as they were. And so then, in 1933, doctors were appealed to – Dr Beckett-Overy and Sir James Purves-Stewart – but the Duke was out of luck again. There was no evidence of any mental derangement nor of drugs.

In the meantime Gladys had of course sent for her solicitor who afterwards reported that he 'distinctly got the impression that the conversation I was having with her Grace [which lasted three hours] was being overheard to a certain extent by a servant. She was in a most distressed state and exceedingly unhappy . . . The condition of the palace', he concluded, 'and the lack of staff struck me very forcibly . . .'

Again, as with Consuelo, so with Gladys, there was no one to turn to. In fact the only member of the family to stick up for her was Lord Ivor Spencer-Churchill, the younger son, who, when he heard about the detective, was indignant with his father and said, 'How could you do such a thing to Gladys? Do you think we are going to stand for another scandal?' (the first having concerned the annulment). To which the Duke answered 'almost in a whisper: "I have to defend myself. You don't know what is being said about me" '.*

Half a century afterwards one wonders whether the Duke himself appreciated the main roots and psychological causes of this tragic rift and whether one of them – for one like himself who worshipped beauty in women, as in landscape – was not the disastrous and disfiguring failure of Gladys's attempts to perfect her all–but–perfect face. This the Duke never mentions and it could be that we should give him credit for it.

On May 29th, 1933 Gladys packed a van and a car with spaniels and such things as belonged to her and, in spite of some feeble opposition on the part of the Duke's agent, who had pretended to sympathise with her, drove off, never to see Blenheim again. The state of the palace, when the Duke returned, was used as evidence of her insanity. He was curious to know whom she had invited in his absence; but Gladys had thought of that and had carried off the visitors' book (later returned).

When in the summer of 1934 the ninth Duke died, his cousin and friend Winston Churchill said at the requiem in Oxford, 'He was never blind to his own failings and in distress sought the consolations of religion.' It was a kind way of putting it.

---

*   Vickers: ibid., chapter 20

As for the rest of Gladys's long, sad story, it has recently been told in detail by Hugo Vickers who, month after month, drove down from London to see her in the nursing home she had literally been dragged to from her farm. In extreme old age (she lived to be ninety-six) she told him: 'Sometimes something happens that is so awful that it cuts you off, and after that you don't care.' She died on the 13th of October, 1977 and was buried in the village churchyard at Chacombe near Banbury where, in a pitiful state of squalor, she had tried to live. In 1978 Christies sold most of her possessions for the astonishing sum of £784,000. None of this found its way to Blenheim!

At Blenheim the tenth Duke, then thirty-seven and always called Blandford by his Duchess, moved into the Coral Rooms in the north-western quadrant, while the rest of the house, as he always called it (never 'palace') was being put in order. The Long Library, converted in the 1914–18 War into a hospital ward, had in the second World War been used first as a boys' dormitory for Malvern College, then by M.I.5 and finally by the Ministry of Supply, who divided it into offices with matchboard partitions. 'Can you imagine', I asked the Duchess, 'what your father-in-law would have said to this?' 'Nonsense', she said, 'we could never have heated the place without them. They're keeping the tapestries warm.' The Library was not restored until later.

When at last the Ministry left, the Duke was faced with the alternative of handing the place over, with endowment, to the National Trust or of keeping it for his family and their posterity and having it shown to the public. Most wisely he chose to keep it and, thanks to the Ministry of Supply's occupation, he was able to draw upon them for materials and labour to make good a great deal of damage and deterioration. The forecourt was cleared of its hideous huts, the staterooms were regilded, the Long Library was later restored; and in the Great Hall it took days and weeks to remove linoleum and the bostik with which it had been glued down.

Even so it was not until 1950 that the owners considered Blenheim fit to be thrown open again to the public.

[159]

VIII

John Albert Edward William Spencer-Churchill
tenth Duke of Marlborough
1897–1972

In the tenth Duke's time, for the period after the last war, I switch to personal reminiscence. I make no apology for this except that, by a set of curious chances, I felt compelled to buy a cottage within four miles of Blenheim and so to transfer my wife and three-year-old son from the wartime purgatory of living in other people's houses to the relative bliss of a primitive place of one's own.

While on leave (demobilisation was slow) I found a large-scale map of our new locality spread open on the kitchen table. 'Take a look at that big patch of blue', said Joyce. 'Why not bike over and see what it's all about?' It was the lake at Blenheim. And so that, for me, was how the wonder that was Blenheim – and still is – really began.

In Blenheim Park (some 2,000 acres of it) we trespassed wildly and were apprehended but once when a keeper with the manners of Versailles touched his cap and said, 'I have to ask you where you are going'. I half expected him to add (as in *An Adventure*) 'Cherchez la maison!' since, had I known it, I was indeed headed for the palace; and when for the first time I saw it, I failed to like it.

I forget now which took longer, getting to know and understand

Blenheim or its owners. No matter. Sometimes buildings and people well worth knowing take a number of years to know.

However in time I did have the good luck to know that vast place, from roof to undercroft, and its owners too, rather well; although it was not until after the death of his duchess in 1961 that I felt I might regard Bert, as he was later to let me call him, as a personal friend; and by that time I had been hopelessly captivated by the whole outlandish building and its setting.

One of the first obvious things to do – and in those days it cost ten shillings – was to fly over Blenheim from the local airport. Palace, lake, island looked wonderful, but I was puzzled at first by the toy castle on the west that was High Lodge: and by the bastioned walls of the kitchen-garden on the south.

High Lodge, once a hip-roofed farmhouse where in 1680 Bishop Burnet had heard the death-bed confession of John Wilmot Earl of Rochester, had nearly a century later been rebuilt by the fourth Duke as a romantic folly. 'Methinks', mused Nathaniel Hawthorne, 'if such good fortune ever befell a bookish man, I should choose this lodge as my own residence, with the topmost room of the tower for a study and all the seclusion of cultivated wildness beneath to ramble in.'

In the Bodleian Library I dug into the lodge's history and suggested to John Piper that we might collaborate in an article on it for *Country Life*. He answered 'Yes, let us do this' and so we did, his style exactly suiting the strangeness and remoteness of that place.

In journalism, with luck, one such article can (or used to) lead to another; and it was Frank Whitaker, then *Country Life*'s editor – short, dapper, smiling –who asked me to write a book on the building of Blenheim. In that high-ceilinged room in Lutyens' building overlooking Covent Garden, he told me: 'If I had wanted an architectural treatise I would have commissioned an architect. I don't. I want a history of Blenheim for the general reader.' I had as it happened a job on *Punch*. It took four years of free time to research and to write the book on the building of Blenheim, now of course long out of print.

Up till then my dealings with Blenheim had, through the Duke's agent, been strictly formal: and on the other hand, via our friend and neighbour

Gerald Horne, who had been hall-boy in the ninth Duke's time, extremely informal. When I applied to the agent for firewood he replied: 'Your message has not yet been conveyed to his Grace but it is in process of being so conveyed'. But there was no such nonsense with Gerald and his buxom wife Nelly (they had married, as butler and cook, from some other great house, though while 'in gentleman's service' she never dared to wear a ring). 'Blenheim was our world', he declared. On first giving the butler his name he was told 'Gerald? Ah no, that won't do. Gerald's a gentleman's name. We will call you Johnny.' And Johnny he remained, even to his wife. 'At one time', he told me, 'I had to work what they called a telephone switchboard, and 'pon me sammy, when his Grace rang through I was petrified.'

On September 18th, 1897, news reached Blenheim that an heir, John Albert Edward William, Marquis of Blandford, had been born in London at Spencer House.

At once [Gerald told me] the steward and his staff climbed to the palace roof [111 steps] and fired a salute; and at night a ball was given for the servants and the people of Woodstock and the rest. The menservants wore dress clothes with special buttonholes and danced with the maids, who looked very nice and graceful in their long dresses. We danced to the organ and a string band. The refreshments, prepared in the palace kitchens, were passed from hand to hand by a row of waiters reaching from kitchen to diningroom. Free beer, free everything flowed like milk and honey, and I can tell you, the beer-cellar at Blenheim (two dozen barrels at a time) was a noted place.

The birth of a royal heir could scarcely have caused more excitement. A life-size bronze of the baby, not altogether flattering, was commissioned from a sculptor called Fuchs; while contemporary photographs show John Albert Edward William, even at a few months old, looking every inch a duke, as indeed he was to look in maturity at six foot four and a half. One can only regret that of all his names the one that clung to him was Bert, a vulgar abbreviation and the least typical thing about him.

In the meantime the Duke's agent had thawed sufficiently to tell me:

'You will find his Grace very pleasant to deal with; and if he lays down the law, just give him his head.'

The high, eastern colonnade, intended by Vanbrugh as the impressive private entrance, had long since been abandoned in favour of a modest door at terrace-level with steps leading down to a gloomy (though now cheerful) corridor and eventually to what in Sarah's day had been known as my lady Duchess's backstairs: elegant enough with a slim handrail and delicate ironwork; but the well of that staircase had been filled with a lift. The general impression was that of a sumptuous rabbit-warren. After climbing the shallow stairs one pushed a heavy swing-door and so entered the vaulted corridor, warm, deep-carpeted, scented, with everything about it on the Blenheim scale: gigantic beaux-pots, elephant-tusks ten feet high, busts on pedestals and, on a polished side-table, a selection of hats and sticks worthy of a well-stocked shop in Bond Street.

In the Duke's study, a northern room once Sarah's, I had time to notice a great many framed photographs, red leather chairs and a large Victorian desk with brass drop-handles in the form of an 'M' before the Duke came in. He too looked to have been built to Vanbrugh's measure, standing six feet four and a half inches; and with, about the face, that symmetry, in features as in buildings, so greatly admired in the age of Anne.

Strangely, for it had leaped ten generations, the face was the face, or nearly so, of the first Duke: the hooded eyes remarkably alert and watchful, missing nothing, the nose elegant and small, the mouth small too, giving nothing away; the hands elegant with a look of alabaster, as though seldom used. Old photographs showed that as Marquis of Blandford he had been dashingly handsome; and now at fifty he was good-looking, ducal, dignified (everyone recognised him on his strolls through Mayfair); indeed, distinguished in everything but dress about which, like his great ancestor, he cared absolutely nothing. In America his mother Consuelo, to whom he was devoted, would order for him a range of matching outfits, only to be faced next morning with a heartbreaking assortment of oddments, some new, some old, topped with an ancient pullover and a favourite jacket which she had hoped had been given away.

At our first meeting he wore an old flannel suit and a white shirt open at

[163]

the neck to show his vest. His voice was well pitched, though a pipe often reduced it to a mumble; but his manner of speaking was unforgettable. He barely parted his lips, added 'What?' to the end of every other sentence, and in general sounded as though he had too often tried to communicate with foolish if not downright boring people. I never heard him laugh aloud, but he frequently spoke with a note of mockery or of incredulity at the pitiful folly of other people. Of his nature he was not unkind, but there were times when, with a solemn face, he enjoyed playing the fool at the expense of others. Then he would deliberately say outrageous things before sitting back to watch the shocked reaction. For myself as a journalist he was – to use a threadbare cliché – out of this world: feudal and altogether extraordinary. And sure enough, as Sacré had promised, he was pleasant, if wary, to deal with.

When I mentioned my book he seemed keen to co-operate. Had I seen the visitors' book and did I know the park? (I had and did.) But he was blowed if he knew what to do with the house when, if ever, the Ministry moved out. When I mentioned the frustrations of the first Duke he said with a faint smile, 'You may say the present Duke's struggle is to keep the rabbits down.' And then, more seriously, 'My main burden at the moment is this bloody roof, what? When we had that heavy fall every man jack in the place had to help sweep the snow off it. One of them disappeared in a drift. I'm told they've found him, but they know I can't go up there because of vertigo . . . By the way, do you know anything about income-tax, what?'

Steering him gently back to the subject of my book I found him vague enough to suppose that it was I who had sketched High Lodge; and when I mentioned the Blenheim archives I thought I could hear thin ice beginning to crack. In the preface to the Nonesuch edition of Vanbrugh's letters Professor Geoffrey Webb had written of the ninth Duke:

Permission was asked of the Duke of Marlborough to examine and copy such originals of Sir John Vanbrugh's MSS as he might have in his possession, and the nature of this book was fully explained to him . . . His Grace not only refused his permission but declared, with doubtful historical sense, that Blenheim Palace was the private house of a private

English gentleman, and went on to express a wish that there might be no discussion of the house or its building history either in the newspapers or in book form. The Editor and his publishers, while fully conscious by reason of the great kindness they have experienced elsewhere of the consideration that is due from them to the owners of buildings and manuscripts . . . yet feel themselves unable to defer to the Duke's wishes in the matter . . .*

Undoubtedly I had been lucky never to cross swords with the tenth Duke's father; but I remember too Winston Churchill's solemn advice to him: 'Admit none but the most eminent authors.' Trevelyan had made the grade, though even he, as legend had it, was expected in the ninth Duke's time to eat below stairs. 'I have a duty to the nation', the tenth Duke now reminded me, 'and so I continue to refuse requests from Tom, Dick and Harry.' While praying for the courage of David when dealing with Goliath, I remembered two other Churchill maxims: 'A young man should never take no for an answer'; and 'Audacity is the only ticket'. All the same it was two years before I could persuade him to admit me to the Muniment Room.

The first time I met Mary tenth Duchess of Marlborough I knew at once that I had never seen anyone remotely like her. In the dim light of a high vaulted corridor smelling of scent and cigars I became suddenly aware of white gloves and then of a remarkably tall, ramrod figure in Red Cross uniform (tailored, it was said, by Dior) which went with them. Though born a Cadogan, she could have passed for the great Marlborough himself. The square jaw gave more than a hint that here was a woman never to be contradicted. And she was handsome too, with huge eyes, and dark hair in a neat bun tucked under a Red Cross hat. At a glance it was obvious that she had as a birthright that quality revered by all the fighting services: the impersonal habit of command; and in fact, for the two years preceding the birth of her youngest son Charles in 1940, she had been Chief Commandant of the A.T.S.

As with the first Duchess so with the tenth, her immense self-assurance

* Webb: The Letters of Sir John Vanbrugh (1928), volume 4, Introduction

[165]

[166]

gave her the conviction that she was right; and whether in fact that happened to be so or not, it was an attitude that often proved useful when chairing dithering committees. I sometimes wondered if she practised this form of discipline on her three dachshunds. 'And now remember, Alex', I hear her telling her favourite, 'mother has this great big ruler beside her *all the time!*' Oh yes, she was not without humour; and luckily for me I usually found her on my side.

In June 1948 I entered Blenheim's Muniment Room for the first time – a breathtaking moment. It had no windows and no heating and not much air. It was in fact a large strongroom with an iron grille inside the thick steel door. Still, none of that mattered. Almost first go off with a spot-check I chanced upon an unpublished letter of Vanbrugh's and it was a good one. Grimed but triumphant I climbed down the ladder and saw a small key-cupboard hung row upon row with neatly labelled keys. This, thought I, is the key of the kingdom; of the kingdom this is the key. Excitedly then I grabbed the first small key that came to hand and read its label. It said: Key to the Key-Cupboard.

Ninety-one boxes, each containing three bundles of letters, were labelled 'Sarah Duchess of Marlborough'. Her spiky writing, at first seemingly illegible, soon became familiar and usually decipherable; but even so there were days when, after hours in that strongroom, I would stagger out on to my bicycle, only to fall off it again: I simply could not see. But at least there was the park to relax in. My favourite picnic place was above Rosamond's Well, my table a beech-stump; and from there, stretched out on deep grass, I could look across the lake to the north front: I had disembarked at Cytherea.

Already we knew the park pretty well, from the Ditchley Gate on the north to the Lince and the Lower Cascade on the far west; but I would wander off on my own to copy endless inscriptions on the Column of Victory. Yet no matter how remote the place I was exploring, the same thing always seemed to happen. I would hear the soft purr of an engine and there sure enough, bucketing over the tussocks, would appear the Duke's

Mary tenth Duchess of Marlborough in Red Cross uniform

Bentley. Climbing out with dignity he would slowly approach – I think he already used a rubber-tipped stick for gout – and would ask: 'What d'you want to know?' He seemed certain that there was some key question which, once he had hit upon it, he would answer; after which he would never need to see me again. In the event he was to be plagued by my company, off and on, for twenty-five years.

One thing that may have foxed him was my social position, which was neither one thing nor the other. Perhaps I fell roughly into the category of a chaplain: 'the sacred domestic', as Dean Jones, the first Duke's chaplain, had been called. We were astonished, in 1947, to be invited to meet the Winston Churchills. But that red-letter day must keep for another chapter.

Certainly Blenheim was bliss compared with research in such mausoleums as Somerset House or the Public Record Office in London, where without Noel Blakiston's patient guidance I might well have been defeated. The British Museum was more peaceful; but even there one waited hours for books and manuscripts and could find oneself entangled in red tape. In all such places there was nearly always a reader, with or without a secretary, who seemed to assume – in spite of all those printed pleas for SILENCE – that all of us were far more interested in his or her subject than in our own. However, cunningly buried though much of it was, treasure was to be unearthed there; and so much of it that I had to take days off to deal with it. There were times when I found myself drifting around like a toad with a jewel in its head, and that jewel was labelled 'Blenheim'.

The seven-acre palace and two-thousand-acre park were so overwhelming, I resolved from the first, with the exception of the first owners, to make no attempt to write then about the Churchill, Spencer and Spencer-Churchill families. Not surprisingly, after four years of this slogging, my Woodstock doctor diagnosed duodenal ulcers and ordered me to bed on a dismal diet. There, though well cared for, I felt jaundiced when I heard from his new agent that the Duke was about to reopen Blenheim to the public and so urgently needed a guidebook. Luckily by then my large book had been published; but it still meant having the printer at my bedside and dictating to him. Luckily again, Alden proved a prince among printers and was soon to become a personal friend; but it was not easy for him; and as for me, it was kill or cure: an odd kind of therapy.

[168]

It was not long before I felt well enough to tackle the palace roof and this I did with that excellent old mason Dan Collett of Wolvercote, who had played a leading part in the building of the ninth Duke's water-terraces. (His name, with others', is inscribed on a stone there.) He had helped too to steady Marlborough's statue, leaning perilously at the top of the Column of Victory, when the ninth Duke had thought that only a man harnessed to a giant kite could have coped with it. With ladders and scaffolding Collett climbed up there, but admitted afterwards: 'It fell on me often at nights when I was in bed'.

As together we tackled the roofs Dan told me, 'You need to be something between a rabbit and a sea-serpent'; and as I posted my long length through a narrow flue, I knew and felt what he meant. 'Colossal job, isn't it?' he gasped, at the top of a tower, 'Marvellous it is, marvellous, and all this enrichment where nobody sees it'. We clambered up the leads to the gilded balls above the Hall and Saloon, and found a wagtail's nest behind the vast marble bust, from Tournai, of Louis XIV.

From the west front we looked down on the fountain-basins of the terraces, where Collett recalled that the Duke had insisted that only the spring-water from Rosamond's Well was to be used. It had meant running a three-inch pipe through the lake to the ram near the Great Cascade, whence the water was pumped up to the terraces, as it still is.

To explore the interior of Vanbrugh's bridge meant borrowing a punt and two men with a ladder long enough to reach an *oeil-de-boeuf* window on the south-east. Having climbed in I found hibernating butterflies, flocks of stock-doves and huge clusters of bats; and on one great Vanbrugh keystone, over a round window, I noticed a bold and deeply incised 'V'.

In St Stephen's, Walbrook, which houses the Vanbrugh vault, there is to our shame no monument to him. But at Blenheim the Grand Bridge alone is enough to set him for ever among the giants of British architecture. As Wren's inscription runs, in the crypt of St Paul's: *Si monumentum requiris, circumspice.*

While in London I consulted Whitaker of *Country Life* about the guidebook, which I had still to finish. 'Oh that's easy', he said, 'all you have to do is to imagine yourself a visitor from the Outer Hebrides, with two hours at most to spend at Blenheim. You want to cream it, to see the

[169]

outstanding things and no more.' This at first sounded sensible, but when I repeated it to the Duke he saw through it at once. It was, he pointed out, founded upon a false supposition, 'for as a matter of fact very few people live in the Hebrides, and those that do are too poor to travel'.

It was then decided that we must all join in a trial-run, a conducted tour of the house or at least of those rooms which were going to be shown to the public. Acccordingly, with the Duke and Duchess leading, we were joined by Lord Cherwell, two Americans, Jenkins the new agent (Sacré had dropped dead in the park), and the Duke's youngest daughter Rosie (later Lady Rosemary Muir). But almost at once a serious controversy arose about lavatories. The Duke, trying hard to be patient, appealed to our common sense. When all was said and done, what was there to prevent men and women from sharing the same loo? The Duchess spoke forcefully against it. Very well then, there were plenty of trees and bushes for men to use in the park.

Self: 'I would have thought you would have been the first to object to that.'

Duke: 'What makes you think so? I'd far rather they went behind a bush than behind the furniture. And after all, considering that my father damned nearly shot a couple copulating in the bracken, what?'

The debate continued as we moved on towards Winston's birthroom; but there again we were faced with the same problem. At the very entrance to the Dean Jones Room there was a water-closet through which, unless it were screened off, visitors would have to pass. So after further argument screens were agreed to. But as to the birthroom itself, dull and depressing at all times, looking into a central well, its wallpaper was in tatters, and the skirting-board disfigured by a large rathole. H'm, that would need thinking about.

Our tour continued by way of the staterooms and library to the chapel, which had been used to store furniture during the war. Queen Mary, on a wartime visit from Badminton, had asked to be allowed to venerate Marlborough's tomb, but no key to the chapel could be found. However, after minutes of panic the key was traced, a path cleared and royal devotion done. Canon Pickles, then Rector of Woodstock, had asked me to ask the

[170]

Duke if, in view of the ninth Duke's conversion to Roman Catholicism, the chapel ought not to be reconsecrated. At the time when I innocently passed on this message I feared the Duke might have apoplexy. I never saw him more angry (he was usually mild). 'Most certainly NOT!' he exploded.

Out on the water-terraces the Duchess, like Duchêne, thought there should be fountains, and I of course supported her. Another altercation ensued. The ninth Duke's heir made no reference to 'the limpidity of still water', but murmured something about expense. Today however, thanks to the present Duke, we find the top terrace lively with fountains which in summertime play all day long.

And so in the spring of 1950 Blenheim was reopened to the public for the first time since 1939. The huge, coroneted key to the main doors shone with Brasso. The Long Library, white as a wedding-cake, was en fête with flowers. There was one professional guide only, whom I had done my best to coach, but he was staffless, so that it was all hands to the pumps when the deluge of visitors arrived. It meant chaos of course, but good-tempered chaos. Family and friends hurled themselves into it and throughout that well-fought day the public, almost to a man, remained in a mood of dogged enjoyment.

'The Great Hall', I shouted feebly, my voice echoing to the painted ceiling and back again, 'is sixty-seven feet high. The ingenious locks to the main doors . . .' They surged towards me, a solid, well-ordered mass, eager to be instructed. I told them all I knew and still they waited for more. 'Any questions?' Oh yes, that immense silver wine-cooler. Was it true that all Marlborough babies were bathed in it? No, I assured them, it was not.

It was then that I noticed, on the far side of the Hall, someone frantically waving. Clearly something was wrong, but what was it? 'You caused bottlenecks', I was told later, 'the crowd behind you was solid, didn't you see?' 'My bottlenecks', I retorted, 'were deliberate. If I hadn't held that crowd back they would have trampled on the birthroom lot and made jam of them. How did things go in the Saloon?' 'Oh', said Lady Rosemary calmly, 'they went like a bomb. I kept telling them the ceiling was flat – it *is* flat, isn't it? – and they couldn't believe it. It does *look* coved, I must say, the way it's painted. They gazed and gazed till their necks ached and asked if I was sure

[171]

and I said yes truly it was *quite* flat; and then they thanked me nicely and moved on.'

Lord Carnarvon ran into unexpected trouble in the birthroom. 'This', he told his audience proudly, 'is the modest room where Winston Churchill was born.' 'Yes', shouted a heckler, 'and it might have been better for the world if he hadn't been.' Carnarvon paused and then with a steady look at the man said urbanely, 'There, sir, I fear we must disagree; because if he hadn't been born I doubt very much if you or I or any of us would be standing here today.'

I must have said my spiel twenty times when the guide whose name was Golden asked if I realised that a queue four deep now stretched, in a howling wind, from the north portico to the clock tower and beyond. So I deserted my army and strode out to the still greater multitude to try to console them. It was bleak and comfortless out there and I marvelled at their endurance. But no, they would not go away and have tea and come back later. They had come to see Blenheim and see it they would though they died in their tracks, like the French infantry at Blindheim.

In the chapel, with one exception, no one challenged my talk on the Marlborough tomb. It was a thing I felt confident about and so my words flowed on, touching here upon the sculptor Rysbrack, and there upon the occupants below, in a tone I hoped was reverent, knowledgeable and assured. I paused for breath. 'But please', insisted a foreigner in a back pew, 'I do not understand. This tomb, how can it be for families? Where are they? Is he here? Is she here? The first ones – where?' 'Why yes', I gently assured him, 'both of them and some of their descendants. Here in the vault, beneath the paving-stones we're standing on.' He looked gravely concerned. 'But how can this be? Beneath us here, so many all together, is it?' Sadly he shook his head. 'In my country', he murmured, 'this could not be.'

As the sun sank behind the stables tower and the crowds still gathered, I had the impression that every living soul west of the Iron Curtain was heading for Blenheim and that, since my voice was all but gone, I would be doomed to speak to them for ever in whispers. It seemed all the more wonderful, then, when of a sudden I found the staterooms empty and, returning to the Great Hall, just one long, limp, familiar figure leaning back with closed eyes in a hooded leather chair. 'Someone left a baby in the hall', said the Duke wearily; 'it cried for a solid hour. Come and have tea in the sitting room.'

Tea at Blenheim was usually a nominal affair at 5.15. Cakes were put on the table but no one dreamed of cutting them. One nibbled a stamp-sized cucumber-sandwich and toyed with a cup of China tea and that was all. This day was no exception and we were going through the motions of eating with Lord Carnarvon and his son Lord Porchester when the Duke suddenly sprang to his feet and rushed into the garden, shouting and waving his rubber-tipped stick. I wondered what on earth could be happening. 'And so did you get them, Dukie?' Porchester calmly asked. 'A couple of sods', fumed the Duke, 'trying to climb the ha-ha.' But he soon calmed and we all relaxed and decided to call it a day.

That summer as I made for the private wing I noticed the electrician at work in the game larder and facetiously asked him to hand me a brace of grouse. 'Ah yes', he said understandingly, 'some get to like them, but for ordinary folk like you and me, give us steak and chips or some really good bangers and we're just as happy.'

In her sitting-room the Duchess asked if I had enjoyed my week in Paris. I said yes except for the strike of taxi-drivers. 'Don't talk to me of taxis', she said, 'I've just been with Queen Mary in Marlborough House. Now it's all very well for her with about fourteen cars to choose from, but for people like you and me, we're lucky to find any transport at all. By the way, do you want to see the Duke? He's in bed with gout.' She showed me to his bedroom and withdrew.

For Blenheim, the Duke's bedroom was a small one (it had been another of Sarah's closets), but with its view over the eastern garden it was less dismal than Winston's birthroom, although in one corner torn wallpaper had been fixed with drawing-pins. Between the windows there was what I took to be a Turkish bath, and near that a wonderfully old-fashioned telephone. It had no mouthpiece. One spoke on to a small wooden board which bore the notice: 'You are on no account to TOUCH OR HIT this thin deal sounding-board which is very delicate and easily damaged'.

A more up-to-date instrument was on a table nearer the bed, a small

[173]

Empire affair that might have belonged to one of Napoleon's lieutenants. In fact all the furniture was Empire, good of its kind but rather depressing. I was cheered to notice an engraving of Vanbrugh, framed above the bed. Another small round bedside table was almost hidden by an astonishingly large assortment of medicine-bottles and pillboxes.

'Just reach me that glass of water, will you?' said the Duke, looking more tousled than usual, 'I'd better take one of these. No I won't, I'll have one of those. What does it say on the label?'

'It says "His Grace the Duke of Marlborough. For pain. One every four hours".'

'That'll do. I say, that opening day did me no good, what? All that noise and those extraordinary people. Even now they keep bursting in and staring at me. I don't know if you've ever been stared at. No, perhaps not. Well, it's not a pleasant experience; and I can tell you in this house one gets little privacy at all.'

I thought it best to change the subject. The new agent, while waiting with me at Hanborough station (then ablaze with flowers) had told me, 'The Duke's grateful for your help in showing the house and wants you, as he put it, to make a good thing out of the guidebook. Hadn't you better come to some sort of written agreement with him?' And so now, at the Napoleonic bedside, I found courage to mention it. 'What? What? Yes of course, why not? You're one of our stagehands now. How's the house?' 'Which house?' 'The one you live in.' 'Thanks, it's a crumbling cottage and, like parts of Blenheim, badly in need of repair. What do you mean to do about the kitchen court?'

'I shall do nothing at all about what you call the kitchen court. There's a building in Rome with the same sort of arcading, arches above arches, all mouldering away. No one thinks of doing anything about that.'

'Well then, how about the south-east tower? Rayson tells me it's so out of true it needs rebuilding from the ground.'

'Let me remind you', said the Duke with a note of triumph, 'of another well-known building in Italy, which has been leaning at a far more acute angle for a great many years. Crowds flock to see it and no one talks of rebuilding that. No, what I'm worried about, as I've told you, is this bloody roof . . . keeps letting the rain in . . . By the way, some film fellow has been pestering me; wants to make what he calls a documentary of Blenheim. I said very well, provided you write the script. That suit you, what?' I thanked him and left.

If as so often happens a film can be damned at birth, then that film was. The script was tough going enough, and when the day came for the Duke to record it, gout had frayed his patience to breaking-point. He shouted into the microphone and made so many slips that the producer said, 'Now we'll just run through that again.' 'What d'you mean?' barked the Duke, 'what's the matter?' 'You fluffed it, your Grace.' 'I WHAT?' 'You fluffed it, made mistakes, you know.' But the second take was if anything worse; and when we sat on the top terrace, for the television-trailer, with the sun on the lake dazzling us, things were no better.

'Mr Green, will you please sit nearer his Grace? You're out of the picture.'

'Sorry, but I can't get any nearer without sitting in his lap.'

'Very well, but when it comes to the take, please don't address the producer as "Mister". There are no misters in the film industry.' 'Oh no', put in the Duke scathingly, 'there are no gentlemen in the film industry.'

At the private view in London the continuity-girl told the Duke that the film had been synchronised but not married. 'But surely', he said, 'it's possible to be synchronised without having to be married?' During the run there was brisk altercation between the Duke and his brother Ivor as to the authenticity of a Van Dyck; but otherwise I could see nothing flagrantly wrong. As we left I heard the backer say, 'It's so byootiful I can hardly believe it's true.' At Bootle however, or wherever it was that that poor little film, made on a shoestring, had its first public showing, it was, I understand, booed off the screen.

When at last my monolithic book on the building of Blenheim was published, I took two copies with me to give to the owners. To Alex, the Duchess's favourite dachshund, it presented no problem. He literally devoured her signed copy from cover to cover. Rufus, however (Winston Churchill's poodle), proved steadier to books, accustomed as he was to them; while his master sent not only thanks but a signed copy of his own masterly biography of Marlborough, a book I regard as my second Bible.

Then late one evening the Duchess telephoned. She had something urgent and serious to say – could I come over at once? Having biked through the park I found her stately and subdued, in Court mourning. A most embarrassing thing had happened. Queen Mary, reading *Blenheim Palace* 'with the utmost interest', had noticed a photograph of the Marlborough fan ('Qui sait quand reviendra?') which she herself, though I had not known it, had given to the Duchess – and in my book there was no mention of her having given it. Of course I apologised and, with Fate still against me, I changed the subject to that of the state bed. 'If you mean the Pink Horror', said the Duchess, referring to Sir William Chambers' domed and gilded triumph, 'the answer's a positive NO, I will not have it in the Third Stateroom. At huge cost I've just renewed the damask curtains there. The bed would clash with them and hide the tapestries. No thank you, that's *not* on.'

Yet on the whole those were days when Blenheim was my playground, whether I read Sarah's *Letters of a Grandmother* while sunning myself on the leads, or strolled the length of an upper corridor peopled, as in *Ruddigore*, by family portraits. Anne Sunderland was there, the mother of them all; and her wilful sister Henrietta and – then in a dark corner but now in a place of honour downstairs – Consuelo, as Veruda saw her, standing in a garden and holding a pink rose: not, like Sargent's, a great painting, but in its way a more engaging one. American friends had just mailed us her autobiography, *The Glitter and the Gold* (unfailingly referred to by her son as *The Gold and the Glitter*). I read it at a sitting and noted, 'She writes intelligently but goes astray on Blenheim, scorning it and missing its meaning . . . And how she loathed her first husband (chosen by her mother) the ninth Duke!'

At the time, I remember, it made good reading (and I have re-read it twice since), but it upset the family including her daughter-in-law and Randolph Churchill. The Duchess declared it anti-British, while Randolph took the tenth Duke to task for having allowed his mother to write such things about her husband. 'I can assure you, Randolph', the Duke told him, 'if I had not blue-pencilled freely it would have been a great deal worse.'

[176]

The Venus Statue in the Italian Garden at Blenheim

The Water Terraces at Blenheim

Mary, tenth Duchess of Marlborough in the Bow Window Room at Blenheim

I met her one late Spring morning, the Vanderbilt heiress, near the walled kitchen-garden, as she sat beside her son who was driving a small Morris. She was in black, an old aristocrat with exquisite nose and profile, the long, graceful neck that had delighted Sargent encircled with four rows of pearls. I told her the Duke had been trying to keep his tulips from flowering before her arrival. She laughed and murmured that in her own little [sic] garden in the south of France the flowers were already parched and over. We exchanged compliments on books before the Duke drove on to the walled garden, and what an elysium that garden then was! Against the high, brick walls figs and nectarines ripened; and in the glasshouses, melons and muscats. Mary Marlborough's favourite flowers – gardenias and huge cream dahlias – flourished as a matter of course; while outside the walls the eighth and ninth Dukes' conservatories, rich with datura and bougainvillea, had grottoes of tufa and clam-shells in which pied-wagtails nested.

In its leaded cupola above a bastion in the fourteen-foot wall hung the gardeners' bell, and how friendly and pleasant were those who answered it. Tompkins the head-gardener was fat and quiet and relaxed; while Page, who was to succeed him, thoroughly understood flowers. Shingler the fruit-manager was smaller and shyer, his rose-covered cottage hidden away and joined to the south-west wall. He too had a garden and a nut-grove, with just room enough for a celestial sundial, a few beehives and an old, propped mulberry still fruiting, not for his benefit (he didn't like them) but for ours.

I often thought how much more enjoyment we must draw from Blenheim than the Duke did himself. Muscats were nothing to him (he grew them for guests), and as for flowers, though he prided himself as a botanist, they seemed only to cause him extra worry. 'What's this, Tompkins?' he would ask as we strolled in the orangery and he prodded some sickly looking plant with his rubber-tipped stick. 'Why, that's one of the lilies your Grace brought back from Mexico.' 'Well then, why isn't it in flower?'

We moved on to the stables and climbed stone stairs to a warren of rooms built for grooms and stable-lads. The Duke limped ahead and turned into the first room he came to. I could hardly believe my ears because from that room there now came fond murmurs and terms of endearment: 'Well well well', I heard the Duke say, 'dear old fellow, fancy finding you here, how are you then, what?' I imagined some aged pensioner, a once-dear retainer perhaps, now mouldering in an attic but nevertheless still high in ducal esteem. And so at last, drawing level with the open door, I looked in; but all I saw, beside an empty chair, was an old and quivering Jack Russell. The Duke was fondling it and stroking its ears.

By the same steep stairs we had begun to leave when without warning the Duke slipped. His stick shot between the rails and went clattering down to distant flagstones. I just managed to grab him. Nothing was said and the rest of the long flight was negotiated with dignity and silence. To falter was not in the Marlborough tradition. One simply pretended that nothing had happened, as indeed nothing much had.

Television had yet to come into its own and in the meantime what were called outside broadcasts had large audiences, the peak period being after the nine o'clock news, the time chosen for what I can only call our state broadcast from Blenheim. Richard Dimbleby, Audrey Russell and I rehearsed all morning, and in the afternoon a strange thing happened, as at Blenheim it often does. It was the 250th anniversary of the battle of Blenheim, and it was the mayor of Höchstädt, a village bordering the battlefield, who materialising as it seemed from nowhere – although he had just come from Chartwell – told us he must, at 5.30 precisely (the time of the last cavalry charge) place a wreath on Marlborough's tomb in the chapel. This ceremony we solemnly attended and at a signal from the chief guide, Illingworth, who held a stopwatch, the mayor laid his wreath, almost as big as himself, upon the tomb, marched backwards, saluted, made a long speech in German, saluted again, bowed and withdrew.

The live transmission seemed to go well enough, although it began badly in the forecourt when Dimbleby, having recited that time-worn jingle beginning 'See, Sir, here's the grand approach . . .', was overcome by a fit of coughing and had temporarily to retire, leaving me with the microphone and Blenheim. I ad-libbed about the roof and upset the timing, but Audrey Russell in the Long Library saved the day and by sheer enthusiasm and professional know-how got things going.

[178]

The author with Richard Dimbleby: a live transmission from the forecourt at Blenheim

My next script was to be translated into French and to be broadcast to Quebec. I wrote long parts for the Duke and Duchess and short ones for the chef and for Lord Charles, on leave from Eton. Surprisingly the Duke's French proved more fluent than his wife's. The word *vieille* defeated her completely. 'It's no good', she sighed, 'Mr Green has put words into my mouth that I would never have thought of.' It was heavy going. Young Charles's French was of the no-nonsense kind favoured by Winston: he disdained to drop the 'h' in *là-haut*. I sometimes wonder what they made of it all in Quebec.

But then of course came television. This, to my alarm, they took

[179]

seriously. 'If you'd stop talking for one minute', said the Duke while the Duchess and I were trying to thrash the thing out, 'I'd like to speak'. My script, he said, was too long; and now he himself had just thought of a little joke about the Malplaquet glass goblet in the Third Stateroom (once a bedroom) being *mal placé*. Now how about that, what? The Duchess countered by insisting that no one except the Duke and herself and Dimbleby was to appear on the screen. At the very end her dachshunds might romp into the Great Hall, but that would be all. How much she would have liked to show her bedroom, but no, that was out of the question. Even with an invisible team of cameramen manoeuvring apparatus the size of a ponytrap, it still would never do to give viewers the impression that she and Dimbleby were alone in her bedroom. 'Now tell me, Mr Green', she asked, switching from a delicate subject, 'what was that well-known phrase of Sarah's about "This pile of stones – where's my Bow Window Room?"'. To that there seemed no answer.

Dimbleby, shown into the Long Library, dominated as it was and is by the eighth Duke's Willis organ, turned to the Duke. 'They tell me', he said, 'that you have the biggest private organ in England?' The Duke allowed himself a smile. 'I would like to think so', he said. But that passage was omitted from the transmission. I did my best to sort it all out.

When the great day came I found myself in a control-van near the north portico, amid batteries of monitors and microphones. On my left the producer, pipe in mouth, kept saying, into various microphones, 'Okay, boy, not to worry'. I gathered we were in touch with an army of more or less attentive and obedient technicians, some in the house, some in London, some in Bristol.

On five of the monitor-screens in front of us huge cameras on wheels moved around in five different rooms, while on the sixth, from London, a couple of comedians were busy with the kind of farce once known as custard-pie. The jumble was quite extraordinary. From the top lefthand screen two eyes blinked at us through a mess of pie; while on that beside it, against a background of tapestry, four engineers were energetically at work on what looked like a flying bedstead. 'What are they doing?' I asked. 'Pumping up the dolly', I was told.

[180]

On one of the lower screens a camera was approaching a twenty-foot window in the Long Library. 'That shot won't do, number four', said the producer, 'sash-bars too thick, can't see the garden. Okay boy, remove window'. 'But chief', came back a faint voice, 'it's good this way. Viewers'll get the idea they're really looking out through the window. Glass a bit smeary, that's all, just needs a rag.' There followed a moment for thought. Then: 'Okay boy, not to worry, clean window . . . and I say, is Stan there? Well just ask him to walk through all the rooms with a mike, testing for sound, will you?'

After which, so much began to happen on all six screens and within the van itself, we would surely have forgotten Stan had not his ghost-voice every now and then drifted back to us. 'I am now in the Duchess's sitting-room. Excuse me, your Grace, I'm just testing for sound. One-two-three-four . . . I am now in the Duke's study. Excuse me, your Grace . . .' and so on. Number three had a nasty accident with a large portrait, luckily by an outmoded painter; though I still wonder how he managed to buckle the frame and the canvas at a single blow.

'By the way', said the producer, addressing me as the Long Library organ swung into view on screen five, 'I'm counting on you to sort out the background music – you are musical aren't you? – for the opening sequence. They've got a mechanical player there, pretty wizard. Be a good lad and get that buttoned up straight away. And don't bother about Dimbleby's piece', he shouted after me, 'he's decided to play *The Lost Chord* just for laughs'.

In the apse behind the organ I found the floor littered with cylinders, most of them labelled with the name of the piece and its composer, but some bore comments in the hand of a dead duke: 'Not good', 'Too quiet', 'Dull' or even 'Not to be played again'. I was hopefully looking for Brahms or Handel, but all I could find was much martial Wagner, Viennese waltzes, some rather woolly Bach, *Land of Hope and Glory* and *The Lost Chord*. Depressed I reached out for a dusty roll in the corner: Dvořák's *New World*, one might have guessed it. 'Oh well, shove it on', I told the electrician, 'at least it won't blast us out of the room.' The roll ran for some seconds without producing a sound. 'How about those notes there?' I asked, pointing to rows of holes which on a pianola would have sounded a fanfare.

[181]

'Those aren't notes', said the electrician, 'that's the organ sorting out the stops it thinks it's going to need.' 'Oh', I said. And when it did reach the opening bars it sounded less formidable than I'd feared. 'Okay, boy', came the voice of the producer, 'Nice work. We'll use it.'

When after countless rehearsals zero hour arrived, I remember being astonished at the noise in the control van right up to the last second. Calls were still coming through from London and Bristol and, within the last half-minute, Dimbleby signalled an alteration to allow of his voice being heard before he appeared on the screen. 'Okay, organ!' commanded the producer, and the *New World* began to seep plaintively through. For better for worse our half hour of Blenheim had begun.

I held my breath while its owners moved gracefully from one glittering room to another. Would they remember their lines? Would the electrician switch off the automatic organ-player in time for Dimbleby's *Lost Chord*? Above all, at the very end would the dachshunds romp joyfully but not too boisterously to the Duchess in the Great Hall? There was one awkward moment when the Duke forgetting his ancestor's comment shook his head at Kneller's portrait of Marlborough in armour and said, 'Surely that isn't me?' But otherwise the programme went smoothly and the dachshunds all but stole the picture.

At dinner congratulatory telegrams began to arrive. One of them read: 'Well done, Dukey!' and was unsigned. The Duchess laughed. 'That's from Porchester, Blandford. No one else calls you that.'

Next day I wrote in my diary:

This morning grey and restful and I feel rather as Sir William Chambers must have when, after coping with the fourth Duke at Blenheim, he wrote to a parson friend at Witney: The transition from a palace to a cot, as you call your habitation, is more agreeable to me than you can well imagine. I shall enter your door with a jovial heart, which I seldom have in the mansions of the great. With you I shall consider myself a welcome guest. With them I am like the Egyptian bird who picks the teeth of the crocodile: admitted and cherished while there is any work to be done, but when that is over the doors are shut and the farce is at an end.

[182]

The publication of my *Gardener to Queen Anne*, the biography of Henry Wise who had helped Vanbrugh lay out Blenheim's park and gardens, must have been the quietest in history. There was a hush as for the burial of a stillborn book. No one wanted to know about formal gardens. And at Blenheim (myself feeling almost as obsequious as Dr Mavor) my call was ill-timed, they had so much else to think of. The Duchess, murmuring 'So kind', put her copy on the sofa she was sharing with Alex and his friends. Alex licked his lips. The Duke put his copy on the floor and gently kicked it with an embroidered slipper. He was not, as his father had been, obsessed with *parterres*. He had just decided to make a garden himself, on the south-east. 'One must have a modicum of privacy', he said.

At a quite early stage in the 1950s [he later explained] I found I needed huge stones, some plain, some sculptured, to add character and to shelter the alpines. These I had brought from a once-elaborate rock-garden [one of the first in England] at the far western extremity of the lake. Some of the rocks weighed fifteen hundredweight or more. With a small crane they were lowered into their places, as were also what remained of the Lion Fountain and a stone trophy by Grinling Gibbons which had crumbled and had had to be re-carved for the eastern colonnade. Further, I created an informal pond and designed a system of grass paths which, winding and intersecting, seem to beckon one on to hidden surprises.

It all of course took years to mature, but it has proved well worth waiting and working for. It has become a source of real delight and a great comfort to me in old age. Unlike men, who with age grow uglier and more gaga, trees and long-lived shrubs improve and become more beautiful. This benevolence of Nature was one of the reasons for my making a garden not only to last my time and afford some solace but, as I hoped, to please those who would come after me. In morbid mood I have been known to refer to it as my mausoleum, because at one time I felt I would like to be buried there. Thinking again however I realise that this might be unfair and selfish, for it would mean having my successors continually conscious of my grave; and it would mean too spoiling what I consider a garden of real beauty, more especially in the spring.

'What would your father have thought of it?' I asked, as we explored the glades together. For answer he trod heavily on a polyanthus. 'Now that's a thing', he said, 'one can never get gardeners to do. You see, the frost pushes them up and you need to tread them in again.' In the midst of it all a seat had been put under an oak tree and on the oak was a plaque with a verse about being nearer to God in a garden than anywhere else on earth. It was signed MARLBOROUGH.

'And will the public see your new garden?' Audrey Russell asked. 'Yes and no. They may see it from a distance, but I regard it as my retreat.' In the eighth Duchess's boathouse we found a skiff and made for Vanbrugh's bridge where Audrey wanted to record the sound of oars and of ducks. Bats brushed our heads as I navigated the south arch and we looked up to see a great swarm of them hanging from the ceiling. 'You were a long time under the bridge with Audrey Russell', said the Duke later. 'I don't know what you were up to. Attractive girl that, what?'

In common with other owners of historic houses the Duke was finding the cost of upkeep onerous; nor was it easy to draw the crowds without appearing to be blatantly vulgar. 'I have no intention of turning the place into a funfair', he said; and in that frame of mind he began to ponder the possibilities of *son et lumière*. If we did it, would I be prepared to write the script?

Having seen the superb show at Versailles I had some misgivings. There for the opening scene Sacha Guitry had conjured romance in a magical way. And then the fountains: that sudden surge of strange sound before seeing them. It had been all so *féerique*; even at Blenheim one could hardly hope to compete with that.

Few things have ever given me more trouble or less reward. Day after day I walked from site to possible site in the park, visualising, imagining and at times getting excited. The scene must of course open with Elizabeth's island and the bridge – nothing could be more romantic – and the palace would remain invisible until later when of a sudden the whole of the north front would leap to the eye, ablaze with light. For the second climax – the making of the lake – I hoped ingenious technicians could somehow contrive the effect of a great mass of water, suddenly released, roaring and rushing through the bridge.

I had begun to enthuse about all this when the Duke murmured 'Cowpats'. 'My father always told me', he explained, 'that when cows have been lying down and decide to get up, ten to one they'll shit. And if you have your audience on that far bank of the lake, either they'll be falling into the water or they'll be sitting on cowpats, possibly both. Moreover', warming to his theme, 'you won't get them out of the park afterwards. They'll copulate and poach the pheasants, what?'

The Duchess had other ideas. At Chambord, she had been told, they could successfully broadcast a whisper. Very well, we must have the whisper. But need we have the show at all? Why not just floodlighting and a band? And why not open the house at weekends? Though there again, there was no privacy as things were. 'If I try to write a letter on the lawn', she said, 'I find them staring at me, so I just get into the car and drive to the top of the bog. After all, if they're so mad keen to see us, they have only to look in *The Tatler*.'

And then too, who was to back us? Winston? Clore? Rothermere? Onassis? 'Good God Almighty!' exclaimed the Duchess, 'we don't want any of your Greek millionaires here. We can manage without them.' As things turned out, no funds for *son et lumière* were then forthcoming, and so it had to be postponed. 'Some day', said the Duchess, 'someone may come along, but remember, we must have the whisper.'

Every writer, every would-be historian needs not only, as Sarah put it, to work like a packhorse. He needs large slices of luck; and these I had at Blenheim, in London and, oddly enough, in Holland where I flew to Rotterdam, that hideous city which happened to be the birthplace of Grinling Gibbons. Well buried among thirty-five bound volumes of Churchill papers in the British Museum I had found detailed bills which proved unquestionably that Gibbons, as Queen Anne's master-carver, had been responsible for all the enrichment of Blenheim, mainly in stone and in marble, within and without. For me it was an exciting discovery and called for a book on his sculpting and woodcarving, including church monuments:

[185]

a book which led me to remote corners of England and Scotland, as well as to Italy and Holland.

At Blenheim Gibbons and his team had done more carving than they had in St Paul's Cathedral, where I spent a great deal of time. I shall never forget the day when, standing in the deserted chancel of St Paul's and seeing the distant western doorway curtained with rain, I heard the thunder slowly advance eastward, the length of the nave, until it was above the dome and then directly overhead. My soul-destroying job near Fleet Street had gone far to destroy me; yet here within walking distance were solace and restoration. So I sat in the Choir, encircled by cherubim, celestial urchins carved with wings but with tousled hair: London choirboys, tough and preoccupied and dedicated at that lasting moment to the job in hand, which was singing.

Back in Punch Office I answered my telephone. 'Mr Green? This is British Red Cross Headquarters. The Duchess of Marlborough would be most grateful if you would be good enough to introduce Monsieur Christian Dior to the Press. It's to do with the dress show she's planning at Blenheim. Yes indeed, this is a personal request from the Duchess. She knows you will be pleased to do anything for the Red Cross.'

I tried to think. The only conceivable link, and that a frail one, was Dryden's *All For Love*, once acted for Marlborough by his grandchildren in the apse of the Bow Window Room. To cheer him, ill as he then was, they had dressed up in the brocades and silks imported from Genoa for Blenheim's covers and curtains, then still to be stitched and hung.

I need not have worried. Of a roomful of tough press-women few wanted to hear anyone but Dior and the Duchess. Still, I made my short speech and at the end of it – 'Any questions?' – noticed among all those women one male American, now ambling towards me like an ape. 'Now, this battle of Blenheim', he demanded, 'who was on which side?'

'Well now, let me see. The Dutch and the Danes and the Austrian and German states were on our side; and the French and the Bavarians were on the other.'

He looked discomforted. 'Listen,' he said, 'were the British on one side and the French on the other?'

[186]

'Yes'.

'Thanks. That's all I wanna know.'

To the feminine show itself I was mercifully not invited; but Audrey Russell, who was, told me it was decidedly the Duchess's evening of triumph. Princess Margaret was there; and Blenheim flying its state flag with the imperial eagle, and floodlit, rose to the occasion like that noble bird itself. 'That place *gets* you, you know.' Oh yes, it had long since got me, hook, line and sinker; so much so that it had begun to haunt my dreams. I dreamt that we were at a grand picnic in the gardens. A footman brought an elaborate cake with a frosted rose on it and the Duchess said yes she *always* got them to make that one, it never went wrong. Then another footman, dark and cadaverous, brought another cake that was an exact model of his own head. It was a nightmare.

Next day I was on Vanbrugh's bridge with Howard Colvin, an old friend who was editing the *King's Works*. He had just discovered evidence of the complex villa Henry II had built for Rosamond Clifford at Rosamond's Well. 'You may think me cynical', said the Duchess, 'but in the Muniment Room Mr Green has discovered Brown's plan for the lake and it shows no trace of any such building at all.' We had now reached the well and were discussing the water. I agreed that recent analysis had shown nothing remarkable; 'but your father-in-law', I reminded the Duchess, 'thought it had a mystical quality.' 'You're absolutely right', she said, 'mystical is the word.'

Sadly, not long after this we heard that the Duchess was mortally ill. There had been unsuccessful operations; and so for fifteen months she languished, at first in hospital, later in her bedroom at Blenheim. Everything in that high room – tapestry (the Triumph of Alexander), chimney-piece in white marble by Vanbrugh and Gibbons, four-poster bed with parchment-and-gold hangings – was grand but not cheering. The eighth Duke's DUST – ASHES – NOTHING, with which he had disfigured the white marble, had been erased and now, over the chimney-piece, hung Kneller's portrait of the Princess Anne in blue. Towards the end the Duchess was moved to an upper room, which was less gloomy and had no unhappy associations. Nothing more could be done for her. When she died, at sixty-

[187]

one, she was buried at Bladon in a new part of the churchyard at some distance from the church and from the rest of the Churchill graves.

In the walled garden, where I had gone for heliotrope and globe-artichokes, the head-gardener told me, 'He's feeling it a bit, I should say. Very quiet. You see, she was always about, she was always there when he needed her.'

For some reason I needed to check something in the east wing where I noticed at once there was no smell of scent, only of cigars. As I was stealing out, the butler stopped me and urged me to go and see the Duke. I found him in his study, acknowledging condolence-letters. 'Sorry I could only top and tail yours', he said. looking over his spectacles, 'there were four hundred of them.' We discussed the memorial services in London and in Oxford. For one of them he had asked for a voluntary which the organist said had been scored for orchestra only. 'I told him', said the Duke, 'I happened to know something about music; and after all, the organ is in itself an orchestra. I mean it provides for all the instruments, the oboe and so on, what? But you see these modern organists can't improvise. Now my father's organist Perkins was in my view the best organist in the world, he could play anything. Otherwise the services went well enough except for the treble solo in an anthem. The boy who sang it, well, I'd say something had happened to him the week before. He just wasn't up to it.'

It seemed a reasonably good moment to ask if a young curate, then staying in our village, might try his hands (and feet) at the Blenheim organ. 'Is he any good?' asked the Duke. 'He's certainly keen,' I said, 'perhaps you'd care to listen to him?' But already his attention had wandered. 'I hear you're another artichoke-fan', he said. 'They tell me they're very good for health and sex. In the former I'm not all that much interested.'

When the day came for the curate to play the organ, I began to hope very much that the Duke had forgotten it, because it was clear from the first that, as the Crown Prince of Germany had found, it was 'like managing an ironclad' – it could easily run out of control. Faced with four manuals and row upon row of stops and couplings (not to mention pedals), Mr Collins fingered this and prodded that until suddenly two stops shot out – *Vox Humana* and *Vox Angelica* – and stubbornly stayed out, resisting his frantic struggles to return them to base. The effect was curious. Whatever he tried to play – the Toccata and Fugue, the Doge's March, the Anvil Chorus – all were superimposed with a piercing falsetto descant. I was praying for him not to be overheard when, just as suddenly, the superfluous stops shot in again and for a time all went calmly. I asked for *Jesu, Joy of Man's Desiring* and he played it well.

We were about to leave when the Duke, in open-necked shirt and with rubber-tipped stick, appeared in a distant doorway and limped towards us. I stood to introduce the organist, but the Duke had been engrossed with the Wimbledon finals on television and could think of nothing else. 'There was this unfortunate girl, don't you see, Christine Truman, she was winnning the finals when she fell . . .' I made a second attempt: 'The Duke of Marlborough – Mr Collins'. 'How d'you do? I've been watching the finals at Wimbledon and the most unfortunate thing happened. This Truman girl, there's no doubt she would have won, but she had the misfortune to fall . . . Oh, but perhaps you're not interested in sport?'

Poor Mr Collins, it was not his day. He was rash enough to ask the Duke if there was some favourite piece he would like him to play. Pause. And then, jerking his thoughts from Wimbledon to music he said, 'The Moonlight Sonata'. In his wildest nightmares, Collins told us afterwards, he had never dreamt of attempting that on anything but a piano. Still, he had to attempt it now, and for a moment or two it seemed as though with prayer he might get away with it; but all too soon his confidence petered out. The Duke's back, as he limped away, expressed everything. Yet once more he had been disappointed and someone he had favoured had let him down. Shades of the perfect Perkins! Shades of that sad Duke whose heart he had beguiled!

When we next found ourselves in the Long Library it was for the reception after the heir's wedding in France to Tina Onassis, a radiantly lovely girl in bright red. When I asked if she liked Blenheim she smiled her wide smile and said yes, she thought the park the loveliest in the world. In the course of a good speech the Duke referred to 'this vast and unruly house' and advised us all to get 'lit up' on his champagne. We did. '*How* Mother would have enjoyed this!' said Lady Caroline, the Duke's second daughter.

[189]

As the party went on, for me at least it grew more and more euphoric, so that at one stage I found myself as it were enthroned with the Duke as, in the middle of it all, we sat on two gilded, Queen Anne chairs. He told me he had bought a house in Jamaica and that he was seriously thinking of writing his autobiography. 'After all, Loelia Westminster has had some success with hers, and I've had quite an amusing life, what?' Would I help him put it together? I said 'Yes, let's do it.' 'It would have to be . . .' he began, 'Dignified?' I suggested. 'No, no, amusing, entertaining.' Lit up as I was, there seemed nothing against it; but of course I had no notion of what I was in for. Nor, I think, had he. However, as time went by, he made no further mention of it, and it was rash of me to remind him. 'Ah yes', he said, 'some day we may get round to it; but just now my man in Harley Street has put me on to a new pill which seems to be doing some good; so you see, there's no urgency, what?'

A few days before Christmas he asked me to lunch in the Bow Window Room. No one else was there and every topic I embarked on died on my lips. 'Such a bore, Christmas trees, don't you think?' he said, nodding towards the forest tree in the apse. I said, 'It always used to have long glass icicles. What happened to them?' He grunted. 'Tinsel doesn't last, you know.'

In desperation I mentioned an old tenant in our village who every Christmas seemed to take on a new lease of life. 'What!' exclaimed the Duke, 'Not dead? Not dead?' I said, 'No, haven't you noticed – people aren't dying any more'. 'All the same', he said mournfully, 'they do die.' Then a prolonged silence. I looked at the butler and the butler looked at me. Was the Duke in a coma? Ought we to send for help? 'Blasted sinus', said my host, coming to, 'do *you* have sinus trouble, what?'

I could hardly make matters worse, I thought, by asking if I might explore the family vault. 'I wish you would', he said with a glimmer of interest, 'and while you're down there, you might find out what sort of room there is left. They tell me it's choc-à-bloc'. And then, after another pause, 'But I don't think I want to be buried there anyway. I'd rather be in the open air.' I dared to say if I were Duke I'd like to lie in the vault among my ancestors. 'What, even if it were crowded?' 'Yes, I'd pull rank or something and tell them to move over.'

[190]

Although by now in the course of field work I had become accustomed to unfamiliar objects on noble tables – silver spikes for corn-cobs or, as at Althorp, a long silver tube for extinguishing a spirit-lamp beneath a tea-kettle – I own I was foxed by the huge uncut Stilton now set before me. Where to make the first incision and how? I seized the only knife I had left and made to plunge it into this millstone at the top. The Duke looked horrified. 'Oh no', he said, 'not like that. Get Wadman to help you.' And so, tactfully and with skill (I shall never know how) the butler made a hole in the monster and then withdrew.

Whereupon the Duke became conspiratorial and asked if I had ever thought of becoming a magistrate. Heavens above! 'I'm not the type', I said. 'Unless cruelty or violence came into it I couldn't send anyone to gaol.' He brushed this aside. 'You must allow me to be the best judge of that. You see I'm retiring from the Bench and although I'm not supposed to nominate my successor, in point of fact I shall.' Yet another long pause. This could have been embarrassing. I could tell his mind was made up and he wouldn't take no for an answer. 'Anyway', he said at last, 'talk it over with your wife and let me know, what?'

In a day or two I sent a note, declining as gently as I could. 'I was thankful to escape', I told my diary. 'He tries to be kind, but anything less like the Christmas spirit . . . I must own though, as Marlborough did of Queen Anne, that I have a tenderness for him, with all his absurdity.'

As for the vault, I found it disappointing: no iron coronets, only bare inscriptions on brass. The first Duke and Duchess, in coffins covered in red baize, lay side by side, and near them another coffin which was Willigo's. In *The Glitter and the Gold* Consuelo remembered how in her time the vault had had to be sterilised and whitewashed, so that now it might be part of some badly-run modern hospital. No doubt a number of coffins had been burned. There was certainly plenty of room to spare.

When I next called I found the Duke about to head a procession consisting of his secretary, his butler and the chief guide, Jock Illingworth. 'Care to join us?' he said. 'We're just going down to the China Room, what?' Much of the Spalding porcelain was still on show, but in the undercroft the China Room had odds and ends which might or might not have been worth a duke's ransom. From among these the Duke now chose a large Kakiemon vase, which he handed to Illingworth, while he himself carried the lid. Our procession then re-formed and made its dignified way to the Third Stateroom, where the Duke took the vase, set it upon the mantelshelf and added the lid. 'Is it very special?' I asked. 'Oh no, nothing much, but I think the public should see these things, don't you?'

The two of us then made for his study, where I told him I had agreed to write a full biography of Sarah. To be definitive, it must mean research in depth, and that in turn must mean my all but living in the palace. But of course, as always, I was welcome to read and write wherever I liked. So I helped myself from the Long Library to a beautifully bound copy of Sarah's *Conduct* and re-read it on the roof. As I came down I met the butler, Ted Wadman. 'I hope you're going to write a more *popular* book this time', he said, 'but there, the most interesting books can never be written, can they?'

'All the same they do die.' Now it was Gerald Horne's turn, with rejoicings no doubt, as he himself had predicted, among Persons of Quality in another world: 'Now we'll be all right', he had said, 'now we'll be properly looked after.' Tompkins the head gardener was next to go and was buried at Bladon, close to the tenth Duchess.

> Sceptre and crown
> Must tumble down
> And in the dust be equal made
> With the poor crookéd scythe and spade.

And then in December 1964 another Duchess, Consuelo Vanderbilt, the Duke's mother who had since become Madame Balsan, died in America. Lord Blandford and his father flew out to bring the coffin home and so she too was buried at Bladon, on a misty day, among the Churchills in that corner beside the church tower.

The more I read of Sarah, the more dismayed I became by what Winston had called the massive range of material. She had been, she owned, a kind of author; and she had gone on writing – letters, endorsements, maxims, Brown Book, Green Book, wills – until she had welcomed death at eighty-four. In her Green Book alone I found a hundred and one foolscap pages of grievances against two of her daughters; and it took me two hours to copy in shorthand one of her 'narratives'.

There could be no doubt about it, I had landed a full-time job; and luckily now I was able to make it so, having most thankfully left *Punch* and *The Countryman* (which latter I had sold to Punch without profit) and literally hurled my bowler into the Thames. A lunch-hour in Blenheim Park, after hours in that stuffy Muniment Room, was worth more than a hundred lunches, in very mixed company, at the Savoy.

All that summer I slaved at collecting Sarah material, not only at Blenheim but at Althorp, the Spencer stronghold in Northamptonshire; and if Blenheim was, as Sarah had maintained, wild and unmerciful, then Althorp seemed at first to run it a close second. At the main entrance lodge there was then a large notice which read:

WHEN THE HOUSE IS OPEN, THE PARK
IS NOT, SO PLEASE DO NOT STOP IN IT.

And when at last my taxi reached the imposing house, which Holland had encased in pale brick, I was met by a stout figure with hands raised to heaven and with quivering jowls.

'WRONG DAY!' shouted the late Lord Spencer, 'WRONG DAY! You gave me no time to tell you it would be inconvenient. This is my day for London . . .' and he continued to simmer audibly as most reluctantly he let me in.

In the event however it proved to be the right day for *me*; for with the knowledgeable owner out of the way I was able to make what Vanbrugh would have called 'an inconceivable progress with the building', gently tearing the guts out of a mountain of material and digesting it, in shorthand, in three and a half days. I never worked faster in my life, fearing that I might be pitched out at any moment; especially when I complained about a servant's loud transistor directly overhead.

But there again, when most needed my luck changed and a slow thaw set in. The late Lady Spencer, whom everyone loved, drove me back to my

[193]

cheerless pub; and on my last day, the best day of all, the Earl himself relented (and after all, we had known each other for years), showed me the house for the third time, let me into the strongroom to see again the Marlborough silver, and finally lent me a microfilm of another nobleman's manuscripts, at that time inaccessible to the public.

On that last day too I made time for Brington and the Spencer tombs (like Blenheim's, sterilised); and in the park for the *cottage orné* with its dairy of slate shelves bearing vast churns and urns and cream-pans, all as Wedgwood had made and left them; while in the next room, where stuffing burst out of chairs, the inglenook was lined with Dutch tiles and above it perched Chelsea doves and parrots. Through the cobwebbed windows I could see swamp-cypress and an island in a small oval lake. And what had all that to do with Sarah? Very little; but I wouldn't have missed it for worlds; and I came home feeling that if my book was not then in the bag it never would be. In fifteen notebooks I took it to Cornwall and wrote most of it in Lamorna, where we had been left a house. Ideas would occur to me as I swam in rock-pools; and of one thing I felt certain: no one would ever be mad or thorough enough to attempt such a biography again.

Thankfully back at Blenheim I found the Duke, in his oldest suit and pullover, under the weather with a cold caught in Scotland. His secretary told him the royal family of Thailand were expected at half-past eleven. 'Let the guides get on with it', he said. And then turning to me, 'You don't think I should greet them, do you?' I thought he should, and so we awaited them in the Hall. They were three-quarters-of-an-hour late. The Duke stomped off, leaving his heir to receive them. When at last they arrived the King, stepping into the Great Hall, looked tiny. His Queen, in violet silk, was beautiful, with high-piled shining black hair and butterfly ear-studs. They was a row of young princesses, a pudding-faced prince and a rabble of oriental thugs loaded with a battery of cameras and, I thought, probably guns.

After smily welcomes and bows Sunny Blandford passed them all on to one of the guides and to me. The King was gentle and quiet, the Queen eagerly interested. She kept asking questions and, for the family, translating the answers in a pretty sounding language and with ballet gestures of slim hands with long silver fingernails. The King was impressed with the Saloon and seemed really interested when I explained about Winston's having been born and buried on the north-to-south axis of the palace. With thanks and waved farewells they left in a beflagged Rolls, a Mercedes and a fleet of security cars and all drove off into the sun. 'I do *hope* they won't be assassinated', I murmured; such a dear little family and so romantically exotic.

Biking back through the park I thought how, as in time one gets to know a village and the names of all its cats and dogs, so now I had come to know Blenheim pretty well. I knew the gardeners and the keepers; and in the house I knew the agent, my friend Bill Murdock, the secretaries, the administrator Paul Duffie, the butler Ted Wadman and, in his modest way perhaps the most important of all, Freddie Brammall, the Duke's valet and chauffeur. As for dogs (no cats at Blenheim, and the dachshunds now pensioned off), Gladys's spaniels were, like herself, never to be mentioned; and now the Duke had acquired a young boxer called Ben and in his offhand way seemed to like him. 'What does he answer to?' I asked. 'He may answer to anything you like to call him', was the answer; 'his name's Ben but for me he answers to nothing.'

However, by Christmas Ben had unquestionably made the grade for there, on the Duke's card, he had hogged the foreground, while his master sat dolefully on a bench at the back of the Temple of Health. 'Did you like it?' he asked me. 'Very much, but do tell me, why did you choose to be photographed like that?' 'Why, don't you see', he said with limited patience, 'when that photograph was taken, I was seventy and Ben was one.' As with Winston and his poodle Rufus, when the Duke drove his Landrover with Ben proudly beside him, the contrast in profiles was wonderful: one elegant nose turned down, the other, pugnacious, up.

For the Duke's seventieth birthday they had hoisted the state flag with the two-headed eagle; but to me it seemed harder than ever to make him rejoice. The chef had made a sumptuous cake, but it didn't do. 'The dog's face', the Duke told me later, 'was a mass of cream.' I thought he might be amused by one of Sarah's remedies for 'ye sinking of ye spirits': milk from a red cow; but no, nothing cheered him. He would spend a couple of days in a

The tenth Duke of Marlborough photographed on his 70th birthday, in the Temple of Health at Blenheim with his dog Ben.

[196]

London nursing home, he told me, and on Saturday go duck-shooting – which he did, in a downpour. He had always been a first-class shot and now in the season shooting was one of the few things he really enjoyed.

Never much of a reader, the Duke dipped into best-sellers or the memoirs of friends. 'Badly written', he said of a book by Princess Alice, 'but about people I used to know.' I said he should be writing the answer (his father's answer perhaps) to his mother's book *The Glitter and the Gold*. He said maybe one day he would. He must think about it. 'By the way that book – *The Gold and the Glitter* – you borrowed it, didn't you? Did you return it? Well, it can't be found.'

I never of course bored him with my troubles with *Sarah*. Luckily it had rave reviews and sold even better in the States than it did here. After that one could afford to ignore being without honour in one's own village. Our licensee, an old woman we were fond of, told me in the mobile library, 'I read your latest book. Wasn't much thrilled though. You see I knew it all before.' I said 'Then you're the very person to help me with my next one, on Queen Anne.'

'I say', said the Duke at our next meeting, 'have you seen my mother's book *The Gold and the Glitter*? I do think people who move books one is reading are the *end*.' That day he was out of sorts and out of temper; and I who had grown used to his hypochondria failed to realise at first how seriously ill he was. A day or two later he told me he had Krohne's disease, with inflammation of the bowel, and might have to undergo two operations.

In a London hospital he was on the operating-table for eight hours. The whole job was done and tidily finished (no colostomy) at one go. 'It was the most horrible place I ever was in', he told me, 'the food was uneatable. If Sunny hadn't brought me smoked salmon every day I would have starved.' He looked older and frailer but still had guts enough to limp the length of the house to show me the redecoration of the Long Library. 'You don't think it looks too much like chocolate cake?' 'No', I assured him, 'it'll tone down. I think we were all a little tired of that wedding-cake effect.'

As we walked slowly back through the Great Hall I told him I was thinking of attempting a definitive life of Queen Anne and hoped to do her justice. 'Not too much justice, I hope,' he said, 'she was an awful bitch, you know.' I said in any case I would like to dedicate the book to him. There was a pause and then: 'I shall be dead long before it's published'. But he was wrong.

> Relying on the usual span
> He thought he'd write a life of Anne.
> Poor devil, if he only knew,
> He'd bitten more than he could chew.

As with Sarah so with Anne, there were times when I seriously thought she would be the death of me. Confound her politics! I cared even less for them than she had . . . And then I began to be interested, not in them but in herself as a fraught and bewildered woman at the mercy of others, including Sarah.

I sought her company in the Long Library – in marble by Rysbrack, in paint by Kneller – but these were frigid indeed compared with her passionate notes to Sarah, then in the Muniment Room. Yes, the manuscripts were fascinating, the printed works less so, for Anne had proved since her death a lodestar for women writers of the type who prefix most of their characters with the adjective 'poor'; and pepper them with screamers: 'Poor Anne!' 'Poor Sarah!' 'Poor Abigail!' After a deluge of such stuff one felt like drowning in a pool of crocodile tears.

Ideas often occurred to me halfway through some tedious sermon; but when it came to writing the book I found it could take two hours to set down one paragraph. I felt like those monkeys typing the whole of Shakespeare. Provided I wrote and rewrote and kept on rewriting, the book might at last, barring misprints and ham-fisted sub-editors, be readable. It might even make sense, if not history.

After many a month at the typewriter I was at long last on the home stretch when the Duke asked me again to help him with his memoirs. I went over to tea. 'Do you like these things?' he asked, helping himself to the last of the prawns. But he looked a lot better and was pleasingly absurd. When he owned he might have thrown one of Winston's letters away, I said 'Shocking!' 'You think I should have kept it?' 'Yes.' 'H'm, by the way, I think you borrowed my copy of *The Gold and the Glitter*. It's nowhere to be found [it had slipped down behind a shelf of novels] . . . Another thing, I've just come from the Bench where we granted Sunny his permit for *son et lumiére*, though I'm not very keen on it.' I said if, as I'd heard, the audience was to be seated on the south lawn, where neither lake, bridge nor island would be visible, let alone the entrance front, it must inevitably be tame if not boring. He agreed but said there were insurmountable difficulties on the north, including cattle (which of course were as sacrosanct as pheasants).

Sure enough, I found the rehearsal on the south front stodgy and seemingly endless, with *longueurs* and monotonous effects, but I liked the fountains on the terraces (one could just glimpse the tops of them), and Nelson's visit, and the end. The ninth Duke too, with Duchêne, came over well (all that stuff I'd unearthed from inches of grime some twenty years before). The Duke limped to the grandstand and when I asked what he thought said, 'Too long and Sarah took too long dying'.

But the first night was far more successful. It still sagged in the middle and needed cutting: ludicrously enough, Winston's birth was given in both versions; and the Gerald Horne part was crude and painfully unfunny. But the show as a whole was adequate – not magical and breathtaking as Blenheim could and should be – but not altogether bad. At the top of the stand I was surprised to find myself neighboured by Sir Charles Ponsonby of Ditchley, whose limp was decidedly worse than the Duke's. 'I don't know how you climbed up here', I said, 'but for God's sake watch that narrow flight of steps where everyone will be pouring out.' 'Don't worry', he said, 'I have my own ambulance. They tell me it ran over a cable and delayed the start of this thing by twenty minutes.'

The one essential for *son et lumière* is of course fine weather, and that we were to have for the first summer only. Indeed, in the cold grey summer that followed there was much to be said for sitting in the smoking-room, as the Duke did in his green leather armchair, under the Stubbs tiger, while the fire, fed with gigantic logs from the park, glowed and rumbled in the depths of its Vanbrughian cave.

For the first few sessions on the memoirs I sat in another armchair, some yards from the Duke's; but finding that hopeless, I moved to the long, embroidered stool before the fire, where at least I stood a chance of hearing what he said.

His own idea for the book's title – *All Things Bright and Beautiful* – I disliked at first, almost as much as (with unprintable comment) he himself disliked the hymn; but my literary agent thought well of it. 'Ha!' exclaimed the Duke triumphantly, 'so you're coming round to it, are you, what?' He handed me some foolscap upon which he had jotted anecdotes, some of the hunting field, some of the army, some of his yawningly boring African safari. 'You can't return from safari and say you haven't shot a lion, you know,' I said. 'But why not begin with parents and childhood? We have the Sargent to kick off with; and it would be fascinating to hear the other side of *The Glitter and the Gold*.' 'That can come later', he said shortly. 'This is not going to be my father's book, it's my book; and this other stuff, the safari and so on, is still fresh in my mind.' I said, 'Have you never kept a diary?' 'Never', he said firmly, 'too dangerous.'

As I set off for Blenheim the following Monday, Joyce called after me, 'Ask him if he took Nanny on safari. I bet you he says, "Yes, look, there's her head up there." ' But then for a while I felt encouraged because some of his recollections of Eton were better than likely.

Self: 'Now, when you were a tea-fag, does that mean that you made the tea?'

Duke: 'Oh no. The maid made the tea. I carried it in.'

Self: 'Splendid, just the stuff!'

Duke: 'I call it trivial detail.'

But there was still better to come. His exploits as a lovesick guards-officer, returning regularly from London leave by the milk-train and pulling the communication-cord as it drew level with his camp, made me laugh.

'You know, I can't understand David Green', he told Lord Blandford. 'He writes serious books about Queen Anne and now he wants me to say *more* in *my* book about pulling the communication-cord.' I said, 'I was thirty years in Fleet Street and I think I do roughly know what the public wants. Every man in this country old enough to remember such things has always longed to pull a communication-cord, and here you are, a duke who has pulled one at least half-a-dozen times!'

Queen Anne was still being troublesome. For the dust-jacket it had been decided that we must have Kneller's full-length portrait of her in blue, with orange-flowers, which then hung, facing the bed, in the Duchess's bedroom; and it took four men to take it down. It needed cleaning. A whole morning was spent on it with a costly camera (I all but died with boredom) – and then the publisher turned it down. When I asked the Duke if it might be lifted down again to be rephotographed he said, 'Oh I say, that would be a frightful bore'; but he allowed it.

As for the index, I could never have got it done to time without my wife who, with a fever, slaved at it all day. We sat in the attic, with the window closed, surrounded by thousands of sticky slips of paper, and kept at it until midnight. It was a desperate business and when at last it was finished we both fervently said, 'Never again!'

After many a hitch, then, *Queen Anne* was published; and when I took the Duke his copy I tucked in a note reminding him that when, three years before, I had told him of my intention to dedicate it to him he had said he would be dead long before it was out. 'I'm delighted to notice', I added, 'that you are very much alive. In fact I never saw you looking better. Long may you remain so. Now we have both to keep alive and well to complete *your* book . . .'

I wondered, next time we met, what he had made of *Queen Anne*, but he could talk only of Peter Townsend's autobiography – 'You know, the fellow that wanted to marry Princess Margaret . . . But this book of his is really first-class and very exciting. In fact I couldn't put it down. And the amount of RESEARCH he must have done! He tells you, don't you see, about a day in the battle of Blenheim: first, how our chaps got on. Then over to Germany and all about their tactics in the battle of Blenheim, I mean the Battle of Britain . . .' He feared he wouldn't have more time for his own memoirs this side of Christmas – 'Shooting, you know, what?'

After that he lost interest and seemed too to be anxious lest his book might be libellous (he who in conversation was entertainingly indiscreet) or even that he might infringe the copyright of his mother's book! To strike any spark out of him seemed impossible, though I tried everything I could think of:

Self: 'When you had that place in Leicestershire, you decided to sell farm produce in a shop in Berkeley Square. What happened? Didn't people, not knowing you were a duke, try to push you around?'

Duke: 'I wasn't a duke then.'

Self: 'Well, a marquis. Surely something funny must have happened?'

Duke: 'I can remember nothing funny at all.'

'I don't mind ghosting his memoirs', I told Joyce, 'though I'd do it for no one else; but I can't be expected to write the reminiscences of a clam.'

Then I remembered his photograph-albums. Couldn't they be useful as can-openers? There were some dozen of them and, like everything else at Blenheim, on the Vanbrugh scale. He seemed to like the idea; so I went through them all, leaving a bookmark wherever a photograph looked promising. There were stacks of them, but they too were to prove a disappointment.

In the smoking-room, as he lounged beneath the Stubbs, I turned page after gilt-edged page. He puffed at his pipe. Ben the boxer did deep breathing. The fire rumbled in its cave. I felt like quoting Winston: 'History cannot proceed by silences.' At one point I heard him mutter, 'Most of these people are dead.' One photograph I had been counting on was of a picnic in the Highlands, for it showed a royal flush: Queen Mary, King George VI, the Princesses . . . all the royals were there. 'And so what happened at that picnic?' I asked. Duke: 'I remember nothing happening at that picnic, absolutely nothing at all.'

I felt in need of air. Might we look at his own paintings in the summerhouse beside the croquet-lawn? And so we did. I particularly liked one he had painted in oils at Montecatini. 'Yes, Winston told me it didn't matter if you made mistakes with oils, you could always paint over them. Watercolour was a different matter.'

The following Monday I found we had reached the Abdication, or rather, that famous weekend just before it when Edward VIII and the Simpsons were staying incognito at Blenheim. But then I discovered that the Duke had already written his account of it (he disliked dictating and hated to be read to) and had left out all mention of his famous guests. 'You'll notice I've said we had some American house-guests', he said. 'I don't think I should particularise. The reader will read between the lines and come to his own conclusions.' I was flabbergasted, but we plodded on, himself now as bored as I was and reduced to a succession of tiny yawns.

In London, when the Duke saw my literary agent about an agreement for the memoirs he was puzzled by the meaning of a publisher's advance. 'Is that taxable?' he asked. 'Yes', explained Richard Simon, 'you see, it's earned income.' 'Oh', said the Duke thoughtfully, 'I never had any of that.'

That May, at the Churchill Memorial Concert in the Long Library, a choir sang the anthem composed by Bononcini for the first Duke's funeral. I thought it magnificent. 'H'm', said the Duke, 'perhaps they'll sing it at my funeral too, when all will applaud.' I said some might feel differently. No comment. Everything just then, even Blenheim itself, seemed to be grinding to a halt. But it was then that he sprang a surprise.

'Look', he said, 'how would it be if you and your wife came out next winter to Jamaica? You know I have a house at Montego Bay. I've an idea we could polish off my memoirs there, what?' I was delighted. Joyce not so. 'It will kill you,' she said. 'You know how you are, always thinking it'll be all right and it never is.' She herself had no wish to go.

I took another look at the Duke's album labelled JAMAICA and noticed everyone wearing coloured shorts; the Duke's were pink. And then what about evenings? 'Oh, some people don't bother to dress and we don't when we're at home. Otherwise, just an ordinary dinner-jacket.' What could be simpler? Yet my dinner-jacket, I decided, was not just ordinary, it was out of date. I had it altered and bought black shoes. All of which, when the time came, were flown thousands of miles to Jamaica and back without once being worn.

Early in 1971 I made a note in my diary:

Duke in friendly mood, twice asked me not to hurry away. Tinkered with Japanese tape-recorder but neither of us could make it work. Moved into his study where we were joined by Laura Canfield, trim in red jersey, light-coloured trousers and head-scarf. She has heavy straight black hair and a husky voice. I liked her. 'So you're coming out to Jamaica?' she said.

[203]

IX

Interlude in the Sun

The flight to Jamaica was an endurance test for which I scored zero. Having flown over most of Europe I thought I could take the Atlantic and the Caribbean in my stride. I was wrong. Only the long-distance flyer knows the nadir of claustrophobia and boredom, the nullifying nothingness of being encapsulated in space hour after hour after hour. I felt ill and uncomfortable and thought at times I must be in endless orbit in outer space. Worst of all – and who could have guessed at such additional horror? – a party of glee-singers joined us at Kennedy and sang and went on singing in close (too close) harmony the songs their grandads had taught them. I prayed fervently that they would vaporise – just quietly disintegrate where they sat or, failing that, that they would vanish at our next touchdown, never to be seen or heard again. The second part of my prayer was granted and the silence surged softly backward when their plunging hooves were gone.

At Montego Bay we arrived in darkness at a tiny airport in, as it seemed, total confusion. There were black men in white uniforms, offering free planter's-punches, while others cross-questioned me as to where I was staying. And then suddenly a friendly face with a broad smile: Freddie Brammall and heavens was I glad to see him! 'Stay as long as you can', he said earnestly in his quiet voice.

Bert and Laura, as I had now to call them, had gone ahead of me and now, as we sped along a road that was no better than a chain of pot-holes, Freddie told me, 'We're staying at Lady Sarah's* and moving to the Duke's place later.' It was the first I had heard of it; and I was still more taken aback to find no one at home on my arrival. I was greeted by two mastiffs and a native butler who showed me to my bedroom downstairs. 'Down, down I go to the base court . . .' With sinking heart I looked about me – and began to feel better; for somebody, even though absent, had taken the trouble to see that everything I looked at was beautiful. Even the flowers matched the lacquered chest they stood on. Except for host or hostess, there was absolutely nothing missing at all.

Sarah's house was called *Content* and it lived up to its name. Next morning when, as Americans put it, I drew my drapes, there was the Promised Land. My room was at garden level: in the foreground plumbago beside old stone steps leading down to a small croquet-lawn enclosed by a low terrace-wall bearing two miniature cannon; and beyond that – far far beyond and miles below us – Montego Bay. A long-tailed bird was balancing on a croquet-hoop, while a jewel-like quit, yellow with a white eyestripe, explored a hibiscus.

House and garden were part of one another. Flowers grew, or so it seemed, as the owner bade them: the cream hybrid bougainvillea was encouraged, the brash amethyst suffered only to nod in at the window. It was the same with hibiscus: vast yellow trumpets were visited by two kinds of humming-bird. Both indoors and out Sarah had, as I was to find later in Greece, a quite remarkable eye for colour.

Meeting her for our first garden-breakfast I found her tall, blonde, heavy-haired, the typical Marlborough features more than becoming. She and Laura Canfield were both in house-coats, and everyone including Bert was most welcoming and relaxed. The mail had arrived and brought a lunatic-fringe letter addressed to the Duke. He handed it round and we all had crooks in our necks as we tried to read it. The mad-looking scrawl went

* Lady Sarah Roubanis, the Duke's eldest daughter

[205]

literally round and round the page and got nowhere. 'She usually begins "Dear David" ', said Bert, 'and signs herself "The Queen". She never stops pestering me. In England I've complained to the police, who of course can do nothing.'

At lunch we were joined by a second Sarah, Lady Brooke, dark and pretty in a yellow head-scarf and a frock patterned with huge links of chain. Completely self-possessed, she managed to appear alert and relaxed, brilliant and witty, charming and sophisticated all in a moment. Did I know, she asked solemnly, that wolves were snobs and looked down on other wolves. 'How do you mean?' I said. 'Do some wolves say "toilet" and "serviette"?' 'Worse than that', she said sadly, 'they keep saying "Pardon?" ' Much of their lunch-table nonsense, accompanied by gasps of incredulity, flew over my head; but who was I to mind with beauty on either side of me and, on my plate, ice-cream sprinkled with fresh coconut? Sarah Roubanis made me promise not to sunbathe before 3.30 in the afternoon. 'I live in Greece all summer', she said, 'so I know what I'm talking about. I promise you the tropics are different.'

'Lady Sarah's husband's filming,' Freddie Brammall told me, 'he's fantastically good looking'; and so indeed Theo was, flawless and in a very un-English way dynamic. Any young man, I suppose, might swim and dive well and be a good shot, but there was a great deal more to Theo than that. He was a master-mariner, navigating the yacht; and he was too a musician with a pleasing voice, who could improvise cunningly on piano or guitar. He could act, he could dance Greek dances, he could paint, he wrote poems. What couldn't he do? As he stood there with his wife, both bronzed, tall and glamorous, I thought of Marlborough and Sarah of whom Bishop Hare had said they were 'handsome to a proverb'. I had never seen a more striking couple.

For the swimming-pool, hidden from the house, one took the gentle slope of the garden amid hibiscus and humming-birds to a chalet-bar-changing-room at the cliff's edge. The pool, blue and kidney-shaped, had long chairs for sunbathing. Laura Canfield, stretched out on one of them in a bikini, of course had a perfect tan, setting off her dark hair. After a swim we had a long talk about Bert's memoirs. For the past week out there he had

[206]

been busy writing, but she feared most of it was prosaic and dull and would need a *cordon bleu* to make it digestible. She had begged him to let his hair down but he wouldn't. He seemed, she said, interested in nothing, 'not in Jamaica, not in the world.'

Sarah too thought I'd find it tough going, trying to make his memoirs entertaining. 'You must be firm with Daddy', she said. But that same evening he was very firm with me. On an ill-starred impulse he had decided that I must partner him in a game of croquet, our opponents being his daughter Sarah and Theo. On rectory lawns I had played the game for fun; but that of course was the last reason in the world a serious player in the professional class would choose for playing.

It was something between a nightmare and the croquet-game in *Alice*. The light was failing, the rough lawn gently sloping and made of Bermuda grass; myself like Alice nervous and uneasy and rightly expecting the worst. Alice, you remember, 'thought she had never seen such a curious croquet-ground in all her life; it was all ridges and furrows'. Just so. I made a hopeless mess of my first shot. 'You must look at the ball', said Bert. I watched the ball and tapped it and did no better. 'You're looking at the hoop', he said crossly, 'you must look at the ball.' I stared it out of countenance and swept it off the lawn. Bert exploded. In all his experience at Blenheim, on Long Island, indeed all over the civilised world he had never known anything so incompetent. Muttering the word 'lavatory' he left. Laura then stepped in to partner Theo, while Sarah and I, thanks to Sarah, just managed to beat them in a hilarious game.

Next day beside the pool Bert handed me not an olive-branch but a leaf from a silver-barked tree he told me was pimento. It tasted delicious. But for Laura he had brought a cable, recalling her to New York. This was a blow not only to him but to me. We could both have done with her lively company at Woodstock House, his place at some distance from Sarah's. That evening, in the cool of my garden-room at *Content*, I wrote in my notebook:

Now Laura and Sarah Roubanis have flown to New York. I was called from the pool to kiss them goodbye. Laura so sweet and sincere, and both

[207]

[208]

so beautiful. This place, perfect though it looks, is certainly glum with no women at all; Bert reading and yawning his head off. At this moment something is making strange burrowing noises in the wainscot. Could it be a mongoose? 'We make an early start for my house tomorrow', Bert is saying. 'I see, and what do you call early?' 'Oh, about ten.'

There was little in common between Woodstock House and Blenheim: a park – of six acres, with cypresses like incense-cedars – and a steep flight of steps up to the house. In the entrance hall I noticed a large engraving of Blenheim's north front; and in the big sitting-room, over the chimney-piece (the fire of course never lit) an oil painting of Vanbrugh's bridge (about 1750), last admired at Blenheim.

And what could be less like the home life of our dear Duke? True, Freddie was ever at hand to respond to his lightest word (almost a whisper); but Malcolm the coloured butler looked nervous, kept calling him 'Issgriss' and bringing him unducal things like book-matches or just not appearing at all. One morning he came to me in agitation and said, 'Misser Green, pliss come. Issgriss is having trouble with telephone.' I heard shouting and found Bert frustrated beyond endurance in his efforts to telephone New York: 'I said NEW YORK! Have you never heard of it? What do you mean, State or City? I WANT NEW YORK. Who AM I? I'm the DUKE OF MARLBOROUGH!' That did it. Almost instantly his number came through.

In the small hours, in the room that was to have been Laura's, I was woken by a barking dog. I switched on the light but could see nothing more sinister than a long and large millipede which was crawling across the headboard of my bed.

In the morning all was radiant and I plunged into our pool at the cliff's edge, with again the distant world of Montego Bay at my feet. 'I bathe only in the tropics', Bert had told me; and what a solitary bathe that was! As I dressed in my louvered room I felt like Peeping Tom as I saw him, with immense caution and dignity, heave himself in.

Woodstock House, Montego Bay: the Duke at his front door, 1971

Woodstock House, Montego Bay: Lady Churchill in the swimming-pool with the tenth Duke of Marlborough, 1965

Breakfast and dinner, when we were on our own, were eaten in dressing-gowns, the breakfast routine on the verandah being always the same. I would arrive first, watching the Doctor Bird (a humming-bird with a long tail of twin feathers) probe the hibiscus, when Bert would appear humming tunelessly and, after 'Good morning', resume his hum while unerringly choosing the larger grapefruit. Breakfast in fact was usually the best meal of the day, himself having the utmost suspicion of all native dishes; and nothing of course in the way of conversation was expected.

He had, I soon found, one obsessive interest and that was the weather, no matter where he happened to be. In England this, though tedious enough, was at least a national pastime. In Jamaica, in March, nothing changes. The sun persistently shines and the wind chases you into the house day after day after day. Except in the autumn hurricanes hardly ever happen. Yet Bert watched every forecast, explained as they were with weather-charts by an earnest native on Jamaican Television, which was, believe it or not, even worse than our own. For Bert no amateur opinion would do. 'A few clouds this morning?' I once desperately ventured. 'Doesn't mean a thing', he growled, and of course he was right. It could only have been total boredom which prompted him to put calls through to Scotland merely to ask what sort of weather they were having there. 'Mist, did you say? Good God, how I envy you. Here? Can't you guess? Just the same bloody sunshine – far too hot – week after week.'

Next to weather, in interest, came television itself. He would sit through it all: plays with all-black casts, talks on how to unkink your hair, commercials about butter – 'New Zealand's best, Jamaica's favourite!' – or even advertisements for what were euphemistically called bathroom-bowls. At dinner I might become aware that my head was obstructing his view of that fascinating screen. Still, attempts at conversation could be even worse:

Duke: 'I notice you eat a great deal of salt. It's very bad for you, you know . . . At home you have a maid?

Self: 'No.'

Duke: 'Oh, just a woman coming in . . . And then how do you get to London?'

Self: 'By train.'

Duke: 'Now let me see, I think the last time I went by train to London was in 1962.'

Once again I had to reassure him about not infringing the copyright of *The Glitter and the Gold*. 'Besides,' I added, 'if the worst came to the worst, I feel certain that an English duke could still get away with murder.'

Duke: 'H'm, I think the day's past when there was one law for the rich and another for the poor, what?'

Self: 'Nonsense. If you murdered me tonight, they'd say, "That poor lonely duke, of *course* he murdered him, he was boring him to death. Why, he couldn't even play bridge or croquet!" '

Duke (smiling faintly): 'I think they'd have to find a better reason than that.'

[211]

'But I do wish I could cheer him up', I told Theo. 'If only I could quickly change my sex.' Like the Duke of Omnium, Bert had 'run through the pleasures of life too quickly and had not much left with which to amuse himself'.

Luckily we had visitors, most of them women. Sarah Brooke teased and amused us. Julia brought lilies and stayed to dinner. She must surely have spent all day in an air-conditioned beauty-parlour. 'Why, Julia', said Bert with his ineffable gift for tact, 'you've gone all albino.' She was staying at a country club where she had her own chalet – 'and I'm told I have a swimming-pool though I haven't found it yet. Why not come over and help me locate it?' 'David will be glad to swim with you', said Bert, 'you can leave me out of it.'

Sometimes we dined out, though never in dinner-jackets, at *Content* or at *The Jetty*, Sarah Brooke's ravishing house designed by Kazimir, the Polish prince she was about to marry. On arrival one looked straight through the house to the Y-shaped tree at the end of the jetty; while in the garden another tall, dead tree was floodlit, beside the swimming-pool. We faced it as we dined on the verandah and, as it chanced, talk turned to garden design. When *Gardener to Queen Anne* was mentioned Sarah, to my amazement, gave a squeal of delight. 'But that's my favourite book of all books!' she exclaimed. 'Does Bert know it?' I said. 'You're my only fan. Say no more, we're twin souls.'

On the way back – always hazardous since at one point on our one-in-four hill half the road had slipped down the cliff – Bert sat in front with Brammall driving. And this is what I overheard:

Duke: 'Lady Brooke will be lunching with us tomorrow. We could have fricassé of chicken.'

Brammall: 'Cheese soup.'

Duke: 'No, egg à cocotte.'

Brammall: 'You wouldn't like a nice fish hors d'oeuvre?'

Duke: 'What? What?'

Brammall (negotiating precipice): 'A nice fish hors d'oeuvre.'

Duke: 'If you would be good enough to address me instead of the windscreen I might be able to hear what you say. What kind of fish?'

Brammall: 'Tunny fish, your Grace.'

Duke (furiously): 'You *know* I *loathe* tunny fish. What vegetable with the chicken?'

Brammall: 'Well, your Grace, there's that tin of asparagus left behind by Lord Porchester's party.'

Duke: 'Very well, we'll have that.'

Yet in spite of everything – the nonsense of trying to entertain without chef or hostess, and the tropical heat – we did between us write and rewrite several thousand words. On a good day he might agree to comparing his father's way of life at Blenheim with his own (though he never did); or again, I might be allowed to mention the unmentionable Gladys Deacon. 'You seem to know more about her than I do,' he said. 'Write what you like and I'll read it through.'

So we made some sort of progress, while green parrots and humming-birds flitted around us and huge, ominous-looking black birds perched on the roof. 'What are they?' I asked. 'They call them John Crows. They're honey-buzzards. Useful scavengers, what?' From James Bond's *Birds of the West Indies* I found that they were turkey-vultures, ugly brutes and disconcerting as they swooped over me in the pool. 'Not yet!' I yelled at them, 'Not yet!' and they seemed to get the message and swerved out to sea.

An amusing thing to do was to charter the small train which ran between Montego Bay and the rum factory. The local silver-band, in uniform said to have been designed by Queen Victoria, went with the train and with the deal. Once, when Lady Churchill was staying with Bert, they went on this trip, which she found great fun. On the return journey the bandsmen, lit up by white rum (the light foundation of planter's-punch), burst into boisterous song. This was jolly enough; but when they were well away with *The Big Bamboo* Lady Churchill, turning to her host, said, 'Bert, as you know, I've lately grown a little hard of hearing, but aren't some of the songs they're singing just a little obscene?'

It was not the done thing to swim in the sea, but of course Jamaicans did and I was happy to join them while Brammall waited for Bert's newspapers to be flown in from Miami. ('Whenever I open a newspaper here', Bert complained, 'it says "Top-Level Talks About the Future of Bananas". I'm

not *interested* in the future of bananas.') The sand was hot to the feet, the sea
lukewarm, but even so I felt refreshed. On one such morning, after a swim,
I lost Brammall and the car and had to ask a tough-looking, smartly
uniformed Jamaican the way. He flashed a huge smile and took my arm so
lovingly I thought he was about to kiss me. Brammall was soon found and,
back in my room, I asked him to mix one of his superb planter's-punches.
Sipping it I noticed an inch-long baby lizard run across Bert's manuscript;
and just then he himself looked in. 'We don't work in the afternoon', he
said, 'and tomorrow Theo's taking you on this picnic, isn't he? I hope you
realise what you're in for, what? It's a *young* people's picnic, you know.'

Theo drove up to Woodstock House in a huge old Buick with two
schoolgirls in the back: his step-daughter Jacqueline (Sarah's youngest)
and her pretty, dark-haired friend Maggie; himself, as always, casual
perfection from black curls to bare brown feet on brake or accelerator. 'We
go first to the airport,' he said as we drove through the park and out among
native shacks (the coloured children waved back), 'I have to collect my New
York ticket. Then we meet the others and all make for Martha Brae Falls.
The film unit follows with the picnic.'

'And who was Martha Brae?'

'No one knows. They are waterfalls in a river. Fantastic. You will like
them.'

Though the heat outside the airport was blistering I was, thanks to
Jamaican air, in euphoric mood and, like Byron, prepared to love anything
that seemed to wish it; and this went for the rest of the party: two trim young
mothers with six remarkably pretty children, who arrived on time in two
large cars, both glossier than our veteran Buick.

It was a day when nothing seemed to matter. Everyone was happy,
enjoying the breeze as we sped along the coast, its beauty ravaged by power-
cables, rusting pylons and mile after mile of cement wall. In England
indignant people would have protested with banners. Not so in Jamaica
where it's far too hot for marching or caring.

But I was glad when we left that road and took to the hills. For a time the
track seemed tolerable, but soon it became a rough bridleway or goat-track
strewn with boulders. There were steep turns too that called for trick-

driving and there was much parched country with very few flowers. Still, Maggie spotted in the bank one small bright orchid, which Theo picked for her. For miles we had seen no one when suddenly we came upon a group of natives working in a small field. They were much more startled and uneasy than we were, had a strange yellow look and gave us shifty glances. 'What are they harvesting?' 'Marijuana.'

After that the track became vaguer and wilder until at last it dipped into a forest, refreshing us with shade and with the sound and sight of a fast flowing river, at least fifty yards wide. We parked in a clearing, changed into swimming gear and left our clothes in a thicket of fifty-foot bamboos.

For a minute we all stood in the aquamarine shallows while Theo shouted instructions above the thunder of the rapids and the sun shone on the white foam below. It was not a deep drop, this first one, and the children made nothing of it. With envy, for I never could dive, I watched the smallest of them shoot neatly down after the others. Then I jumped and seemed to sink a very long way. I knew there were no crocodiles but gave a thought to snakes as I bobbed up in the rapids and was carried down to a lake.

'What happened to the picnic?' I shouted to one of the mothers, swimming strongly beside me.

'Don't know,' she shook her wet head, 'hope it turns up though. We've nothing with us but a tin of peanuts.'

Oh but this was fun – or was it? We had reached another fall, just that bit higher and more rugged than the first. Ah well, here goes . . . H'm, not too bad, but how many more? 'Society' (I felt with Firbank), 'oh it's a vocation – yes and a very strenuous one too.' Theo in white briefs was far ahead but, as I soon realised, he knew the height of each fall, the depth of each pool and the position of every rock. We were all of us, children included, strong swimmers, but Theo was in the professional class. He missed nothing of our muddles, his shouts reaching us clearly above the roar of the most thunderous cascade. And this last – a narrow chasm into which most of the river leaped and foamed – we had now to my horror reached. The smaller children, yelled Theo, were not to attempt it. They must take the gentler stream which skirted the main fall and bypassed it. After an appalled glance I decided to go with them and then, in a moment of shame and madness,

[215]

changed my mind. There was but one wet rock to leap from and even as I hesitated, Theo's muscular brown body vanished amid clouds of foam. What a pity the film unit had missed it! I jumped and hit foam and sank and thought I'd never surface; and when I did my head was under a rock shelf.

'David, are you all right?' I heard Theo shouting. 'No', I yelled back, but I very soon was. The current was fierce but the overhang was nothing and in a few moments we were all swimming in calm water towards a giant flamboyant-tree, rooted in the water between two pools. Among those roots stood Theo who, when we reached him, explained that we were to climb the tree and let ourselves drop into the far pool which, he said consolingly, would be the last pool of all. He then climbed into the fork and beckoned us to follow.

As a boy I had been proud of my tree-climbing, but now I was exhausted and careless and I slipped. I would have fallen into the shallows, perhaps with nothing worse than a broken ankle. As it was, in that split-instant I was caught and held, seemingly without effort, until I had my breath and could swing down from a bough and drop into deep water.

After that, having swum the last lake and found the riverside path, we could take in the beauty of it as we wandered back: green parrots, yellow butterflies, writhing lianas, humming-birds and the huge-leaved creepers they call vines . . . Cars and clothes were where we had left them. The one thing missing was the picnic. Where was the food and where (we had been promised it) the chilled wine? I was not much surprised that the film unit in charge of it all had lost its way, but with one tin of peanuts between the lot of us, one could hardly blame the smallest and youngest for bursting into tears.

There were miles of rough riding before Theo found in the midst of nowhere a strangely pretentious restaurant with deplorable service and uneatable food. The children made do with ice-creams, and we with planter's-punches.

'Let's talk food', said Jacqueline dreamily to Maggie in the back of the Buick, speeding along the coast road to our hills. 'You like banana-split?' 'In Nassau I do.' 'Tell you what I don't like, I don't like a three-minute egg, but Theo eats raw eggs and animals' eyes, don't you, Theo? Now why don't you sing? Please sing to us, Theo.'

'Listen, darlings', he said, 'I have to catch the five o'clock plane. It's now four and I'll never make it; and if you two sing, please try to keep in the same key.'

'Well then, why don't we ask Mr Green to sing to us?'

I sang *The Silver Swan* – 'More geese than swans now live, more fools than wise'. After a thoughtful pause (we were doing eighty with Theo's bare foot flat on the accelerator), there was gentle clapping.

'You've had a very long day,' said Bert, back at Woodstock House, 'I expected you hours ago. What happened?' I began to explain. 'H'm', he said gloomily, 'I did warn you it was to be a young people's picnic. Let me see, what are you, forty-five? In your fifties? Ah well, best years of a man's life, what?'

While I was in my bath he opened the bedroom door and I thought I sensed some excitement. 'Just heard on the news', he called, 'that they're scrapping surtax altogether . . . Oh but you're in the bath', and he withdrew.

Next morning I drove with Sarah's butler to the farmers' market for mangoes, paw-paws and so on to take home. While the butler was bargaining (they shook large black insects out of a bunch of bananas) I stood in a pocket of shade, soon to be shared by a black bible-banger and his pathetically small congregation. 'Ah'm not a rich man,' he told us, 'Ah'm a poor black man jist like all of you, dear friends'; and he went on to harangue us about Jesus and something he called the Woolly Ghost. I think the others were hoping I was in some way part of the show and might testify, but I didn't.

Bert, suffering from what he called dysentery, couldn't wait to be back at Blenheim (he never could); and Julia had promised to help see him off at Montego Bay airport. So there the three of us were in the small VIP lounge, jets roaring; and it didn't much help that that plunge into the chasm had deafened me in one ear. There was an hour to wait and I really thought Bert wanted to be alone. Julia said no, we had come to see him off and that was what we must do, and she was right. As we talked he relaxed and when his flight was called he seemed better. One last thought though: 'Where', he asked the air-hostess, 'is the closet?' Momentarily she looked mystified.

'The closet?' she said, raising elegant eyebrows, 'why, this is the closet' –
and she flung open the doors of the drinks-cupboard.

For a few days I stayed on, but Woodstock House seemed desolate
indeed. Even Freddie had left to look after his boss. Sarah Brooke drove me
to see the bird lady ('Try not to tread on the mourning-doves') and let me
swim in her pool with Kazimir.

The flight back was far less tedious than the other had been and, while
over the Atlantic, I scribbled doggerel:

On bottom dollar and in final ditch
I still feel richer than the very rich.
Crumbling a crust and sitting on the floor
I pity them as relatively poor.

My lot, which must to them seem drab and dismal,
Is not as low as theirs, which is abysmal.
Who would be rich and sick and full of cares
When some though penniless are millionaires?

'What did I tell you?' said Joyce, welcoming me at the gate of our
crumbling cottage, 'it costs a lot to be rich, but anyone can afford to be poor
– you can do it on a shoestring.'

Bert was back in hospital. Theo told me that when he and Sarah visited
him there, everyone talked at once until he said firmly, 'And now we'll talk
about ME. These are my symptoms . . .' But when I went I was saddened
and thought his hands, those fine alabaster hands now tremulous, especially
pathetic. He was pleased with the herbs Joyce had sent him and told
Brammall to put them in water. I told him about his garden – the snowball
viburnum, the yellow tree-peony – and he asked if the tulips were over. I
was anxious not to tire him and soon left.

On his return to Blenheim we arranged a film show in the Grand
Cabinet; and there he sat in his dressing-gown, with Sarah on his right and
Theo in the chair Winston had lolled in; while old Dr Tothill tinkered with
his antiquated projector . . . 'By the way', said Bert suddenly, 'what
happened to my medicines, all those pills and things on my bedside table,

what?' 'I told Wadman to throw them away', said Sarah calmly. 'Oh I say,' protested her father, 'but they might have cured half of Woodstock. And my Montecatini Water – it arrived only yesterday!' 'Too late, Daddy', said Sarah, 'they're down the john.'

The film was of the 1938 Blenheim pageant in which Bert had played the brief part of the great Marlborough arriving in his coach. For reasons of his own he had fond memories of it and wanted to make much of it in his book. Alas for nostalgia, something was very wrong with the film or the projector or both, so that on screen everything moved backwards, not just coach wheels, but everything and everybody; so that as with something between horror and hilarity we watched, men ran down flags instead of running them up, until at last, when we came to the longed-for climax, the coach with four horses backed briskly towards us and a heavily uniformed Marlborough, instead of emerging, climbed into it and was swiftly driven off screen with wheels in reverse as in a very old Western.

I broke the appalled silence by asking Sarah what she really thought of her namesake, the first Duchess. 'I think she was a marvellous woman,' she said firmly, 'after all, but for her we wouldn't be here.' She then for the fourth time pressed me to visit them in Greece and I promised to go. That was to be in October; but in the meantime I had two new guidebooks to write, one on the park and gardens at Blenheim and the other on the grounds of Hampton Court.

Every Monday we tried to resume Bert's memoirs but as before they went haltingly. Had I written about the pageant? Yes, but it made only half a page. Well then, his long term as Mayor of Woodstock, surely something could be made of that? I had to go gently. Couldn't we, I suggested, hear more of Winston? We had nothing about his funeral and nothing about his son. 'The funeral? I'm coming to that. And as for Randolph, no, I shall make no mention of him.' 'But surely you could say something in his favour? Everyone's busy whitewashing him just now.' 'Not while Clemmie's alive. There's a saying, you know: let sleeping dogs lie.' Yes, I seemed to have heard of it, but I still thought that that old dog's ashes, now mouldering at Bladon, might be glad of a ducal pat. 'I shall write more later', said Bert, 'but not while I'm feeling so awful. I have to go back to hospital for a slight operation.'

'Thursday', he told me afterwards, 'was the longest day I ever remember; and on Friday, before the Pentathol, they gave me something that was supposed to make me very happy. I felt gloomier than ever.' He was convalescing when I flew to Greece.

We arrived by night, Sarah driving the Mercedes; and the house, built round a courtyard filled with huge earthenware jars overflowing with flowers, welcomed us with open arms. From that moment I knew there was to be no happier part of my Blenheim adventure. Indeed, I felt better and happier even than in Jamaica. In my mind's eye now I see a rough road zigzagging down from the hilltop house Aitos Katakali (near Corinth) to the private cove where we swam or boarded the yacht. Now I'm in the sea and looking up see dwarf pines on the cliffs and, on a rock where I'd flung it, a pink towel embroidered with two capital C's, interlaced back to back.

And now my dream switches to the verandah where, over *langoustines*, Sarah is telling me – and she's a wonderful *raconteuse* – about her grandmother Consuelo. 'And so there she was in Cartier's and the man who always looked after her there asked if she had ever thought what an elegant monogram could be made with two interlaced C's. After which she had them put on everything.'

Theo was filming, but would dash home and relax at the piano. I hear and see him singing duets with his mother; and I hear too her lullaby, which he accompanied and which moved me to tears. Then he told me to choose three notes – any three – on the piano and so I chose them and on those he improvised. I said his catchy tune deserved a lyric, and that night in my bedroom I made one up:

When these notes have died away,
I shall think I hear you play
In that house beside the sea
Where you made this song for me.

Those who have a feeling heart
Know the pain it means to part.
Paradise can never last.
Death itself can't snatch the past.

[220]

Life is more than what it seems;
Truth can linger on in dreams;
Gone the player, gone the play;
Love shall live another day.

What could be more trivial? But his tune was a good one and still runs through my head.

And so through the Corinth Canal we sailed to the port of Delphi, that fishing village where Pisces Theo had been born; and while he looked up old friends there, we drove half-way up the mountain and poured a libation for him at the spring of the oracle. One thing I had looked forward to seeing, having read so many lyrical descriptions, was the statue of the charioteer, but I was disappointed. Compared with Theo, whether at the wheel of the yacht (driving again with bare feet) or flung down asleep on a bunk, the statue was a thing of metal, a dead effigy, no more.

We were all so happy, they begged me to stay, but I had a lecture date in England and had to fly back for it. At Christmas they called me:

Theo: 'Our song is a great success, everyone loves it. They may record it.'

Sarah: 'You must join us in Greece next year. I think Daddy will marry Laura. He says yes, she says no . . .'

Bert was certainly looking better and wanted to hear about Greece. I told him how, on what was supposed to be a partridge-shoot with Theo, I had played the part of Duke and said, 'Well, Theo, I suppose you know your ground, but I've seen nothing bigger than a jenny wren.' He managed a smile and later agreed it was true that he meant to marry. 'But the tapestry must come down in her bedroom. She says she can't sleep with tapestry, and I'm wondering where to put it . . . We shall be in residence here in February and I must do something about the memoirs. Can you manage that, what?'

'I do think he's marvellous', said Joyce when I told her, 'the apotheosis of Mother Hubbard's dog.'

Towards the end of January they married. 'Someone tied a boot to the back of the car', Bert told me, 'but I said what I needed was Boots the chemists.'

[221]

At Blenheim a fleet of pantechnicons, photographed in the forecourt, their white-overalled drivers proudly beside them, spoke of the new duchess, Laura, moving in. But too soon I was writing in my diary:

March 2nd, 1972. My last talk with Bert, by telephone to London hospital. Told him Blenheim was miserable without him and he said, 'I'm miserable without it, but I can't tell you when I'll be back. They keep making more tests.'

March 3rd. As I looked at the bare flagstaff at Blenheim this morning, grey clouds scudding behind it, I had a feeling of misgiving – *Qui sait quand reviendra?* Later I was told he's to have another operation and Sunny's flying back. One of the secretaries said to me, 'Dukey doesn't *know* how many of us here are thinking of him and wishing him well.' I dashed off a note to Laura and told her.

March 11th. The Duke is dead.

At Blenheim this was for me my strangest time of all. I had borrowed one of the Coral Rooms, a kind of ducal broom-cupboard behind the north-west quadrant, with a typewriter and two coronets on the table before me. The coronets were waiting to be cleaned and altered. The typewriter was for my first draft of *The Battle of Blenheim*.

Bert's coffin lay in the chapel where Laura had asked for the doors to be left open so that any of us who felt like keeping him company could go down for a while, which of course we did. Would I, suggested Sarah, go back with them to Greece, after the funeral, to help look after Laura, who was desolate and must have rest? I so longed to, but it was out of the question.

Woodstock church was of course full for the funeral on March 15th. There were the usual arrangements of arums, and swags of evergreens on the screen. Theo in morning dress strode in, shepherding a flock of children, some looking like peeled shrimps, others like frightened rabbits. It stopped raining. The sun came out and the bishop in white linen mitre advanced with Father James to welcome the coffin borne by the head keeper and others and with two wreaths on it, one of white daffodils, one of lilies of the valley. When the procession halted and the great coffin was lowered beside the new Duke and Laura, I thought 'This is a grisly business.'

Laura had said, when I asked about the private committal at Bladon, 'I want you to be there'; so I went on through the park and found the wreaths beside the path full of bees; past Consuelo's grave, past Winston's and so to the young cherry trees beneath which Mary Marlborough had been buried. Two trumpeters of the Guards Division sounded the Last Post and the Reveille. The family bowed to the coffin while the rest of us stood at a distance; and one of the daughters stooped to pick a pink hyacinth from her mother's grave and let it fall on her father's coffin. Sarah looked distressed.

Next day on the water-terraces I felt deprived and conscious, amid pheasants and collared doves, of the remoteness of the dead. Then I walked in Bert's garden: the empty seat and the empty Temple of Health in western sun. (A home had been found for Ben, who had once hogged the foreground.) Never again, never again. Yes I know he was the least sentimental of men but . . .

His memoirs remained unfinished: we had written about half the number of words the publisher had asked for. I returned to my own battle in the broom–cupboard. It rained and rained. From my window the north front looked more than ever like a stage set awaiting some noble spectacle now unlikely to happen. I could hear the wind howling in the Long Library. Everything seemed theatrical, even the wind.

I flew to Munich and took a train to Donauwörth, for the battlefields. Nothing could be more moving than the Schellenberg (the hill of the bell) – the memorial chapel, the Calvary, the *Via Dolorosa* – nor anything more flat, arid and daunting than the battlefield of Blindheim and Höchstädt, since the diversion of the Danube.

Back at Blenheim I tried to write about the prisoners and the wounded in that walled, hospital town called Nördlingen. But the palace teemed with ghosts. Some of them of course had always been there: Marlborough ('That was once a man'); Vanbrugh reminding Sarah, 'You cannot see all things from all places'; Hawksmoor: 'I cannot help thinking of Blenheim'; and Sarah herself:' 'Tis a chaos only God Almighty could finish.' But now there

[223]

were others – the ninth Duke telling Duchêne: 'It is only by thought, constant thought and mature reflection that artists have left their great works for the enjoyment of posterity'; the tenth Duke: 'Tinsel doesn't last, you know'; and his first Duchess: 'We must have the whisper.'

I thought I could hear Sir William Chambers too: 'The doors are shut and the farce is at an end'; and in our own village another ghost voice – Gerald Horne in his beekeeper's hat, asking Joyce: 'Tell me, my dear – nobody knows nothing in this village – are the lime trees in flower?' Yes indeed, 'Shadows we are and like shadows depart'; and yet it's good to remember that, as Gerald Horne said, Blenheim was our world – at least it seemed to belong to us, as we belonged to it.

X

The Winston Churchills at Blenheim

'It does seem extraordinary', I wrote to Randolph Churchill in December 1967, 'that none of us can now be certain about the circumstances of Sir Winston's birth. I mean why that gloomy little room had to be chosen, and whether there is anything at all in the legend that Lady Randolph was, just before the event, either at a ball in the Long Library or out with the guns in the park whence she was "hastened into the house" (I quote Sir Winston) and made comfortable in the first available room.'

To which Randolph replied: 'It is interesting to record that my father never said anything to me either about a ball or a shooting party or even about a dismal little room – only about the prematureness of his birth; but, when in later years he was asked why he was born in so small a room he was wont to reply that the room was quite in keeping with his standing as a member of the Cadet branch of a ducal family.'* Interesting too that for many years – until the birth of the tenth Duke of Marborough in 1897 – Winston was the heir to the Marlborough dukedom.

---

* When, for the filming of *Jennie*, a baby was needed to play the part of the infant Winston, to be christened in the Blenheim's chapel, the only one available was the new-born daughter of the chef. 'You do appreciate', warned the Rector of Woodstock, 'that if I baptise her "Winston Leonard", she must bear those names for life?' In the event the baby was christened twice over, once in church and once unofficially at Blenheim.

[225]

We can look back now on the pattern of Sir Winston's life [wrote the tenth Duke] and see or think we see a pleasing inevitability. His birth at Blenheim, his proposal of marriage here beside the lake, his burial at Bladon – these things form a mosaic which seems almost too neat to be true. Yet it was only by chance that he happened to be born in the house built for the man John first Duke of Marlborough whom he so much admired.

Sir Winston had a strong sense of family. If he did not worship his ancestors he came near it in his protagonism of Marlborough and of his own father Lord Randolph Churchill. His affection was strong for his family and for his friends of whom my father was one. When I was a boy he visited us often at Blenheim. My father invited too Sir Winston's brother Jack and Lord Birkenhead and they livened things up with wild games of 'French and English' in the Hall.

Beyond question Blenheim made for Sir Winston the ideal background, and I don't mean only for his paintings. At times, for example when he was researching for his life of Marlborough, it must have given him inspiration; but although before I was born he was heir to the dukedom, I doubt if he hankered much for the place itself. He had other and better ideas.

Vanbrugh's north-to-south axial line for the palace passes through Marlborough's Column of Victory, the Great Hall (adjoining the birth-room), the Saloon and the tower of Bladon Church, which may be seen from the Saloon and beside which tower Sir Winston is buried. Thus physically and symbolically are linked the places of his birth and burial.

By choosing to be buried beside his parents in a village churchyard Sir Winston made Bladon a place of pilgrimage for ever. The remains of his dearly loved wife Clementine, Baroness Spencer-Churchill, who died in December 1977, now lie there peacefully beside him, as they both would have wished.

In the Churchill Exhibition at Blenheim, near the birth-room, one sees his painting of the Great Hall. Before he had finished it the tenth Duchess expressed her admiration. 'Do you like it, Mary?' he said. 'Then you shall

[226]

have it for Blenheim.' Other paintings of his – of the staterooms with their tapestries, of the lake – are to be seen there also.

The late Margaret Jourdain (an authority on furniture if not on pictures), dropping her spyglass after a long stare at one of his lake paintings, said: 'H'm, curious about Winston's painting, isn't it? Not so bad but it mightn't be worse'; a criticism which Sir Winston could be said to have answered in his *Painting as a Pastime* when he wrote: 'Do not turn the superior eye of critical passivity upon these efforts. Buy a paint-box and have a try . . . We must not be too ambitious. We cannot aspire to masterpieces. We may content ourselves with a joy ride in a paint-box. And for this, audacity is the only ticket.'

In *The Glitter and the Gold* Consuelo, writing as Madame Balsan from her house in the south of France, remembered: 'His departure on these expeditions was invariably accompanied by a general upheaval of the household. The painting paraphernalia with its easel, parasol and stool had to be assembled, the brushes, freshly cleaned, to be found; the canvases chosen, the right hat sorted out, the cigar-box replenished. At last, driven by our chauffeur, accompanied by a detective the government insisted upon, he would depart with the genial wave and rubicund smile we have learned to associate with his robust optimism. On his return he would amuse us by repeating the comments of those self-sufficient critics who congregate round easels. An old Frenchman one day told him, "With a few more lessons you will become quite good" – a verdict connoisseurs have already endorsed.'

In the pleasure grounds of the palace there are two late-eighteenth-century temples: the Temple of Health on the south-east and, on the south-west, the smaller, Ionic Temple of Diana, designed by Sir William Chambers and his protégé John Yenn. It was in the Temple of Diana, built for the fourth Duke, that on August 11th, 1908 Winston Churchill proposed to Clementine Hozier.

As Dr Mavor observed, 'Though every part of the garden has peculiar charms, this terrace [overlooking the lake] – this point in particular, as a Home View – combines more than all and exhibits almost every different excellence of each.'

[227]

The temple was restored by the eleventh Duke of Marlborough and was reopened by Lady Churchill, who unveiled a plaque, in April 1975. We had always been given to understand that, on that August day in 1908, there had been a sudden storm which had caused the couple to seek shelter in that temple; but no, that was wrong. When I asked Lady Churchill about it she said, 'Do you mean when my husband proposed to me?' 'Yes'. 'Oh no, it was a fine day and we had been walking in the rose garden when Winston said, "There's a rather nice summer-house near here (he called it that). Why not rest in there?" There was a bench there then', she remembered, 'and we sat on it for half an hour and nothing happened.' 'Tell him about the beetle, Mama', interposed Lady Soames, her youngest daughter and biographer. 'Ah yes, the beetle', said Lady Churchill. 'Well now, I looked down at the stone floor and noticed a beetle slowly moving across it, and I thought to myself, "If that beetle reaches that crack and Winston hasn't proposed, he's not going to."' But he did propose, and was accepted.

'Now that I've got you', Miss Hozier is reported to have said, 'the trouble will be to keep you.' To which Churchill replied, 'My dear, you will find that no trouble at all.'

'It is a good marriage for both of them', commented Wilfrid Blunt, 'for Clementine is pretty, clever and altogether charming, while Winston is what all the world know him to be and a good fellow to boot.'

As the Blenheim visitors' book shows, they both revisited Blenheim often and were there when Edward VIII and the Simpsons were fellow-guests. There were, as we know, strong links of friendship between the Winston Churchills and the ninth Duke, in spite of occasional differences about politics. In the autumn of 1913, while Clementine Churchill was one of a house-party at Blenheim, there was what came to be known and deplored in the family as 'that foolish row'. As the tenth Duke told me, 'Clementine had received a letter (or was it a telegram?) from Lloyd George. We were at lunch in the Green Writing-room and she insisted upon answering it at once. My father asked her not to write on Blenheim paper, and she flew into a temper and left the house. It could hardly happen today, but there, at that time Lloyd George had not been highly complimentary about dukes'. The rift lasted for nearly two years, but then came reconciliation. 'My brother and I', the Duke continued, 'were delighted to see them together again, as Winston had been so friendly to us both as children and we had keenly felt his absence the previous Christmas.'

The only other ripple on the surface of the lifelong friendship between the ninth Duke and his cousin occurred many years later when, from 1924 to 1929, Winston as Chancellor of the Exchequer imposed taxation which laid a heavy burden on the rich. In a cartoon still at Blenheim Max Beerbohm showed Winston with both hands upon the shoulders of a crestfallen ninth Duke. 'Come, come', says Winston, 'as I said in one of my speeches, "There is nothing in the Budget to make it harder for a poor hard-working man to keep a small home in decent comfort."' A sketch of Blenheim's north front serves as background.

In August 1947 Mr and Mrs Winston Churchill, as they then were, were staying at Blenheim for an important Conservative rally; and to our great excitement and pleasure we were asked to tea with them. In the usual course of things, as I've said, tea at Blenheim was a nominal affair; but not so that day. In the Grand Cabinet (the first Duke's room, hung with red damask and enriched with gilded pelmets by Chambers) the table was laid almost as though for a banquet. 'I do so enjoy these austerity teas', said the Duchess's sister.

We were all seated when the great man came in, relaxed that hot afternoon both in speech and dress (every shirt-button undone, showing pale sandy hair), and sat beside the unlit fire in a vast red–damask chair which just about fitted him. Someone of course had to mention the weather, but Winston pooh-poohed the idea of a heatwave. 'We have only to experience one or two warm days', he said, 'for farmers to climb down on their knees and for the cry to go up: "When will these brazen skies relent?" While in the House someone rises to ask what the Thames Conservancy is doing about it. These people will always have their whack.'

He was in good form and, between puffs of a large cigar, clearly enjoyed giving his words the air. Tea was declined – he had had 'something better upstairs'. And even that was a cue for telling 'Prof' (Lord Cherwell) that he had a first-class brain and would be really wonderful if only he would drink something stronger than water. 'Prof' was fiddling with a slide-rule. 'The

higher mind', observed Churchill, 'has no need to concern itself with the meticulous regimentation of figures.' Someone with the ticket of audacity then wondered aloud how Churchill had managed as Chancellor of the Exchequer; and that of course sparked off his tale of a Budget Day eve when the Chancellor had asked for an explanation of the labyrinth of statistics set before him: 'Well, gentlemen, what does it mean? What does it mean? Can no one tell me?' Clearings of throat and shufflings of feet made it plain that the Chancellor's expert advisers knew no better than himself; and so 'They sent for a little man from the basement who in words of one syllable told me exactly what those figures meant. I thanked him. He went back to his basement and was never seen again.'

The tea-party continued, our hostess eating cucumber while striding around the table, making sure that her guests were as happy as she was. 'Yes, Mary', said Mrs Churchill, 'I *would* like a fork for this delicious cream bun.' 'I know', said Lord Charles (then seven), who had just lifted a silver dish-cover at his place and quickly replaced it, 'you don't want to get your fingers mucky.' 'Charles!' said his mother severely. 'You are *not* to use that word.' Charles: 'Muck mucky mucky mucky MUCKY!'

It was not a moment to be shocked; nor, I decided, was it a time to cross-question the great man about his youthful reminiscences of Blenheim. The Duke had already introduced me twice, the second time to explain that I was writing a book about Blenheim. 'How interesting,' murmured Winston, his mind obviously full of the speech he was due to make the next day. 'Well, what do you want of me?' 'Anything, sir, about your early days at Blenheim would be more than welcome,' I stumblingly said. 'I am rather busy, you know', he said gently, 'but have you read my books? It's all in there.' Lord Blandford was to show him to his room.

'Well?' asked the Duke, 'did you get what you wanted?' I had to own I hadn't. 'Then why not follow him to his room?' But no, I was not feeling brazen enough for that. 'Anyway', the Duke added, 'I can tell you all you need to know about hide-and-seek in the house and all that.' I thanked him

Sir Winston Churchill at Blenheim

Mary Duchess of Marlborough at cards, in her sittingroom at Blenheim, with Sir Winston Churchill: 'I won't say he's a bad loser, but he much prefers to win'.

and wondered if Winston, who had said he was proud to have been born at Blenheim, was then polishing his speech. There was one sentence, when next day he delivered it from the Saloon steps, which I particularly liked: 'The Socialist belief is that nothing matters so long as miseries are equally shared, and certainly they have acted in accordance with their faith.'

Those were red–letter days as, strangely enough, was my first meeting there with Randolph Churchill. Though I had not, like Curzon, reached the stage of dining at Blenheim once a week, I never knew when I might receive a sudden summons. In my London office I might be fainting from boredom (we were always overstaffed) when the telephone would ring and a call from

Lady Churchill beside the croquet lawn at Blenheim (1947)

[233]

The Freedom of Woodstock: the Winston Churchills with Mary tenth Duchess of
Marlborough and her youngest daughter Lady Rosemary

Blenheim would change all my plans. Would I please come over that
evening?

A nearly full moon glimmered on the lake and on the island; I could
barely see the bridge; the palace all gloom except for twinkles from the
housemaids' heights and dim illumination from the private wing. I was
admitted by a foreign footman in livery, who suggested I might make
myself comfortable in the smoking-room while her Grace finished
dressing. I had the ever welcome company of Stubbs's tiger; the room itself
fragrant with growing narcissi and hyacinths, and rich too with sprays of

[234]

pink and white orchids. I flipped through Randolph's potboiler on the royal household and looked at the photographs.

Then Randolph bustled in, hugely fat in blue velvet smoking-jacket, his slippers embroidered with forty-point silver Rs and leafy chaplets. He mixed Martinis. Then came the Duchess in wine-coloured silk, the Marlborough pearls (once Catherine of Russia's) and for ear-studs large white daisies. Exclamations of delighted surprise, and introductions; Randolph cooing about my Wonderful Book, which he had had time only to glance at in the car.

We dined in the apse of the Bow Window Room, the centre-piece of red cyclamen acting as a net to catch words as they flew across the table. For once I was glad the Duke was not with us: I hadn't to strain to hear him and could enjoy the other two, who had plenty to say. In fact as Randolph warmed up, his hostess was all but shouted down. She raised her voice: 'If I *may* speak in my own house, if I could be allowed just *one* word, if that wouldn't be expecting *too* much . . .' Altogether there was quite a lot of hilarity.

Throughout the meal the Duchess nursed a dachshund bitch on her lap and cooed to it: 'And after the Coronation we're going to have a wonderful wedding, aren't we? Yes we are. It's the very next thing after the Coronation, a lovely little wedding.' She then told us what Winston had just said about dogs – that they must always have water beside them at meals. At Chartwell he had had his man set places at table, with water, for her Alex and for his own poodle Rufus who, put in Randolph, was a fool.

I was of course more than content to listen and to look about me at Gibbons' carvings and Moore's pier-glasses; but over liqueurs Randolph and the Duchess had another brisk battle on the subject of modern youth, Randolph insisting upon its irredeemable decadence. I agreed but suggested that it might be less obvious if there were not still a few giants among us. But at this Randolph bridled. 'I am only too well aware', he said huffily, 'that my father is head and shoulders above me.'

Over port, in the absence of the Duchess, Randolph showed his business hand. He had been commissioned to write a book on famous English houses. Would I help him? I said willingly if I had time; but I had, I explained, a footling job in London; and besides that, the Oxford University Press had just asked me to write a book on Henry Wise and the formal garden. 'Most interesting', he said, 'but *our* book should be painless for both of us. You will merely act as consultant while I drift from house to house, making notes and, for my own satisfaction, awarding marks as I go.' 'And how many marks', I asked, 'have you so far awarded to Blenheim?' 'H'm, it has still to be totted up; but yes, there has already been some score. For absence of host in America: one mark.'

I was Wise-hunting at Melbourne in Derbyshire – that wilderness of sweets – when a sudden call from Randolph demanded my immediate presence at Chatsworth. It seemed out of the question; but by working half that night and, next morning, taking a taxi for twenty miles, I made it; and of course I was glad I had. But Chatsworth, wonderful as it was and is – and its owners couldn't have been more welcoming and entertaining – belongs to another story, much of which has recently been told.* In the park, where the Duchess had just planted a serpentine beech-avenue, Randolph, in ginger tweeds, his abdomen forming a domed annexe in a yellow pullover, said, 'Debbo, you'll be known as the Planting Duchess.'

While Randolph drove northward I was able to get on with my own work; but all too soon came his summons to Oving, a large house he had rented near Aylesbury; and so once again I dropped everything and went. We met at White's for whiskies (my least favourite drink) before driving down. 'Now we mustn't take this book too seriously', Randolph warned me, passing a sports car, 'as a book it'll hardly boil one pot. No, the thing is, where I'm hoping to make a little is in the serialisation – for the knitters, you know, in some woman's magazine.'

On arrival at Oving, the house he had rented and was hoping to buy ('But that oak must come down, ruins the view'), I was of course handed a king-sized whisky which, while Randolph was reading his daughter Arabella her bedtime story, I managed to feed to a potted plant. 'My dear fellow!' he exclaimed jovially, returning to the smoking-room, 'your glass is empty', and he kept generously refilling it.

* *In the House* by Deborah Duchess of Devonshire (Macmillan, 1982)

After dinner we talked and worked till one in the morning. Around midnight he telephoned Garter King of Arms (a regular habit) and browbeat his secretary till she burst into tears. I had a lukewarm bath and slept poorly between sheets boldly embroidered in red with the name of June Churchill.

Breakfast was eaten in silence while Randolph fed spoonfuls of peach to Arabella. Not once but twice the butler knocked, put his head round the door and said, 'You rang, sir?' When it happened the second time Randolph was cross until he realised that his house-guest was so dim-witted as to have his foot upon the bell beneath the table.

I was thankful when he grew as bored with his pot-boiler as I was and began to talk of writing a biography of the late Lord Derby. It was a subject which held no interest for me, but then I was to have nothing to do with it: lucky again. However, when we next met at Blenheim, he graciously drank a toast to Henry Wise and I drank one to Lord Derby.

In green corduroy Randolph sprawled in the smoking-room and talked of portraits; Van Loo's Charles third Duke, who in defiance of Sarah had donned that red uniform and died of dysentery, staring down at us woodenly from the chimney-breast. Randolph volunteered that his father disliked his own portrait by Sutherland so intensely that he couldn't bear to hear it mentioned. It was still in a packing-case, he said, in a basement.

Randolph of course was the perfect mimic of his father: 'When it comes to my funeral, dear boy, your mother may have modest ideas . . . But I want troops, I want *troops*!' Though hard to believe now, at that time (1953) the place of burial had still to be settled; so that when I asked Randolph about Bladon he said no, 'a place with a view, on the lawn at Chartwell'. 'And then', Winston had told Lord Camrose, 'for the National Trust we'll throw in the corpse too – that'll fetch 'em.'

We were soon joined by the Duchess in Red Cross uniform and black stockings. With her came three dachshunds, one of them trembling. 'You're at Blenheim', I told it, 'we can't do more for you than that'; while another climbed on my lap. The Duchess was worried about redecorating. 'I lie awake at night', she said, 'wondering where to put a grandfather clock.' Randolph soon tired of this and asked which rooms his father had used

[237]

when writing at Blenheim. I said I had been told the Arcade Rooms, beneath the Long Library, but I was not sure. 'Well, I'm working in the Coral Rooms', he said. 'Like to come and have a look?' It was a long dark walk from east to west – such cavernous gloom in hall and corridor – and all I could see was the glow of his cigarette and at every few yards the pale blur of a white marble bust.

Sure enough, two of the Coral Rooms had been rigged up as a writer's office and muniment room; a third for a secretary. There were rows of filing-cabinets and piles of black deed-boxes all filled, he said, with wads and bundles of Derby material. Why, I asked, had he chosen Lord Derby, and which aspect of the man was he taking? 'He had no aspect', said Randolph, 'he was a booby.' As for the reason, that was easily answered. While staying at Knowsley for 'our' book, the suggestion had been made to him by one of the family and, to Randolph's astonishment, his agent had since told him there might be some money in it. That was enough. At the very start however he had struck a most awkward snag. His hero's widow, still very much alive in her nineties, declared that, not having been consulted before all was settled, she positively declined to have anything to do with it. What was worse, she sat upon a small mountain of important letters and refused to budge.

I still wondered why Blenheim had been chosen for writing the life of a booby. Perhaps it was the only house big enough to take all those files and boxes, let alone the outsize author; in which case it would surely presuppose hospitality on a munificent scale. Alas, calling a month later I found a dejected Randolph still in the Coral Rooms, where he had recently been joined by his wife; but in his own blunt words they had just been given a week's notice. If only they could have stayed another fortnight, groaned Randolph, Lord Derby would have been rendered down and made digestible. 'He came here in a pantechnicon', he said, 'and was to have left in a suitcase.' But the Duchess was adamant. The Coral Rooms, she insisted, must be redecorated before the reopening of the house for the season.

After Randolph had left I thought it might be an idea to edit an anthology to be called *Sir Winston Churchill at Blenheim Palace*; for after all, he was one of the main reasons for hundreds of thousands of visitors flocking

[238]

there. For that slight work I had imagined a stack of first-class material – photographs, paintings, anecdotes – but when I came to look into it, the stack at Blenheim was not as high as I had hoped. I questioned the tenth Duke. 'He was always writing', he said, 'when he wasn't painting, all the years I have known him, and he does most of his writing in bed. For the past twenty years or so it has been his habit not to rise until late; though what exactly he does in bed I don't know, I never went to look.'

But surely, I suggested, there must be photographs? Oh yes of course, masses of them, all in those albums on the windowsill. The Duchess would look through them and show me the best ones 'after church'. But when after the church I biked over I found the Duchess displeased. 'Here I've been all morning heaving around these huge albums', she said, 'and you turn up now'. She had found excellent prints, but I could see nothing of Winston being given the Freedom of Woodstock. 'I think I know where that is', she said, 'just follow me'.

Feeling small as a dachshund I followed her tall figure along that shadowy, vaulted corridor until of a sudden I realised that she had vanished. Then, muffled by masonry, came the commanding voice: 'Mr Green?' 'Yes, Duchess, where are you?' 'I'm in the bathroom.' Her bathroom, hewn as it seemed from the living rock, windowless and gloomy, had a bath and wash-basin and, except for the odd towel-rail, little else from floor to ceiling but framed photographs, and of them there were many covering the walls. There were children and grandchildren with perambulators and nannies; there was Princess Margaret at a daughter's wedding; there was the Duke at Ascot; and sure enough, there was the Duchess in mayoral robes presenting Winston with the Freedom of the borough. This last, in triplicate, was in various poses. 'You can take your choice', she said.

By this time the Duchess seemed calmer and so I dared to ask if I might photograph Winston's painting of the Hall. 'Yes of course', she said, 'I asked "Prof" to do it but I've never seen a print. As I think you know, I told Winston it would be nice if we could have the painting for Blenheim and he said, "Would you like it, Mary? Then you shall have it, but I must touch it up a bit first." Well, I don't like it as much as I did before he finished it, but it's still pretty good. Come and have a look.' I thought his Corinthian

[239]

columns a little wobbly but didn't say so.

It may have been then that she told me how Winston insisted upon playing bezique with her far into the night. 'I wouldn't say he's a bad loser', she added, 'but he much prefers to win.' Bezique bored the Duke, but Winston had chosen the same game when they had crossed the Atlantic in the *Queen Mary* at the end of the war. 'It was certainly boring', said the Duke, 'but I managed to take quite a bit of money off him; and the one thing that saved us both was that, in the bowels of the ship, they found an excellent Montrachet. They said it had been there for the whole of the war.'

Thanks to the Duchess and her editor, the anthology was published but, in spite of the Churchill Exhibition there, it was too much to expect a busy staff to show it and sell it. The public knew nothing of its existence and so it soon died an unnatural death.

Some months later Randolph Churchill returned to reconnoitre for his father's biography. The Duke kindly passed him on to me; although as one who cared little for politics and had found Winston's *Lord Randolph* dull, it was doubtless as well that Randolph the second preferred a more learned helper.

But now, as the tenth Duke told me, Randolph had to be asked to leave Blenheim for the second time. It happened like this. They had been about to dine informally in the smoking-room when Randolph noticed a television set still switched on and asked for it to be turned off. The Duke objected and Randolph said, 'But how can you watch such stuff? You know it's only for the hoi-polloi.' Lady Rosemary Muir, the Duke's youngest daughter, due to have a baby next day, then put in with 'Randolph, why don't you leave Daddy alone?' Whereupon Randolph rounded on her and told her to shut up.

Duke: 'Randolph, I think you had better leave the house.'

Randolph: 'Very well, Bert, ask your minions to pack my bags.'

Duke: 'If my minions feel the same way about you as I do, I'm not sure that they will.'

He left next morning. 'I won't have him in the house again', the Duke told me, 'and I shall do nothing to help him.' Later however, when he heard that he was mortally ill and was prepared to apologise, he forgave him and

At the Temple of Diana. The Duke of Marlborough and David Green assist Lady
Churchill to her car.

let him return. The Duke had in fact a sneaking regard for him. 'He had
great courage', he said, 'both moral and physical.'

And indeed, on that bitterly cold day when Winston was buried at
Bladon, Randolph, sitting with cadaverous eyes beside his heavily veiled
mother, at the back of a black car, looked like death itself.

Early that morning we had walked down the station hill to Hanborough
Lodge. It was strange, the frosted road empty of traffic, and nearly
everyone walking towards Bladon, itself sealed off. There were hundreds of
policemen and St John's Ambulance people in uniform, but no crowd
needing control. When the train was due we stood under an apple-tree in

[241]

old Tompkins' garden and from there watched the engine steam slowly towards us from the edge of Burghley Wood. There was a long pause before the cortège appeared: a procession of Rolls Royces, some of them looking old. I noticed the Duke and Lord Blandford who told me afterwards how much those groups of men standing hatless in the fields, as the train passed, had moved him.

As we left, some of the mourners from London were returning by train. Glancing down towards the station – the flowery halt we knew so well in summer – we were amazed to see two guardsmen in full uniform, bearskins and all; while the little station itself was entirely swathed in white and purple, tricked out with laurel wreaths and daffodils.

Later I queued for an hour at Bladon to see the grave and when I reached it it was hard to tell which it was, since the whole of that corner by the tower was a mass of flowers, topped by the Queen's white wreath. Consuelo's mound, I noticed, had its cross of flowers; and in the distance I could just make out another on the grave of Mary Duchess.

At Blenheim that week I found the Duke in his garden. The funeral had of course upset him. 'Had to take a pep pill', he told me, 'I rode in a brougham. The wind was bitter and the cold went to my stomach. Spent yesterday in bed.' He then turned to the head-gardener and asked suspiciously if those irises – mere blades – were going to flower. 'Oh yes, your Grace, they'll flower all right.' 'Are you SURE?' I then left him and tried to get on with writing.

But let my last memories be of Lady Churchill. The first when, after unveiling the plaque in the Temple of Diana ('I must read what it says – oh yes, I'm glad that was put'), we lunched and, over coffee, the Duchess* asked, 'Shall we have Edward in here or in the garden?' 'Oh do let's have him in here', said Lady Soames. And so Nanny Highmore, treasure of treasures, brought him in. He was in blue and white wool and at eight months seemed bursting with life and spirit, round head, round face like Winston's. When I asked Nanny if she was trying to make his hair curl she

---

* Rosita eleventh Duchess of Marlborough and her son Edward Albert Charles Spencer-Churchill (born 1974).

Hanborough station, dressed overall for the funeral of Sir Winston Churchill

said, 'Well no, this is his *party* hair'. After being danced on the table he lay and kicked on the carpet; and when Lady Churchill asked what he was up to, he was lifted and they gazed closely at each other until she said, 'You're a very nice little boy, very charming.'

My last memory of all is of Lady Churchill's memorial service in Westminster Abbey on January 26th, 1978, which I attended with Audrey Russell. The flowers made white and green pyramids. The faces were fascinating: Arabella now a handsome young woman with long shining blond hair. Her brother Winston read part of the address which had been given at his grandfather's funeral: prophetic and telling. Sarah Churchill, Randolph's sister, was there and at the end of the order of service had written:

[243]

Tears are never too late to sow,
Some seedling in the dark may grow.

In a strange way I was reminded of a verse written by Mary Godolphin,
the second Duchess of Marlborough's daughter, at the age of twelve:

I hear the voice you cannot hear
That says I must not stay.
I see the hand you cannot see
That beckons me away. . . .

Appendix

The first Duke and Duchess of Marlborough and Blenheim
by Charles ninth Duke of Marlborough*

Only Sarah Jennings could command the confidence of John Churchill. Only John Churchill could command the confidence of Sarah Jennings, and Providence made them husband and wife. That confidence was never broken.

John Churchill was a true romantic . . . his romance lasted as long as his life and was even unaffected by the pitiful quarrels between his wife and his children.

Sarah was a most efficient woman of the world, but to her husband she was a radiant and wonderful being whom he was reluctant to place in the world at all. He worshipped intellect in his wife. Her masculine qualities made her the dearer in his eyes because they were the complement of his own nature. He exalted her for her brains and because of them he placed her even above his Queen.

The harsh fate which clouded the domestic happiness of John and Sarah with overwhelming grief for the loss of their two sons ironically decreed that their vast possessions should descend through their daughter named after

---

* Reprinted from *John and Sarah, Duke and Duchess of Marlborough* by Stuart Reid (1914), to which the ninth Duke of Marlborough added an introduction.

their benefactress the Queen.

Charles Spencer, upon whom the family estates eventually devolved, was the son and grandson of first ministers. The twenty-fourth of his line, he brought the tradition of statecraft to a house built to commemorate military achievement, and the compound name of his descendants is emblematic of the union of the two qualities. It may be that his rollicking spirit would have preferred the simple delights of the chase at Althorp to the responsibility of administering the nation's magnificent gift to its victorious hero, but he accepted his duty and his descendants have striven to act in his spirit . . .

It has been said and with a certain truth that Marlborough was ambitious. It was as it were an impersonal desire for fame. It seemed to him a special mercy of Providence that his talents should have been placed at the disposal of England and not of any other country; that because of him England was enabled to wreck the plans of the great Sovereign who threatened her liberties, and to shatter the nightmare of the junction of French and Spanish power in one man's hand.

That such a boon should pass without formal thanks offended his sense of piety. Therefore he set himself to see that his exploits were worthily commemorated, and took it as a matter of course that no memorial could be too magnificent. The talent that won Blenheim must be honoured; and it was, as he felt it, only incidental that the honour should be bestowed upon his own person. It was his achievements, not himself, that were to be recognised by a grateful country.

For this reason he determined that the stately palace which his countrymen intended to build should be named after the first and most dazzling of the victories that it recalled. But he felt that his fame would be the special heritage of his descendants, and he determined that they should be in a position to maintain it. For them he saved money – which however he spent again generously enough when the needs of his country demanded it – and for them he collected pictures and tapestry in his travels through Europe. It seemed to him entirely fitting that his descendants should live in the building which was to bear eternal witness to his genius.

For personal glory, on the other hand, he cared not at all. It is true that Blenheim, as it stands today, is a memorial of the first Duke much more

[246]

than a thank-offering for his victories. That however is not due to any conceit of Marlborough's. The house was only partially complete at the time of his death, and it was the Duchess who really changed his intentions in endeavouring to carry them out. It was not by any desire of hers that Blenheim was planned on so gigantic a scale; and she never quite understood what was in her husband's mind when he planned it. But she obeyed his wishes the more closely because she did not understand them; and, as she was incapable of drawing the distinction of which he was so conscious himself between his personality and his genius, she converted the house he had projected into the stateliest personal memorial that has ever been raised to any Englishman, and so helped to blind posterity to the modesty that was really one of her husband's qualities. Blenheim suggests the Duke as a man rather too ready to make his less fortunate fellows realise their own inferiority. It was thus that the Duchess would have behaved had she been a man possessed of all the qualities that were hers and of her husband's military gifts besides; and Blenheim enshrines her ideal and rather subjective version of him. But the man himself was other and finer.

Blenheim, April 18th, 1914   MARLBOROUGH

Select Bibliography

MANUSCRIPT SOURCES

Althorp, Northamptonshire: The Marlborough Papers
British Library: Blenheim Papers, Add. MSS 61101–61710.
   Chambers, Sir William, Add. MSS 41133–6
   Godolphin Papers, Add. MSS 28071
   Leeds Papers, Add. MSS 28052, 28057
   Marlborough Papers, Add. MSS 19591–19618, 9123, 9125
Hertfordshire County Library: Dr Hamilton's Diary
R.I.B.A.: The Letters of Sir William Chambers

PRINTED SOURCES

BALSAN, CONSUELO: *The Glitter and the Gold* (1952)
BATTISCOMBE, GEORGINA: *The Spencers of Althorp* (1984)
BLAKISTON, GEORGIANA: *Woburn and the Russells* (1980)
BOYDELL, JOHN and JOSIAH: *The River Thames* (1794)
BROWN, B.C.: *The Letters of Queen Anne* (1968)
BURNET, BISHOP: *History of My Own Times (1724–34)*
CHURCHILL, RANDOLPH: *Biography of Sir Winston Churchill* (Vol 1, 1968) since concluded by Martin Gilbert
CHURCHILL, LADY RANDOLPH: *Reminiscences* (1908)
CHURCHILL, PEREGRINE (with JULIAN MITCHELL): *Jennie* (Lady Randolph Churchill), (1974)
CHURCHILL, SIR WINSTON: *Marlborough, His Life and Times* (1947)
— *Lord Randolph Churchill* (1906)
— *Painting as a Pastime* (1949)

COLVIN, H.M.: *A Biographical Dictionary of British Architects, 1660–1840 The King's Works* (1983)

COXE, W.C.: *Memoirs of John Duke of Marlborough* (1820)

Dictionary of National Biography

EVELYN, JOHN: *Diary*

GREEN, DAVID: *Battle of Blenheim* (1974)

— *Blenheim Palace* (1951)

— *Gardener to Queen Anne* (1956)

— *Grinling Gibbons* (1964)

— *Queen Anne* (1970)

— *Sarah Duchess of Marlborough* (1967)

— *Sir Winston Churchill at Blenheim Palace* (1959)

GREEN, V.H.H.: *Oxford Common Room* (1957)

HAWTHORNE, NATHANIEL: *Our Old Home* (1863)

HISTORICAL MANUSCRIPTS COMMISSION

LEVER, SIR TRESHAM: *Godolphin, His Life and Times* (1952)

MARLBOROUGH, SARAH DUCHESS OF: *Conduct* (1742)

   Letters from Madresfield Court (1875)

   Private Correspondence (1838)

MARSHALL, EDWARD: *Woodstock Manor* (1873)

MAVOR, DR W.F.: *New Description of Blenheim* (1787–1846)

REID, STUART: *John and Sarah, Duke and Duchess of Marlborough* (1914)

ROWSE, DR A.L.: *The Early Churchills* (1969)

   The Later Churchills (1971)

SCOTT-THOMSON, GLADYS: *Letters of a Grandmother* (1943)

STROUD, DOROTHY: *Capability Brown* (1950)

VICKERS, HUGO: *Gladys Duchess of Marlborough* (1979)

WEBB, GEOFFREY: *The Letters of Sir John Vanbrugh*, vol. 4 (1928)

WHISTLER, LAURENCE: *Sir John Vanbrugh* (1938)

   The Imagination of Vanbrugh (1954)

Index

Page numbers in *italics* refer to illustrations

Account of the Cruel Usage of my Children, An (Sarah, Duchess of Marlborough), 64, 71

Addison, Joseph, 18

Adelaide, Queen, 105

Alex (dachsund), 175, 183, 235

Alexandra, Queen, 138, 141; (as Princess of Wales) 114, 115, 130, *131*

Alice, Princess, 197

All for Love (Dryden), 44, 186

Althorp, 34, 94, 120, 193–4

Anne, Queen, 26, 42; and right of succession, 30, 33, 52; sufferings of, 33, 34; accession, 35, 52; favours to Marlboroughs, 35, 38, 39, 52, 53; Rysbrack's statue of, *36*, 85; dismissal of Marlboroughs, 39; death, 40; early friendship with Sarah, 51–2; worsening relations with Marlboroughs, 53–6; transfers affections to Abigail Masham, 54–5; final break and dismissal of Marlboroughs, 55–6; interest in Marlborough children, 60; Green's biography of, 197–8, 201

Ansidei Madonna, 107, 119

Arbuthnot, Mrs Harriet, 104

Armstrong, Colonel John, 85, 89

Aylesford, Lord, 114

Aylesford, Edith, Lady, elopement with Marquis of Blandford, 114–15, 121

Balfour, Arthur, *131*

Balsan, Jacques, 144, 145

Battle of Blenheim, The (Green), 15, 222, 223

Beaconsfield, Benjamin Disraeli, Lord, 114, 115

Beaverbrook, Lord, 142

Beckett-Overy, Dr, 157

Bedford, 3rd Duke of, 81

Bedford, John Russell, 4th Duke of, 80, 89

Beerbohm, Sir Max, 229

Ben (boxer dog), 195, *196*, 202, 223

Berners, Lord, 156

Bernini, Giovanni Lorenzo, 103, 151

Berwick, James FitzJames, Duke of, 26, 31, 40

Bhumibol, King of Thailand, 194

Birkenhead, F. E. Smith, Lord, 142, 226

Birkenhead, Frederick Furneaux, 2nd Lord, 156

Bladon, 90, 91, 137; Churchill burials at, 121–2, 123, 188, 192, 219, 223, 226, 241–2

Blandford, George Charles Spencer Churchill, Marquis of – see Marlborough, 8th Duke of

Blandford, George Spencer Churchill, Marquis of – see Marlborough, 5th Duke of

Blandford, Bertha, Marchioness of, 111; divorce, 115

Blandford, John Churchill, Marquis of, 31, 33, 76; death, 52, 53, 60; statue on Blenheim monument, 59, 66, 71

Blandford, John George Vanderbilt Henry Spencer Churchill, Marquis of – see Marlborough, 11th Duke of

Blandford, Tina Onassis, Marchioness of, 189

Blandford, Willigo Godolphin, Marquis of, 63, 191; Continental travels, 75–7, 82; weak character, 76, 78; marriage, 77–8; alcoholism, 78, 81, 100; death, 78, 81

Blandford, Maria de Yonge, Marchioness of, 78

Blenheim, battle of (1704), 37, 39, 53, 178, 223

Blenheim Palace: foundation and building of, 38–9, 41–2, 44, 56–7, 58–9, 70, 71; payment for, 38, 41, 94; work stopped on, 41, 56–7; Marlborough's move into, 44, 47; as his memorial, 46–7, 246–7; Sarah's dislike of, 47, 89, 146; Marlborough monument in chapel, *48*, 59; canalization of river, 85, 89; diversion of river

and creation of lake, 91–2; neglect of, 89; repairs, decoration and additions to, 90–91, 103–4, 107; landscaping of park, 91–2, 93n, 94, 102, 103, 147, 187; launching of gondola on lake, 92; amateur theatricals, 93, 95; enlargement of estate, 94; staff and running expenses, 94–5; George III's visit, 95–7; Nelson's visit, 98; extravagant celebrations on 5th Duke's succession, 102; creation of exotic gardens, 103, 104; complaints over admission fees, 107–8; styles of living, 110–11, 113, 126, 130–2, 135, 137–9; dispersal of library, 116; sales of treasures and heirlooms, 116, 117–20; Willis organ, 120, 180, 181, 188–9; dredging of lake, 124; restoration of gardens and trees, 127–9, 134–5, 147, 148–55; 'sleeping policeman', 129; royal shooting-parties, 130–2; record rabbit-shoot, 132; gate-keeper, *133*; redecoration, 133–4; limited comfort, 134, 135, 137–8; morning prayers, 135; Planting for Victory, 142; water terraces, 147, 148–55; restoration after wartime occupation, 159; Green's book on building of, 161, 164, 167–8, 175; guidebooks to, 168, 169, 174; reopening to public, 168, 170–3, 174; problem of lavatories, 170; documentary film, 175; walled garden, 177; gardening staff, 177; broadcast from, 178–9; television transmission from, 180–2; new garden created by 10th Duke, 183–4, 223; *son et lumière*, 184–5, 199; family vault, 190, 191; film of 1938 pageant, 219; Arcade Rooms, 103–4, 238; Bernini fountain, 151, 155; Bow Window Room, 44, 59, 85, 91, 102, 120, 134, 190,

235; bridge, 57, 85, 89, 91, 93n, 169, 184; chapel, *48*, 59, 71, 85, 170, 172; Churchill birthroom, 113, 170, 172, 226; Churchill Exhibition, 142, 226, 240; Column of Victory, 24, 58, 76, 85, 167, 169; Coral Rooms, 113, 159, 222, 238; Druid's Temple, 103, 147; Flagstaff Lodge, 90, *133*; Godolphin Rooms, 34; Grand Cabinet, 90, 102, 218, 229; Great Cascade, 92, 103, 169; Great Hall, 59, 102, 132, 159, 171, 172, 226, 239; High Lodge, 42, 66, 92, *131*, 161, 164; Long Library, 17, *36*, 58, 85n, 102, 103, 113, 116, 134, 159, 171, 180, 181, 189, 203; Red Drawing-room, 17, 93, 130; Rosamond's Well, 91, 167, 169, 187; Saloon, 59, 102, 113, 132, 171; Spring Lock, 103; Sunderland Library, 76; Temple of Diana, 16, 90, 227–8, *241*, 242; Temple of Flora, 90, 103; Temple of Health, 90, 97, *196*, 223, 227; Venus fountain, 135, *136*
Blenheim Palace (Green), 161, 164, 167–8, 175
Blenheim Settled Estates Act (1880), 116, 117
Blindheim (Blenheim), 37, 172, 223
Bobart, Tilleman, 56
Boehm, Sir Joseph, 117
Boldini, Giovanni, 141
Bolingbroke, Henry St John, Viscount, 41, 49; and downfall of Marlboroughs, 54, 56, 58; panegyric on Marlborough, 58
Bolingbroke, Diana, Viscountess, 98
Bononcini, Giovanni Maria, 70, 77, 203
Brammall, Freddie (10th Duke's valet and chauffeur), 195, 204, 205, 206, 209, 212–13, 214, 218
Bridgwater, Scroop, Earl of, 81
Bridgwater, Elizabeth Churchill, Countess of, 31, 74n; death, 40, 62, 65; Kneller portrait, *62*
Brooke, Sarah, Lady, 206, 212, 218
Brown, Lancelot, 14; and

landscaping of Blenheim, 91–2, 93n, 94, 102, 103, 147, 187
Burnet, Bishop, 33, 42, 161
Burney, Fanny, 97

Cadogan, William, 1st Earl, 37, 40, 42, 47
Campbell, Lady Colin, 121
Campbell, Mrs Patrick, 123
Camrose, Lord, 238
Canfield, Laura – *see* Marlborough, Laura Canfield, Duchess of
Cardigan, Mary, Countess of, 81
Carlisle, Charles Howard, 3rd Earl of, 39
Carlisle, Henry Howard, 4th Earl of, 74n
Carnarvon, Henry Herbert, 6th Earl of, 156, 172, 173
Carnarvon, Countess of, 156
Carolus-Duran, C. E. A., 134
Carson, Sir Edward, 142
Cavendish, Lady Arabella, 74n
Cecil, Lord Alfred, 108
Cecil, Lord David, 156
Cecil, Lord Hugh, 117, 140
Chambers, Sir William, 90, 176, 182, 224, 227
Chaplin, Henry, *131*
Charles I, 27, 116, 119
Charles of Denmark, Prince and Princess, 130, *131*
Chartwell, 92
Chatsworth House, 236
Cherwell, Lord, 178, 229
Chesterfield, Earl of, *131*
Churchill, Anne – *see* Sunderland, Anne Churchill, Countess of
Churchill, Arabella, as James Duke of York's mistress, 26, 28
Churchill, Arabella (daughter of Randolph), 236, 237, 243
Churchill, General Charles, 27, 37
Churchill, Charles, 31, 59
Churchill, Diana, 156
Churchill, Elizabeth, Lady (mother of 1st Duke of Marlborough), 27, 29
Churchill, Elizabeth – *see* Bridgwater, Elizabeth Churchill, Countess of
Churchill, Admiral George, 27, 37

Churchill, Harriet, 29
Churchill, Henrietta – *see* Marlborough, Lady Henrietta Godolphin, 2nd Duchess of
Churchill, Jack, 115, 121, 226
Churchill, John – *see* Marlborough, John Churchill, 1st Duke of
Churchill, Lord Randolph, 110, 135; 'poppy eyes', 111; courtship and marriage to Jennie Jerome, 111–12; and Blandford scandal, 115; in Ireland, 115; political career, 115, 122; objection to sale of Marlborough heirlooms, 116, 117; downfall and death, 122–3; burial at Bladon, 123
Churchill, Jennie Jerome, Lady Randolph, 109, 125, 132; on life at Blenheim, 110–11, 115–16; courtship and marriage, 111–12; first sight of Blenheim, 112; birth of Winston, 112–13; in Ireland, 115; and Randolph's last years, 122–3; later marriages, 123; in shooting-party, *131*
Churchill, Randolph, 113, 176, 219, 225; Green's first meeting with, 233–6; literary work, 235–8, 240; asked to leave Blenheim, 238, 240; and Winston's funeral, 237, 241
Churchill, Sarah – *see* Marlborough, Sarah Churchill, Duchess of
Churchill, Sarah (Lady Audley), 243
Churchill, Sir Winston (father of 1st Duke of Marlborough), 27–8
Churchill, Sir Winston Spencer, 13, 92, 116, 122, 132, 156, 218, 235; attitude to Blenheim, 16, 226; on dispersal of Marlborough heirlooms, 17, 120; his *Life of Marlborough*, 24, 28, 30, 35, 44, 46, 51, 54, 56, 176; birth at Blenheim, 112–13, 170, 172, 195, 199, 225, 226; in Ireland with parents, 115; as heir to dukedom, 125, 225, 226; uncertainty as to how to address 9th Duke, 127; 'in love with own image', 141;

support for 9th Duke, 141,
142; escape from shrapnel,
142; tributes to 9th Duke, 155,
158; maxims, 165, 202, 229;
burial at Bladon, 236, 237,
241–2, *243*; his paintings,
226–7, 239; proposal of
marriage to Clementine, 227–
8; later visits to Blenheim,
228–33; card-playing, *233*,
240; and Freedom of
Woodstock, *234*, 239; funeral,
237; anthology on, 238–40
Churchill, Clementine, Lady,
210, 213, 219; in Jamaica, *210*,
213; burial at Bladon, 226;
Churchill's proposal to, 227–8;
'foolish row' with 9th Duke,
228; later visits to Blenheim,
229–31, *232*; and Freedom
ceremony at Woodstock, *234*;
at Temple of Diana, *241*, 242;
memorial service, 243
Churchill, Winston Spencer,
MP, 243
Clayton, Mrs (later Lady
Sundon), 47
Clifford, Rosamond, 38, 187
Closterman, John, 31, 60
Cockerell, Sir Charles, 104
Collett, Dan, 169
Colvin, Howard, 187
Compton, Henry, Bishop of
London, 51
Congreve, William, 39; affair
with Henrietta Godolphin, 66,
68–70; portrait, *69*, 70;
Henrietta's effigy of, 70
Cornwallis-West, George, 123
Cowper, William, 18
Coxe, Archdeacon William, 47,
88, 100
Curzon, Viscount and
Viscountess, *131*
Curzon, George Nathaniel (later
Marquis), *131*, 138, 139, 233
Curzon, Mrs George Nathaniel,
131

Derby, Edward Stanley, 17th
Earl of, 237, 238
Devonshire, Deborah, Duchess
of, 236
Dimbleby, Richard, and
television programme from
Blenheim, 178, *179*, 180, 181,
182

Dior, Christian, 165, 186
Dryden, John, 44, 81n, 186
Duchêne, Achille, 133, 143, 199,
224; and Blenheim garden and
water terraces, 127, 134, 147,
148–53
Duffie, Paul, 195
Duleepsinhji, Prince, 132

Edward VII, 140, 141; (as Prince
of Wales) 122, 138; at
Blenheim, 113, 138, 139–42;
and Blandford scandal, 114–
15; godfather to 10th Duke,
127
Edward VIII, 202, 228
Egerton, Lady Anne, 74n, 75, 81
Ellis, General, *131*
Epstein, Jacob, 146
Eugene of Savoy, Prince, 37, 56
Evelyn, John, 53
Everest, Nanny, 116

Fish, Captain Humphrey, 82, 83
Fitzharding, Barbara, Lady, 31,
32
Frederick William, Crown Prince
of Germany, 139–40, 188
Fuchs, Emil, 162

Gardener to Queen Anne (Green),
183, 212
Garth, Sir Samuel, 42, 44;
Kneller portrait, *45*
Gay, John, 68
George I, 41
George III, 90; at Blenheim, 96–
7
George of Denmark, Prince, 35–
7, 51, 54–5
George of Greece, Princess, 146
Gibbons, Grinling, 42, 44, 59,
89, 90, 151, 185
Glitter and the Gold, The
(Balsan), 15, 125, 126, 137,
138, 139, 176, 191, 197, 200,
211, 227
Gloucester, William, Duke of,
33, 34, 52
Glover, Matilda, 105
Glover, Richard, 23
Godolphin, Francis, 2nd Earl of,
34, 64, 66; portrait of, *65*; as
complaisant husband, 68, 70;
and son's 'improper marriage',
77, 78; and Marlborough
Trust, 88

Godolphin, Henrietta – *see*
Marlborough, Lady Henrietta
Godolphin, 2nd Duchess of
Godolphin, Mary, Duchess of
Leeds, 68, 75, 78, 244
Godolphin, Sidney, 1st Earl of,
34, 35, 39, 60, 70; as Lord
Treasurer, 53, 55; dismissal,
56
Golden (Blenheim guide), 172
Gosford, Earl and Countess of,
131
Green, V. H. H., 105
Grenfell, Mr and Mrs William,
131
Greville, Hon. Sidney, *131*
Guest, Lady Cornelia, 122
Guest, Ivor, 125
Guitry, Sacha, 184
Gunning, Gunnilda, 101

Hakewill, John, 91
Hamilton, Sir David, 56
Hamilton, Sir William, 98
Hamilton, Emma, Lady, 98
Hanborough station, 174, 242,
243
Hare, Dr Francis, 60, 206
Hawksmoor, Nicholas, 39, 85,
223; and building of
Blenheim, 57, 58, 116
Hawthorne, Nathaniel, 161
Henry II, 38, 187
Herbert, Lord (later Earl of
Pembroke), 58, 85
Highmore, Nanny, 242
Hill, Abigail – *see* Masham,
Abigail
Holywell (St Albans), 41, 46, 50,
51, 75
Hordley, 94
Horne, Gerald (butler), 15, 130,
162, 192, 199, 224
Horne, Nelly, 162
Hudson, Thomas, 87, 237
Hyde, Anne (Duchess of York),
27, 29

Illingworth, Jock (Blenheim
chief guide), 178, 191–2
In the House (Devonshire), 236n

James II, 28, 34; Churchill's
desertion of, 26, 29, 30;
abdication, 29, 51; Churchill's
correspondence with, 30
Jenkins, Edward, 170, 174

Jennings, Frances, 28, 50, 51
Jennings, Richard, 50
Jennings, Sarah, see
    Marlborough 1st Duchess of
Jerome, Leonard, 111, 120
Johnson, Dr Samuel, 23, 107
Jones, Dean, 59, 68, 168
Jourdain, Margaret, 227
Joynes, Henry, 56, 107
'Julia', 212, 217

Keeble, Sir Frederick, 156
Keeble, Lady (Lillah McCarthy),
    156
Kent, William, 59, 85
Kingscote, Lady Emily, *131*
Kit-Cat Club, 39, 55, 57, 58, 62
Kneller, Sir Godfrey, 31

Laguerre, Louis, 59
Langley (Bucks), 41, 86, 89, 91,
    97
Lansdowne, Henry Petty-
    Fitzmaurice, 5th Marquis of,
    142
Lediard, Thomas, 24, 27
Lee of Fareham, Lady, 148
Leslie, Sir Shane, 112, 155
Lloyd George, David, 228
London, George, 51
Londonderry, 6th Marquis and
    Marchioness of, *131*
Longford, Lord, 156
Lutyens, Sir Edwin, 152

Manchester, Bella, Duchess of
    (later Countess Beaulieu), 81
Mann, Sir Horace ('governor' of
    Willigo Blandford), 75–6, 82
Margaret, Princess, 187, 201
Marlborough, James Ley, 1st
    Earl of, 30
Marlborough, John Churchill,
    1st Duke of, 13, 103, 135, 191;
    books about, 23–4; Kneller
    portrait of, *25*; embarrassing
    facts, 26, 28, 30–31; switch of
    allegiance from James to
    William, 26, 29–30; ancestry
    and birth, 26–7; early life, 28;
    marriage to Sarah, 28, 50, 51;
    his religion, 30; earldom, 30;
    dismissal by William, 30–31,
    52; in Tower, 31, 52; change
    of fortunes, 33, 52; tutor to
    Duke of Gloucester, 33, 52;

daughters' marriages, 34; wins
Anne's favour, 35, 38, 53;
dukedom, 35; Blenheim and
other victories, 37, 39; granted
manor of Woodstock, 38;
dismissal by Anne, 39, 56;
retirement abroad, 39–40, 57;
deaths of daughters, 40, 42,
73; return and restoration
under George I, 40–41, 57;
sued for debt over building of
Blenheim, 41; London home,
41; illnesses, 42, 66, 73, 75;
partial recovery, 44; move into
Blenheim, 44–7; desire for
Blenheim to be his memorial,
46–7, 246–7; death, 47, 66;
monument in Blenheim
chapel, *48*, 59, 71, 85, 172;
covetousness, 49; devotion to
his children, 53, 59–62, 63–4;
pension, 101n; treasures
collected by, 116, 119, 120,
151
Marlborough, Sarah Jennings,
    1st Duchess of, 13, 191; desire
    for Marlborough's biography
    to be written, 23, 26, 27;
    ancestry and birth, 26, 50;
    early experiences at Court, 28,
    51; marriage, 26–7, 50, 51;
    agnosticism, 30; disgust with
    appearance in Closterman
    painting, 31; Kneller portraits
    of, 31, *32*; her one surviving
    love-letter, 33; dislike of
    Blenheim, 34, 44, 47, 89; as
    favourite of Anne, 35, 39, 52,
    53; duties at Court, 35, 39, 53;
    parsimony, 39, 59, 67, 85;
    building and embellishment of
    Blenheim, 39, 41, 44, 56, 57–
    9, 70, 71, 85, 89, 247; in
    Holland, 40, 57; disputes with
    Vanbrugh, 39, 41, 42, 44, 57–
    8; and Marlborough's strokes,
    42, 44, 66; move into
    Blenheim, 44; and
    Marlborough's death, 47, 67;
    covetousness, 49; early
    friendship with Anne, 51–2;
    worsening relations with
    Anne, 53–6; final break with
    Anne, 55–6; dismissal, 56;
    Green Book of children's
    alleged misdemeanours, 60–66,
    71, 73, 193; estrangement

from daughters, 68, 70–71;
care of grand-children, 71, 74,
78–86; last years and death,
71–2, 80; her will, 71;
rejection of suitors, 79;
matchmaking, 80, 86; lack of
interest in arts, 81, 82;
concern at grandsons'
extravagance, 82, 83;
estrangement from grandson
Charles, 84–5; final memorial
to Marlborough, 85;
protection of Marlborough
heirlooms, 86, 116, 120;
letters, 167, 192; Green's
biography of, 192–4, 197
Marlborough, Lady Henrietta
    Godolphin, 2nd Duchess of,
    13, 31, 42, 59, 78; marriage to
    Francis Godolphin, 34; Lady
    of Bedchamber, 35; as a child,
    60, *61*, 63–4; Kneller portraits,
    61, 63; misdemeanours, 63, 64;
    alienation from Sarah, 65, 66–
    8, 77; and father's illness and
    death, 66–7; affair with
    Congreve, 66, 68–70; birth of
    daughter Mary, 68; death, 84
Marlborough, Charles Spencer,
    3rd Duke of, 11n, 34, 71, 73,
    75, 89, 246; Continental travel,
    82; gambling and
    extravagance, 82, 83, 88;
    mumble, 83, 84; marriage, 84;
    military career, 84, 86;
    estrangement from Sarah, 84,
    85; move to Bray, 85; at
    Langley, 86; fond letters to
    wife, 86–7; death, 87
Marlborough, Elizabeth Trevor,
    Duchess of (wife of 3rd
    Duke), 84, 86, 87, 88
Marlborough, George Spencer,
    4th Duke of, 14, 41, 105; as
    Lord Blandford, 87;
    succession to dukedom, 88;
    marriage, 89; alterations and
    additions to Blenheim, 90–91,
    94–5, 97, 119, 161; intelligence
    and culture, 90, 97;
    landscaping of park, 91–2, 99;
    Reynolds family group of, 93–
    4; public and political life, 94;
    financial worries, 95;
    retrenchment, 95, 97–8, 100;
    elopement of daughter, 95;
    entertainment of George III,

95–7; death, 99

Marlborough, Caroline, Duchess of (wife of 4th Duke), 89, 93, 94, 96; illness and death, 98–9

Marlborough, George Spencer Churchill, 5th Duke of, 89; as Lord Blandford, 88, 92, 94, 98, 100–101; estrangement from parents, 98; succession to dukedom, 100, 102; bibliophile and botanist, 100, 101, 102–3; weakness and extravagance, 100, 101, 102, 104–5, 114; in blameless scandal, 101; marriage, 101; adds Churchill to surname, 102; creation of new gardens at Blenheim, 103, 147; redecoration of Blenheim, 103–4; mistresses, 104, 105; death, 105; his will, 105

Marlborough, Susan Duchess of (wife of 5th Duke), 101, 105; flower paintings, 104

Marlborough, George Spencer Churchill, 6th Duke of, 104; destruction of papers, 14, 106; marriages, 106; speeches in Lords, 106; comments on Mavor, 107; and admission of visitors to Blenheim, 108

Marlborough, Jane, Duchess of (first wife of 6th Duke), 106

Marlborough, Charlotte, Duchess of (second wife of 6th Duke), 106

Marlborough, Jane Stewart, Duchess of (third wife of 6th Duke), 106

Marlborough, John Winston Spencer-Churchill, 7th Duke of, 13; sale of heirlooms, 17, 114, 116; self-righteous dullness, 109–11, 117; lavish entertaining, 113–14; Viceroy of Ireland, 115; and Blenheim Settled Estates Act, 116, 117; death, 117; his will, 117

Marlborough, Frances, Duchess of (wife of 7th Duke), 109, 110, 114, 123; dislike of Lady Randolph Churchill, 116; dislike of 'little upstart Winston', 125

Marlborough, George Charles Spencer-Churchill, 8th Duke of, 110, 187; sale of heirlooms, 17, 116, 117–20; as Lord

Blandford, 111–12; disastrous marriage, 111; elopement with Lady Aylesford, 114–15; divorce, 115; succession, 117; family group, *118*; second marriage, 120; death, 120–1; his will, 121; burial at Bladon, 121

Marlborough, Lily, Duchess of (wife of 8th Duke), 120–1

Marlborough, Charles Richard John Spencer-Churchill, 9th Duke of, 14, 90, 94, 199, 224, 226; auction of Sunderland Papers, 17; devotion to Blenheim, 18, 124, 126; marriage to Consuelo, 124–5, 144; at mealtime, 126; restoration of gardens and trees, 127–9, 134–5, 147, 148–55; political life, 130, 142; painted by Sargent, 130, 155; shooting-parties, 130–2, 138; redecoration of Blenheim, 133–4; takes local loyalty for granted, 137; first meeting with Gladys Deacon, 139; failure of marriage, 140–1, 142; separation, 141; growing friendship with Gladys, 141–2; escape from shrapnel, 142; divorce, 143–4; conversion to Catholicism, 145, 155, 171; marriage to Gladys, 145, 146; sculpted by Epstein, 146; rudeness to Gladys, 147; gift of plovers' eggs to grandchildren, 148; disappointment in second marriage, 148; his Water Terraces Garden, 148–55; breakdown of marriage, 156–8; death, 158; defence of Blenheim privacy, 164–5; friendship with Winston Churchill, 228–9; tribute to first Duke and Duchess, 245–7

Marlborough, Consuelo Vanderbilt, Duchess of (first wife of 9th Duke), 122, 177, 220; marriage, 124–5; her autobiography, 125, 126, 135, 137, 143, 176, 191, 197, 227; first meeting with family, 125–6; and dullness of life at Blenheim, 126, 132, 147; birth

of sons, 127; portraits, *128*, 134; at shooting-party, *131*; as Lady Bountiful, 135–7, 142; as Blenheim hostess, 137–8, 139; failure of marriage, 140–1, 142; separation, 141, 143; war charity work, 142, 143; divorce, 143–4; second marriage, 144, 145; burial at Bladon, 192, 242

Marlborough, Gladys Deacon, Duchess of (second wife of 9th Duke), 213; flirtation with German Crown Prince, 139–40; friendship with 9th Duke, 140, 141–2; opinion of Winston Churchill, 141; face-lifting experiments, 141, 156; marriage, 145, 146; attempts to enliven Blenheim, 146; boredom, 147, 155; miscarriages, 147; gardening and spaniel-breeding, 147; as Sphinx, *153*, 155; sensationalism, 155; break-up, 156–7; alleged insanity, 157–8; leaves Blenheim, 158; last years, 159

Marlborough, John Albert Edward William Spencer-Churchill, 10th Duke of ('Bert'), 106, 147, 159, 160 *et seq.*; character, 14–15; his memoirs, 15, 190; attitude to Blenheim, 18, 165; sense of humour, 17, 180; birth, 127, 162; as a baby, *128*, 162; as Lord Blandford, *129*, 143; painted by Sargent, 130; war service, 143; marriage, 143; appearance, 162, 163, 195; carelessness in dress, 163, 203; manner of speaking, 164; desire to shock, 164; worry over roof, 164, 174; interest in Blenheim guidebook, 168, 170, 174; and opening of Blenheim to public, 170–3, 174; his bedroom, 173–4; making of documentary film, 175; and mother's autobiography, 176, 197, 199; worry over gardens, 177, 218, 242; affection for dogs, 178, 195; French broadcast, 179; television programme, 180–2; making of garden, 183–4; considers *son et lumière*, 184–5; on dangers of cowpats and copulation, 185; and the Blenheim organ, 188–9; purchase of house in Jamaica, 190, 203; attempt to write autobiography, 190, 198, 199–200, 201–3, 206, 213, 219, 223; attempt at Christmas spirit, 190–1; interest in family vault, 190; doleful 70th birthday, 195; comments on books, 197, 201; operation, 197; attends *son et lumière*, 199; in Jamaica, 203, 205–17; nightmare croquet game, 207; bathing, 209, *210*; obsessive interest in weather, 210–11; addiction to television, 211, 240; small talk, 211; in hospital again, 218, 220, 222; second marriage, 221; death, 222; funeral, 222; burial at Bladon, 223; on Winston Churchill, 226, 239, 240; rift with Randolph, 240; at Winston Churchill funeral, 242

Marlborough, Mary Cadogan, Duchess of (first wife of 10th Duke), 159, 173, 176, 183, 231, *234*; marriage, 143; personality, 165–7, 235; in Red Cross, 165, *166*; and opening of Blenheim to public, 170, 171; opinion of mother-in-law's autobiography, 176; favourite flowers, 177; French broadcast, 179; television programme, 180–2; and proposed *son et lumière*, 185; and Dior dress show, 186–7; mortal illness, 187; burial at Bladon, 188, 242; memorial services, 188; and Winston Churchill's painting, 226, 239; card-playing with Winston Churchill, *233*, 240; as Mayor of Woodstock, *234*, 239; concern with redecorating, 237, 238; and Churchill anthology, 239–40

Marlborough, Laura Canfield, Duchess of (second wife of 10th Duke), 203, 221; in Montego Bay, 205, 206–7; marriage, 221; and Duke's

death and funeral, 222–3

Marlborough, John George Vanderbilt Henry Spencer-Churchill, 11th Duke of, 16, *241*; restoration and upkeep of Blenheim, 11–12, 18, 228; marriage to Tina Onassis, 189; as Lord Blandford ('Sunny'), 192, 194, 197, 199, 200, 231, 242; and father's death and funeral, 222, 223

Marlborough, Rosita, Duchess of (third wife of 11th Duke), 15, 16, 242

Marlborough Gems, 105, 114

Marlborough House (London), 41, 77, 81, 89, 91, 97, 119; Sarah's death at, 71; reversion to Crown, 100

Marlborough Trust, 78, 88

Mary, Queen, 170, 173, 176

Mary II, 26, 29, 30, 33, 52

Mary of Modena, 29

Masefield, John, 156

Masefield, Constance, 156

Masham, Abigail, 34, 41, 86; ascendancy over Anne, 53–5, 56

Masham, Samuel, 41, 54, 84

Mavor, Rev. William Fordyce, 92–3, 96, 103n, 104, 107, 183, 227

Millais, Sir John, 119

Montagu, John, 2nd Duke of, 47, 66

Montagu, Mary Churchill, Duchess of, 31, 59; alienation from mother, 65, 66–8, 70–71, 80, 81; and father's death, 67; Kneller portrait, *67*

Montagu, Lady Mary Wortley, 68

Montego Bay, 203, 204–18; Woodstock House, *208*, 209–18; river picnic, 214–17

Moore, John, Archbishop of Canterbury, 88, 95, 96

Morrell, Lady Ottoline, 129

Morris, Roger, 58, 85, 86

Muir, Lady Rosemary, 170, 171, *234*, 240

Murdock, William, 17, 195

Nelson, Horatio, Lord, 98

New Description of Blenheim (Mavor), 92–3, 103n, 107

Newcastle, Thomas Pelham-

Holles, 1st Duke of, 57, 75

Newcastle, Harriet Godolphin, Duchess of, 68, 78, 80, 81; marriage, 57, 75; and Marlborough's death, 67; and brother Willigo's marriage, 77

Onassis, Tina, 189

Oving, 236–7

Oxford, Robert Harley, Earl of, 41, 42, 84; and downfall of Marlboroughs, 54, 56

Oxford Common Room (Green), 105

Page, Tom (head-gardener), 177

Painting as a Pastime (Churchill), 227

Pembroke, Betty, Countess of, 88, 97

Perkins, C. W., organist, 120, 130, 138, 188

Piper, John, 161

Polignac, Princesse de, 146

Ponsonby, Sir Charles, 199

Porchester, Henry Herbert, Lord, 173, 182

Purves-Stewart, Sir James, 157

Queen Anne (Green), 197–8, 201

Quelch, Eileen, 123

Rayson, Thomas, architect, 174

Reid, Stuart, 245n

Reid, Whitelaw, 141

Relapse, The (Vanbrugh), 17

Reynolds, Sir Joshua, 93–4

Ridley, Grace, 72, 86

Rochester, John Wilmot, Earl of, 42, 161

Rosebery, Archibald Primrose, 5th Earl of, 122, 123

Roubanis, Lady Sarah, 218–19, 222, 223; at Montego Bay, 205, 206–7; Grecian home, 220–1

Roubanis, Theo, 206, 207, 212, 214–16, 218, 220–1

Rowse, A. L., 88, 105, 109

Rufus (Winston Churchill's poodle), 175, 195, 235

Russell, Audrey, 178, 184, 187, 243

Russell, Jacqueline, 214, 216

Rysbrack, John Michael, 59, 66, 71, 85

Sacré (agent), 164, 170
Sarah Duchess of Marlborough (Green), 192–4, 197
Sargent, John Singer, 94, 130, 155, 176, 177
Shingler (fruit-manager), 177
Simpson, Ernest, 202, 228
Simpson, Wallis Warfield, 202, 228
Sir Winston Churchill at Blenheim Palace (ed. Green), 238–40
Sirikit, Queen of Thailand, 194
Sitwell, Sir Sacheverell, 91, 154
Soames, Mary Churchill, Lady, 228, 242
Somerset, Charles Seymour, 6th Duke of, 79
Somerset, Lady Elizabeth Percy, Duchess of, 56
Sophia, Electress of Hanover, 40, 105n
Spalding (porcelain collector), 119
Spencer, Albert Edward, 7th Earl, 193
Spencer, Cynthia, Countess, 193
Spencer, George John, 2nd Earl, 104
Spencer, Lady Anne (later Lady Bateman), 73, 74, 84
Spencer, Lord Charles, 95
Spencer, Lady Diana (later Duchess of Bedford), 73, 74n, 75; as Sarah's favourite granddaughter, 78–80; marriage, 80; death, 80
Spencer, Lady Frances (later Countess of Carlisle), 74 and n
Spencer, Lady Georgina, 86
Spencer, John, 34, 73, 75, 81, 84; Continental travel, 82, 83; extravagance, 82, 83; marriage, 86; death, 86
Spencer, Lord Robert (later Earl of Sunderland), 73, 75, 76
Spencer-Churchill, Lady Caroline, 189
Spencer-Churchill, Lord Charles, 165, 179, 231
Spencer-Churchill, Lord Edward Albert Charles, 242

Spencer-Churchill, Lord Ivor Charles, 127, *129*, 130, 143, 175; support for stepmother, 158
Spencer-Churchill, Lady Lilian, 125, *131*
Spencer-Churchill, Lady Norah, 125
Staël, Madame de, 98
Stewart, Lady Helen, *131*
Story, Waldo, 135
Strong, Edward, 41
Stroud, Dorothy, 91
Sturt, Lady Mary Ann, 104
Sunderland, Charles Spencer, 3rd Earl of, 56; marriage to Anne Churchill, 34; second marriage, 76; losses in South Sea Bubble, 76, 82; his library, 76, 101, 104, 116
Sunderland, Anne Churchill, Countess of, 31; marriage, 34; Lady of Bed-chamber, 35; death, 42, 62, 65, 73, 74, 79, 81; Kneller portraits, *43*, *61*; as a child, 60, *61*, 73; popularity with Kit-Cat Club, 62; letter to husband on care of children, 74
Sunderland, Judith Tichborne, Countess of, 76
Sunderland House (London), 143
Sutherland, Graham, 237

Thornhill, Sir James, 59
Time Clipping the Wings of Cupid (Van Dyck), 119
Timms, Bert (gardener's boy), 147, 150
Tompkins (head-gardener), 177, 192
Townsend, Peter, 201
Trevelyan, G. M., 165
Tyrconnel, Frances Jennings, Lady, 28, 31, 50

Van Dyck, Sir Anthony, 116, 119
Vanbrugh, Sir John, 17, 64, 70, 164, 223; and building of Blenheim, 38–9, 41, 42, 44,

57, 58, 89, 90, 91, 103, 116, 148; disputes with Sarah, 39, 41, 42, 44, 57–8; his bridge, 57, 85, 89, 91, 93n, 169, 184
Vickers, Hugo, 139, 146, 156n, 158n, 159
Victoria, Queen, 113, 114, 115, 122, 138
Victoria, Princess, 130, *131*
Villiers, Barbara, affair with John Churchill, 26, 28
Villiers, Elizabeth, 31

Wadman, Ted (butler), 191, 192, 195, 219
Wales, Frederick, Prince of, 80
Walker, Thomas, 90
Walpole, Horace, 88, 89
Walpole, Sir Robert, 80, 85
Waterford, Lord William Beresford, Marquis of, 121
Wellington, Duke of, 104
Westminster Abbey, 47, 70, 243
Whitaker, Frank, 161, 169
Whiteknights (Reading), 98, 101, 104
William III: John Churchill's switch to from James II, 26, 29, 30; dismissal of Churchill, 30–31, 52; and death of wife, 33; death, 35
Willis, Ward, 155
Wilson, Lady Sarah, 125
Windsor Lodge, 41, 44, 83, 85, 89; Marlborough's death at, 47, 67
Wingfield, Colonel and Mrs Maurice, 156
Wise, Henry, 237; and Blenheim gardens, 52, 57, 58, 134; Green's biography of, 183, 236
Woodstock, 112, 157, 222; Freedom conferred on Winston Churchill, 16, *234*; manor of, 38, 57; Hensington House, 90; town hall, 90, 94; narrow-gauge railway to Oxford, 117, 126
Wren, Sir Christopher, 41
Wyndham, Sir William, 78

Yenn, John, 90, 91, 227
Yorke, Sir Philip, 71

The Marlborough (Spencer–Churchill) line of descent

Sir Winston Churchill b.1620 = Elizabeth Drake of Ashe, Devon

John
b.1650 or Duke of Marlborough *
and KG 1702
or Prince of the Holy Roman
Empire 1705 d.16 June 1722

= **Sarah**
dr. of Richard Jennings of
St Albans
b.1660 m.1678 d.18 Oct 1744

* Duke of Marlborough : a title which John
Churchill is believed to have taken in consequence
of a connection on his mother's side, with
the family of Ley, earls of Marlborough,
extinct ten years previously.

Henrietta
Duchess of Marlborough
1722 s.p.m d.1733

= **Francis**
2nd Earl of
Godolphin

Anne = **Charles Spencer**
b.1684   KG 3rd Earl of
d.1716   Sunderland

Elizabeth = **Scroop**
b.1687   1st Duke of
d.1714   Bridgewater d.1751

Mary = **John**
b.1689   2nd Duke of
          Montagu

John
Marquess of Blandford
b.1686 d.1703

Robert Spencer
b.1701 suc. as Earl of
Sunderland 1722
d. unmarried 1729

Charles Spencer
b.1706 suc. as Earl of Sunderland
1729 and as 3rd Duke of
Marlborough 1733 KG d.1758

= **Elizabeth**
dr of Earl
Trevor

John Spencer
(Ancestor of the
Earls Spencer)

= **Georgina**
dr. of Earl
Granville

Diana Spencer = **John**
b.1708 d.1735   4th Duke
                 of Bedford KG

† The fifth Duke was authorized in 1817
to 'take and use the name of Churchill,
in addition to and after that of Spencer...
in order to perpetuate in his Grace's
family a surname to which his illustrious
ancestor, John, first Duke of Marlborough,
added such imperishable lustre'.

George Spencer
4th Duke of Marlborough
KG, LLD, FRS
b.1739 suc. 1758 d.1817

= **Caroline**
dr. of Duke of Bedford
b.1743 d.1811

George Spencer-Churchill †
5th Duke of Marlborough
b.1766 suc. 1817 d.1840

= **Susan**
dr. of 7th Earl of Galloway
b.1767 d.1841

George Spencer-Churchill
6th Duke of Marlborough
b.1793 suc. 1840 d.1857

= 1. Jane, dr. of 8th Earl of Galloway d.1844
  2. Charlotte, dr. of Viscount Ashbrook d.1850
  3. Jane, dr. of Hon. Edward Stewart d.1897

b.1822 MP suc. 1857. Governor
General of Ireland 1876-80 d.1883

George Charles Spencer-Churchill = 1. Albertha
8th Duke of Marlborough   dr. of Duke of Abercorn
b. 1844 suc. 1883 d.1892   2. Lilian
                                  dr. of Cicero Price (USA)

Randolph Henry Spencer-Churchill = Jennie
b. at Blenheim 1849   dr. of
PC, LLD, etc d. 1895   Leonard
buried at Bladon, Oxon   Jerome
                                   (USA) d.1.1921

Charles Richard John   = 1. Consuelo
Spencer-Churchill   dr. of William Vanderbilt (USA)
9th Duke of Marlborough KG   m. 1895 d.1964
b.1871 suc.1892 Secretary   2. Gladys
of State 1903-5 d.1934   dr. of Edward Parker Deacon (USA)
                                  m. 1921 d. 1977

Winston Leonard Spencer-Churchill = Clementine
KG, OM, CH, MP, etc   dr. of Sir
b. at Blenheim 30 Nov 1874-   Henry
d. 24 Jan. 1965 buried at Bladon,   Montagu
Oxon   Hozier KCB.
                                    d. 12 Dec 1977

John Albert Edward William   = 1. Alexandra Mary Cadogan
Spencer-Churchill   dr. of Viscount Chelsea
10th Duke of Marlborough JP   m. 1920 CBE JP
b. 18 Sept. 1897 suc. 1934   Chief Comdt ATS 1938-40 d.1961
DL, etc Mayor of Woodstock 1937-42 2. Laura
Lt Col Life Guards (ret.) d. 1972   dr. of Hon. Guy Charteris m. 1972

Ivor Charles Spencer-Churchill
b 14 Oct. 1898 d. 1956

John George Vanderbilt   = 1. Susan Mary
Henry Spencer-Churchill DL, JP   dr. of Michael
11th Duke of Marlborough   Hornby m. 1951
b 13 April 1926 suc 1972   2. Athina Mary
                                  dr. of Stavros G.
                                  Livanos m.1961
                                  3. Dagmar Rosita
                                  dr. of count Carl
                                  Ludwig Douglas
                                  m.1972

Charles George
William Colin
Spencer-Churchill
b.13 July 1940
m.1) 1965 Gillian
Spreckels Fuller
2.) 1970 Elizabeth
Jane Wyndham

Sarah Consuelo
Spencer-Churchill
b. 17 Dec. 1921
m.1) 1943 Edwin
F Russell (USNR)
2) 1966 Guy Burgos Waterhouse
3) 1967 Theodorous
Roubanis

Caroline
Spencer-Churchill
b. 12 Nov 1923
m. 1946 Major
Charles Hugo
Waterhouse

Rosemary
Mildred
Spencer-Churchill
b. 24 July 1929
m. 1953 Charles
Robert Muir'

Charles James
Spencer-Churchill
Marquis of Blandford
b. 24 Nov. 1955

Henrietta
Mary
Spencer-
Churchill
b. 1958
m. 1980
Nathan Gelber

David Aba
Gelber b. 1981

Richard Spencer-
Churchill
b. 1973 d. 1973

Edward Albert
Charles Spencer-
Churchill
b. 1974

Alexandra
Elizabeth Mary
Spencer-Churchill
b. 1977

John David Ivor
Spencer-Churchill
b. 1952 d. 1955